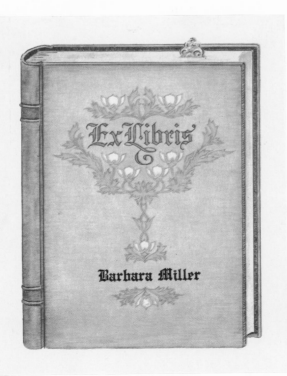

Ex Libris

Barbara Miller

Outline of
PRICE THEORY

Outline of
PRICE THEORY

Albert M. Levenson

Babette S. Solon

QUEENS COLLEGE OF THE CITY UNIVERSITY
OF NEW YORK

Holt, Rinehart and Winston, Inc.

New York   *Chicago*   *San Francisco*   *Toronto*   *London*

To E and I and TFT

Preface

This text on intermediate price theory the authors hope will fill a lack felt by them in their experience in teaching intermediate price theory courses. Concisely presenting the topics usually covered in a one-semester course, it avoids the encyclopedic approach and thus permits the instructor to introduce relevant readings and empirical material as he sees fit. A companion workbook, *Exercises and Problems in Price Theory*, is composed of sets of exercises designed to foster proficiency in the use of the theoretical tools, and sets of problems drawn from empirical investigations to which the theory is applied by the student.

We assume no mathematical knowledge on the part of the student beyond first-year high school algebra, which is reviewed in the first chapter. Anything requiring more advanced mathematics is treated in footnotes or in short appendixes to some of the chapters.

We thank our colleagues in the Queens College Department of Economics for their friendly assistance, especially Professor William Hamovitch, who was kind enough to read some of the chapters. Professor Persia Campbell, chairman of the department, gave particular encouragement to this enterprise. Students in our price theory classes have made valuable suggestions on the earlier drafts.

We gratefully acknowledge our indebtedness to Mrs. Evelyn Nagdimon, Miss Elke Meldau, Mrs. Evelyn Levenson, Miss Lillian Mittleman, Mrs. Lynn Alcosser, Mrs. Rose Kraus, and Miss Gloria Natale for their able typing and clerical assistance in the preparation of the manuscript.

A. M. L.
B. S. S.

New York, March 1964

Contents

PREFACE   vii

INTRODUCTION   1

1 Mathematical and Graphical Techniques   3

2 Demand, Supply, and Price under Perfect Competition   31

3 Total, Average, Marginal, and Elasticity Concepts
     as Applied to Demand   44

4 The Theory of Demand: Classical Utility Approach   63
     APPENDIX 4A   74
     APPENDIX 4B   76

5 The Theory of Demand: Indifference Curve Approach   78
     APPENDIX 5   107

6 Market Structures   108

7 The Theory of Production   116

8 Costs of Production   139
     APPENDIX 8   151

9 Pricing and Output Decisions under Perfect Competition   154
     APPENDIX 9   174

10 Pricing and Output Decisions under Monopoly   175
      APPENDIX 10   190

11 Pricing and Output Decisions under Monopolistic
      Competition and Oligopoly   192

12 The Determination of Factor Prices   212

13 General Equilibrium   231

14 Introduction to Linear Programming   237

INDEX   249

Outline of

PRICE THEORY

INTRODUCTION

Price theory is concerned with the operation of the market mechanism under conditions of free enterprise. Free enterprise is taken to mean an economic system in which individuals are substantially free to sell the services of their resources to the highest bidders and to spend their incomes thus obtained by buying from the cheapest sources of supply those goods and services that yield the greatest satisfaction; and businessmen are substantially free to combine resources in enterprises and to produce goods and services that are sold on markets to the highest bidders.

In such an economic system, the interaction of consumers and producers in resource and product markets solves the economic problems of the society without any central direction. Economic problems all arise from the fact that resources are scarce relative to the human wants for the goods and services produced with these resources. Therefore, every society is faced with the problem of allocating those scarce resources among their competing alternative uses. First, the society must set up priorities concerning what goods and services should be produced, since scarcity of resources prevents all desired goods from being produced. Second, given the fact of scarce resources, society will desire to make the optimum use of these resources; this involves choosing the most efficient techniques of production. Third, once the national output has been produced, it must be distributed to the members of the society in some fashion.

While all societies face these problems, the manner in which they are solved depends upon the institutions of the society. In this book we shall be concerned with market economies, such as that of contemporary America. There is not now, nor has there ever been, a completely free enterprise economy. In contemporary economies, government impinges on producer and consumer free choice to varying degrees. Nonetheless, it is impossible to understand the operation of the modern American economy without understanding how a free enterprise system works, for even with the growing importance of government, the salient feature of the American economy is that of free enterprise. It is to an improvement of this understanding that we now invite the student.

MATHEMATICAL AND
GRAPHICAL TECHNIQUES

1

Mathematical and graphical techniques are widely used in economic analysis. Their use has been partly responsible for the growing insight into the workings of the economic system. Today, one of the major frontiers in economics is the application of advanced mathematical techniques to economic problems.

Fortunately for the student who does not have a mathematical background, intermediate price theory can be adequately explained with relatively few and simple mathematical concepts. In order to prevent the student from getting bogged down in later chapters because of inadequate mathematical knowledge and to enable him to concentrate instead on the economic concepts, this chapter is devoted to a presentation of the necessary mathematical and graphical techniques. Those who are familiar with basic algebra and geometry may find the chapter a useful review.

Functional Relationships

In economics, as in all branches of science, we are concerned with relationships among variables. Variables are quantities that may take on different values; that is, they are not fixed or constant. The land area of New York City is a constant over time, but its population is a variable, as is the total income of the inhabitants. Population is an example of a discrete variable; its value must be one of the whole numbers — fractional people are an oddity even in New York. Total income is a continuous variable, since it may assume both whole and fractional numbers.

Some of the variables with which we are concerned in economics are quantities produced of various goods and services, the prices of these items, the national income, and the supply of money.

A functional relationship exists when the value of one variable depends on the value of one or more other variables. When a variable, y, is a function of a variable, x, then given a value of x we can associate with it a unique value of y.

SIMPLE FUNCTIONAL RELATIONSHIPS

In some instances the value of a variable depends only on the value of one other variable. In general terms, this may be written as

$$y = f(x) \tag{1.1}$$

which is read: "y is a function of x." For example, New York State's yearly receipts of tax revenue from the cigarette excise is a function only of the total number of cigarettes sold in the state during a year, given the tax rate. We can state this functional relationship as follows:

$$\text{Tax receipts} = \$0.05 \text{ x number of packs of cigarettes sold} \tag{1.2}$$

or in symbols

$$T = \$0.05 \ C \tag{1.2a}$$

FIGURE 1.1

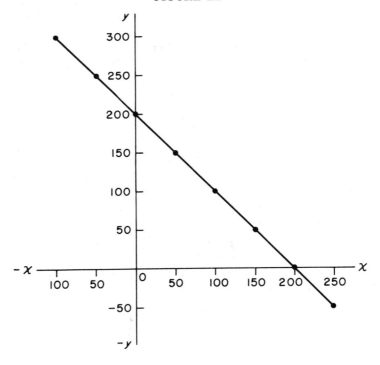

A positive relationship is said to exist between the two variables since as the number of packs sold increases so do the tax receipts. The variable we are trying to predict is called the dependent variable — in this case, tax revenue; and the variable upon which it depends is the independent variable.

Another example should suffice to clarify the concept of a simple functional relationship. If a household regularly consumes three pounds of coffee a week, its total expenditure on coffee would be a function of the average weekly price of coffee. In functional notation we can write:

Total weekly expenditure on coffee = 3 lbs.

$$\times \text{ average weekly price of coffee} \quad (1.3)$$

or

$$TE = Q \times P \quad (1.3a)$$

In addition to stating simple functional relationships algebraically, we can also express them in tabular form and graphically. To demonstrate these methods, we assume the continuous functional relationship

$$y = 200 - x \quad (1.4)$$

We may express this relationship in tabular form by choosing convenient values for the independent variable, x, and computing the corresponding values of y. Such a table has the disadvantage, of course, of giving us only a limited range of information. It is only the algebraic expression that can give us the completely general relationship between the two variables. There is always the danger, therefore, that, when the tabular form is used, values of x are omitted that would have given critical[1] values of y.

We may use our table to construct a picture or graph of the function, as shown in Figure 1.1. This is done on a set of perpendicular coordinates on which we measure the values of our variables. We designate a point as the origin; above it we measure the positive values of y, and below it the negative values of y. To the right of the origin we measure the

[1]For instance, suppose that a functional relationship between x and y looks as follows:

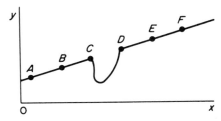

If by accident we chose to tabulate the relationship between x and y for points A through F we would get a false picture.

positive values of x and to the left of the origin the negative values of x.
(It is the usual procedure to place the independent variable on the
horizontal axis and the dependent variable on the vertical axis. However,
in later chapters we shall see that this procedure is sometimes reversed
in economics.) All this is a matter of convention, just as the direction

TABLE 1.1

$$y = 200 - x$$

x	y
-100	300
-50	250
0	200
50	150
100	100
150	50
200	0
250	-50

on a map is a matter of convention. As in map reading, we must have
a scale with which to measure distance; these scales are marked off on
the axes, keeping in mind that equal distances represent equal magnitudes
on each axis. If we want to locate a point we must have its longitude
(y-value) and latitude (x-value), which will uniquely locate it on our
graph.

The points plotted in Figure 1.1 correspond to the set of discrete
pairs of x and y in Table 1.1. Since we have assumed a continuous function
we may join these points to give the curve (in this case, a straight-line
curve) that appears in Figure 1.1.

FUNCTIONAL RELATIONSHIPS AMONG MORE THAN TWO VARIABLES

There are many instances in which the value of one variable is related
to the values of two or more other variables. For example, the weight
of an individual is dependent upon the number of calories he consumes,
the kinds of foods he eats, the rate of his metabolism, and the amount and
kind of exercise in which he indulges. Or the number of pounds of steak
that a housewife purchases in a week depends on the price of steak, the
tastes of her family, the income of the family, and the prices of other
goods (most importantly, the prices of substitute foods — such as chops,
hamburger, or fish, and of complementary foods — such as potatoes or
mushrooms).

This type of functional relationship can be expressed algebraically
in the following way:

$$v = y(w,x,z) \tag{1.5}$$

which reads, "the value of y is dependent upon the values of w, x, and z."
We write $y = y(w,x,z)$ simply to identify the function and the y has the
same meaning as the f previously used.

There are occasions when it is desirable to isolate the relationship
between one of the independent variables and the dependent one. For
example, if it is desired to determine the effect of a change in the value
of only x on the value of y, and it can be assumed that the other independent variables remain constant at given levels, then we can write

$$y = y(x) \; ceteris \; paribus \tag{1.6}$$

Graphical representation of functional relationships where more than
two variables are involved is more difficult than it is for the simple
relationship shown above. If our dependent variable is a function of
two independent variables, we can attempt to show the relationship
by a graph. But an equation with three independent variables requires
four dimensions; whereupon graphical methods fail us. (Of course, if
it is permissible to make the *ceteris paribus* assumption, a two-dimensional
graph can be used.)

Table 1.2a presents a series of related values that fit the function

$$y = x + \frac{z}{2} \tag{1.7}$$

This function, which is plotted in Figure 1.2, has two independent
variables and is a plane.[2]

TABLE 1.2a

x	1	1 1	1 2	2 2	2 3	3 3	3 4	4 4	4
z	1	2 3	4 1	2 3	4 1	2 3	4 1	2 3	4
y	1½	2 2½	3 2½	3 3½	4 3½	4 4½	5 4½	5 5½	6

TABLE 1.2b

x	0 1 2	0 2 4	0 3 6	0 4 8
z	4 2 0	8 4 0	12 6 0	16 8 0
y	2 2 2	4 4 4	6 6 6	8 8 8

We can often bring a three-dimensional relationship of this sort down
to two-dimensional representation by drawing a contour map that shows
the y-"elevation" at various combinations of x and z. As on a geological
map, where each contour line connects points of equal elevation, the

[2]This three-dimensional graph is plotted in the following manner: the x- and y-axes
are the same as before; the z-axis has a common origin with the other two and is
placed at an appropriate angle to show perspective. Take the 9th set of related values
in Table 1.2a and see how the corresponding point is plotted. Go along the x-axis to 3;
down parallel to the z-axis, to 1; then vertically up to $y = 3\frac{1}{2}$. This is labeled pt. A.

FIGURE 1.2

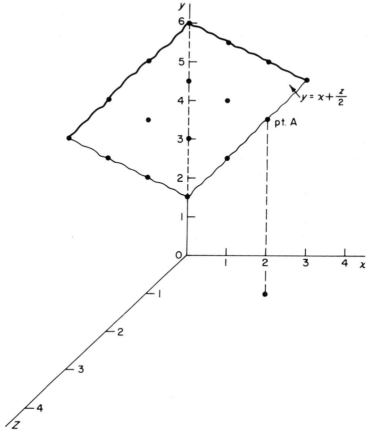

lines in Figure 1.3 give all the combinations of x and z that will yield a given value of y. Since Figure 1.2 is a plane surface, these contour lines are straight lines. For each of the contour lines drawn in Figure 1.2, Table 1.2b gives three (of the infinite) combinations of x and z that yield the constant level of y.

The Concept of Slope (The Marginal Concept)

DISCRETE CHANGES

In the preceding section we saw that the value of the dependent variable is based on the value of the independent variable; that is, as the value of x changes, the value of y will change. In this section we shall compare changes in y with the initiating changes in x. We shall measure the rate of change of y in relation to changes in x.

We show the function

$$y = 10 - x \qquad (1.8)$$

FIGURE 1.3

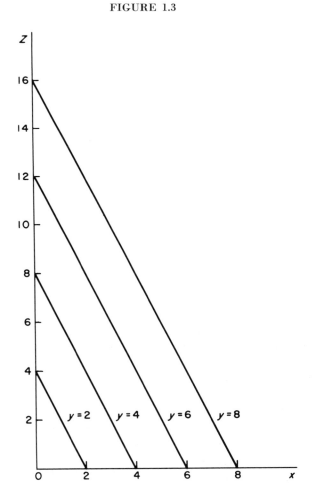

in tabular form in Table 1.3 and as a graph in Figure 1.4. Assume that the initial value of x is 4; the related value of y is 6 (point A). If the value of x changes to 5, we know from the functional relationship and the graph that y will change to 5 (point B). For this given change in x, we wish to determine the rate at which y changes. We do this by dividing the change in y by the change in x; or, in notational form,

$$\frac{\Delta y}{\Delta x}$$

where Δ represents a measurable (or finite) change.

TABLE 1.3

$y = 10 - x$

x	y
0	10
1	9
2	8
3	7
4	6
5	5
6	4
7	3
8	2
9	1
10	0

Thus, between points A and B

$$\frac{\Delta y}{\Delta x} = \frac{-1 \text{ unit of } y}{1 \text{ unit of } x} = -1 \text{ unit of } y \text{ per unit of } x \qquad (1.9)$$

This means that the average rate of increase of y, as x changes from 4 to 5 units, is -1 unit per unit increase in x. The minus sign before the 1 indicates an inverse relationship between x and y; that is, as x increases, y decreases. This is shown graphically by the downward-to-the-right pattern of the line.

This measure of the rate of change of y is, in graphical terms, the slope of the function between points A and B. We could have measured the slope between any two points on the line and our answer still would have been -1 unit of y per unit of x. For example, between points B and C in Figure 1.4, the slope can be measured as follows:

$$\frac{\Delta y}{\Delta x} = \frac{-3 \text{ units of } y}{3 \text{ units of } x} = -1 \text{ unit of } y \text{ per unit of } x \qquad (1.10)$$

For any straight line, the slope between any two points on it is always a constant. In algebraic terms, the standard equation for a straight-line function is of the form

$$y = ax + b \qquad (1.11)$$

FIGURE 1.4

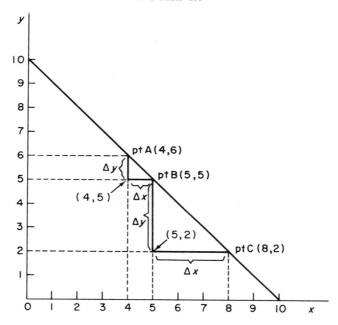

where y is the dependent variable

x is the independent variable

a is a constant whose value is equal to the slope of the line

b is a constant whose value is equal to the y-axis intercept of the line

Therefore, we can rewrite equation (1.8) in standard form as

$$y = -1x + 10 \quad \text{or simply} \quad y = -x + 10 \tag{1.8a}$$

and we see that the slope a is -1 and the line crosses the y-axis at 10.

The quickest way to plot a straight-line function is to first assume $x = 0$ and find the related y-value that would be plotted on the y-axis, since the y-axis is the locus of points where $x = 0$; then assume $y = 0$ and find the related x-value that will lie on the x-axis. Two points are sufficient for determining the straight line, or one point and slope.

We now determine the slope of another function:

$$2y = 5x - 1 \tag{1.12}$$

We can rewrite this in standard form as

$$y = \frac{5}{2}x - \frac{1}{2} \tag{1.12a}$$

The slope of this function is $\frac{5}{2}$ (or $2\frac{1}{2}$ units of y per unit of x), and the line has a y-axis intercept of $-\frac{1}{2}$. The positive slope would be reflected graphically in an upward-to-the-right direction of the line.

Many functions to be discussed in later chapters are curvilinear rather than linear. The treatment of nonlinear functions is basically the same as that for the straight-line ones, both algebraically and graphically, but the measurement of the slope between two points on a curve deserves special mention. Consider the following relationship presented in Table 1.4 and shown graphically in Figure 1.5.

$$xy = 24 \quad \text{or} \quad y = \frac{24}{x} \tag{1.13}$$

TABLE 1.4

x	y	x	y
1	24	13	$1\frac{11}{13}$
2	12	14	$1\frac{5}{7}$
3	8	15	$1\frac{3}{5}$
4	6	16	$1\frac{1}{2}$
5	$4\frac{4}{5}$	17	$1\frac{7}{17}$
6	4	18	$1\frac{1}{3}$
7	$3\frac{3}{7}$	19	$1\frac{5}{19}$
8	3	20	$1\frac{1}{5}$
9	$2\frac{2}{3}$	21	$1\frac{1}{8}$
10	$2\frac{2}{5}$	22	$1\frac{1}{11}$
11	$2\frac{2}{11}$	23	$1\frac{1}{23}$
12	2	24	1

Obviously, the slope of this curvilinear function (or any curvilinear function) is not a constant, but varies along the curve — being large (either positive or negative) where the curve approaches the vertical and nearing zero as the curve approaches the horizontal.

To find the slope between two points on the curve, we assume a straight line exists between the two points and proceed as before. This gives us the average slope along the curve between the two points. Thus, the slope between points A and B is

$$\frac{\Delta y}{\Delta x} = \frac{-12 \text{ units of } y}{1 \text{ unit of } x} = -12 \text{ units of } y \text{ per unit of } x \tag{1.14}$$

Between points B and C the slope is

$$\frac{\Delta y}{\Delta x} = \frac{-4 \text{ units of } y}{1 \text{ unit of } x} = -4 \text{ units of } y \text{ per unit of } x \tag{1.15}$$

The slope is -2 between points C and D and $-\frac{6}{5}$ between points D and E. To test his understanding, the student can compute the slope between the other points.

FIGURE 1.5

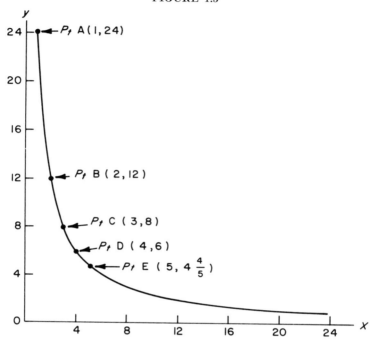

CONTINUOUS CHANGES

We have discussed the slope of a function when the change in x was a finite quantity. We again consider a nonlinear function. In Figure 1.6 we can measure the average slope of the curve between points P_1 and P_2' by finding the slope of the straight line between those points. Now visualize that P_1 is fixed but that P_2 moves closer to it along the curve. We can determine the slope between P_1 and P_2^2 and between P_1 and P_2^3 by computing the appropriate $\Delta y/\Delta x$. Notice that as P_2 gets closer to P_1, Δx gets smaller and smaller. As Δx approaches zero the line between P_1 and P_2 approaches the line AB. Thus, we can consider the slope of a curve in the vicinity of a point, rather than between two points along the curve. And this continuous slope is the value that the discrete slope approaches as P_2 approaches P_1 (or as $\Delta x \rightarrow 0$; to be read as Δx approaches zero). This continuous slope may be written as

$$\lim_{\Delta x \to 0} \frac{\Delta y}{\Delta x} \quad \text{or} \quad \frac{dy}{dx}$$

The slope of the curve at P_1 is measured by determining the slope of the line AB, which is the tangent to the curve at P_1. Since the slope

FIGURE 1.6

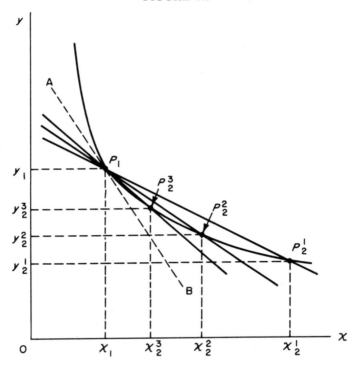

of a straight line is a constant, to get the slope at P_1, $\Delta y / \Delta x$ can be computed between any two points on this line and this is the same as computing dy/dx at P_1 on line AB. Thus, the discrete slope of the line tangent at P_1 and the continuous slope of the curve at P_1 are the same.

The Concept of Elasticity

We are interested in measuring the responsiveness of y to changes in x. It must occur to the reader that we have discussed such a measure in the concept of slope. The need for another measure will be made clear in the following example. Consider the $y = 10 - x$ function once again but this time we shall specify the units in which x and y are measured. In Figure 1.7a the y-axis is measured in pints and the x-axis in dollars-per-pint. The same function is shown in Figure 1.7b, but here the dependent variable is measured in quarts and the independent variable remains in dollars-per-pint. If we compute the slopes between $4 and $5 on each graph we get the following results:

$$\text{slope} = \frac{-1 \text{ pint}}{\$1 \text{ per pint}} \qquad \text{(Fig. 1.7a)} \quad (1.16)$$

$$\text{slope} = \frac{-1/2 \text{ quart}}{\$1 \text{ per pint}} \qquad \text{(Fig. 1.7b)} \quad (1.17)$$

We can see, therefore, that slope is a measure that depends upon the units in which the variables are measured. We should be wary of a

FIGURE 1.7

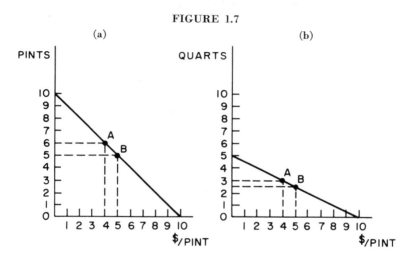

measure of responsiveness that changes simply because of a change in the units. If we desire to make comparisons of responsiveness using the slope as the measure, we must always be sure that the units of measurement are the same, so that differences in the measure will be due to differences in responsiveness rather than to differences in units.

POINT AND ARC ELASTICITY

The concept of elasticity obviates this difficulty and has certain virtues of its own. To make our measure independent of units, we use a ratio of the percentage change in y to the percentage change in x, instead of taking a ratio of the absolute change in the dependent variable to the absolute change in the independent variable. Thus, as compared with slope, which is $\Delta y/\Delta x$, the elasticity coefficient is computed as[3]

$$E = \frac{\Delta y/y}{\Delta x/x} \qquad (1.18)$$

The elasticity between the points for which we determined slope in Figures 1.7a and b can be computed with this formula. For Figure 1.7a we have

$$E = \frac{-1 \text{ pint}/6 \text{ pints}}{\$1 \text{ per pint}/\$4 \text{ per pint}} = -2/3 \qquad (1.19)$$

For Figure 1.7b we have

$$E = \frac{-5 \text{ quarts}/3 \text{ quarts}}{\$1 \text{ per pint}/\$4 \text{ per pint}} = -2/3$$

Notice that the use of a ratio of percentage changes results in the cancellation of units of measurement; or, in other words, the elasticity coefficient is a pure number. Thus we have a measure that is independent of units and frees us of the necessity of converting our functional relationships into comparable units before we can make comparisons of responsiveness.

The elasticity formula can also be written as

$$E = \frac{\Delta y}{\Delta x} \cdot \frac{x}{y} \qquad (1.20)$$

and we can see that elasticity is the product of (1) the slope between the two points and (2) the ratio of the initial values of x and y; that is, the location on the line of the two points.

Some problems do arise with the elasticity formula given above. If we were to measure the edge of a table, we would expect to get the same measurement whether we placed the ruler from left to right or from right to left. In the same way, we would expect to get the same elasticity coefficient between two points whether we measured from left to right along the graph or from right to left. Let us return to the two points we used before in Figure 1.7a, but this time we shall compute elasticity for a change in x from 5 to 4, rather than from 4 to 5.

$$E = \frac{1 \text{ pint}/5 \text{ pints}}{-\$1 \text{ per pint}/\$5 \text{ per pint}} = -1 \qquad (1.21)$$

[3]In the discussion of elasticity that follows, we compare the percentage change in the dependent variable with the initiating percentage change in the independent variable. However, in later chapters we shall find it more useful to find the reciprocal of this ratio; that is, the percentage change in the independent variable divided by the percentage change in the dependent variable.

The answer is -1, compared with our previous answer of $-\frac{2}{3}$ in equation (1.20). We are thus faced with the anomalous situation that our results differ, depending upon the direction in which we decide to measure the change. To see the cause of this result, let us compare our elasticity measures:

$$E_{4\to5} = \frac{-1 \text{ pint/6 pints}}{\$1 \text{ per pint/\$4 per pint}} \text{ and } E_{5\to4} = \frac{1 \text{ pint/5 pints}}{-\$1 \text{ per pint/\$5 per pint}}$$

Our difficulty exists, it is clear, because the base for computing our percentage changes is different for the two computations.

The way out of this dilemmna can be seen if we visualize point B as getting closer and closer to point A in Figure 1.7a. As the distance between A and B approaches zero, Δy and Δx approach zero and the differences between the initial and subsequent values of x and y approach zero. Therefore, the difference between the two elasticity measures will also approach zero. Hence our elasticity formula should be written as

$$E = \frac{dy}{dx} \cdot \frac{x}{y} \tag{1.22}$$

which is called point elasticity.

It should be remembered that dy/dx represents the rate of change of y with respect to x in which the change in x is infinitesimally small. Thus, in Figure 1.7a, the elasticity at point A is

$$E = -1 \cdot \frac{4}{6} = -\frac{2}{3} \tag{1.23}$$

Although we now have an exact formula for computing elasticity, we are still faced with a problem. Most of the changes in variables that arise in economics are finite rather than infinitesimal. So we must still devise a method for finding elasticity between two points on a function (called arc elasticity) that will give us the same results no matter in which direction we measure. As we saw before, the reason that we obtained different answers is the fact that different bases were used, depending on the direction in which we measured. We can overcome this problem in the following way: in computing the percentage change in y, instead of using the original y quantity as a base — Δy/original y — use the average of the initial and the new y values as the base; the same applies to computing the percentage change in x. Thus

$$E = \frac{\% \text{ change in } y}{\% \text{ change in } x} = \frac{\Delta y/[(y_1 + y_2)/2]}{\Delta x/[(x_1 + x_2)/2]} = \frac{\Delta y}{\Delta x} \cdot \frac{(x_1 + x_2)/2}{(y_1 + y_2)/2} \tag{1.24}$$

where the subscripts 1 represent initial values and subscripts 2 represent new values. Since division by 2 appears in both the numerator and the denominator of the ratio, we can cancel out the 2's without changing the value of the fraction. In simplified form, then, the arc elasticity coefficient is

$$E = \frac{\Delta y/(y_1 + y_2)}{\Delta x/(x_1 + x_2)} = \frac{\Delta y}{\Delta x} \cdot \frac{x_1 + x_2}{y_1 + y_2} \tag{1.25}$$

To test this new arc elasticity formula, we shall once again measure elasticity between points A and B on Figure 1.7a in both directions. Going from A to B, we find

$$E = \frac{\Delta y}{\Delta x} \cdot \frac{x_1 + x_2}{y_1 + y_2} = -1 \cdot \frac{4 + 5}{6 + 5} = -\frac{9}{11} \tag{1.26}$$

Going from B to A, we find

$$E = -1 \cdot \frac{5 + 4}{5 + 6} = -\frac{9}{11} \tag{1.27}$$

The elasticity between various points on the function $y = 10 - x$ is presented in Table 1.5. Note that elasticity (arc or point) varies along a straight line, while the slope is a constant. This is perfectly logical

TABLE 1.5

x	y	E
0	10	
		$-1/19$
1	9	
		$-3/17$
2	8	
		$-1/3$
3	7	
		$-7/13$
4	6	
		$-9/11$
5	5	
		$-1\frac{2}{9}$
6	4	
		$-1\frac{6}{7}$
7	3	
		-3
8	2	
		$-5\frac{2}{3}$
9	1	
		-19
10	0	

because elasticity depends only partly on slope; its other determinant is the location of the points or point being considered, and this varies along a straight line.

The elasticity concept requires further discussion, but this will be reserved for those chapters where specific applications of the concept are discussed.

Relationships among Total, Average, and Marginal Concepts

We discussed the concept of a marginal quantity in pages 8 – 14. It is the purpose of this section to elucidate some extremely useful relationships that hold between a marginal quantity and its corresponding total and average quantities. This will be done with reference to a specific example.

THE TOTAL CONCEPT

We are told by the engineer of a company that the total costs of producing various levels of output of a particular product are those given in

FIGURE 1.8

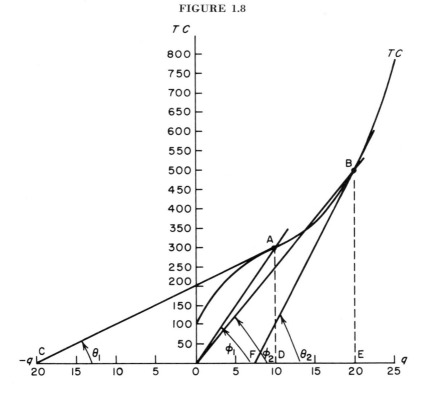

TABLE 1.6

(1) Output q	(2) Total Cost TC	(3) Average Cost AC	(4) Continuous Marginal Cost MC	(5)* Discrete Marginal Cost MC
0	$100.00		$40.00	
				$37.10
1	137.10	$137.10	34.30	
				31.70
2	168.80	84.40	29.20	
				26.90
3	195.70	65.20	24.70	
				22.70
4	218.40	54.60	20.80	
				19.10
5	237.50	47.50	17.50	
				16.10
6	253.60	42.30	14.80	
				13.70
7	267.30	38.20	12.70	
				11.90
8	279.20	34.90	11.20	
				10.70
9	289.90	32.20	10.30	
				10.10
10	300.00	30.00	10.00	
				10.10
11	310.10	28.20	10.30	
				10.70
12	320.80	26.70	11.20	
				11.90
13	332.70	25.60	12.70	
				13.70
14	346.40	24.70	14.80	
				16.10

column 2 of Table 1.6 and shown graphically in Figure 1.8. We assume all levels of output can be produced; that is, we assume a continuous function. Note the following characteristics of total costs. When output is zero, total cost is equal to $100. Total cost increases over the entire range of outputs, but it increases at a decreasing rate until 10 units of output, and after 10 units it increases at an increasing rate.[4]

[4]In Chapter 8 we shall discuss in detail the reason for fixed costs and the shape of the total cost function.

TABLE 1.6 (continued)

15	362.50	24.20	17.50	
				19.10
16	381.60	23.85	20.80	
				22.70
17	404.30	23.78	24.70	
				26.90
18	431.20	23.90	29.20	
				31.70
19	462.90	24.40	34.30	
				37.10
20	500.00	25.00	40.00	
				43.10
21	543.10	25.90	46.30	
				49.70
22	592.80	26.90	53.20	
				56.90
23	649.70	28.20	60.70	
				64.70
24	714.40	29.80	68.80	
				73.10
25	787.50	31.50	77.50	

Column 2 was derived using the function

$$TC = 1/10q^3 - 3q^2 + 40q + 100$$

Column 3 is then derived as

$$AC = \frac{TC}{q} = \frac{1}{10}q^2 - 3q + 40 + \frac{100}{q}$$

Column 4 then is $MC = dTC/dq = 3/10\ q^2 - 6q + 40$
Column 5 is the discrete marginal cost defined as $\Delta TC/\Delta q$, and since $\Delta q = 1$ it is simply ΔTC.
*Since discrete MC is actually the average MC over an interval, it is listed between the two relevant output levels. When discrete MC is shown graphically (Figure 1.10), it is plotted at the mid-point of the interval.

THE AVERAGE CONCEPT

An often-used concept is cost-per-unit of output, or simply average cost, which can be expressed in algebraic terms as

$$\text{Average Cost} = \frac{\text{Total Cost}}{\text{Output}} \quad \text{or} \quad AC = \frac{TC}{q} \qquad (1.28)$$

Average cost is presented in column 3 of Table 1.6 and is plotted in Figure 1.9. It is possible to derive average cost graphically from the total cost curve. This is done in the following way: To find the AC at

FIGURE 1.9

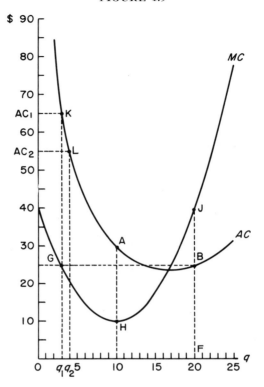

any level of output, find the point on the *TC* curve that corresponds to this level of output. Construct a line from the origin to that point on the curve. Drop a perpendicular from the point to the horizontal axis. Since average cost is Total Cost/Output, on the graph it can be measured as the ratio of (1) the perpendicular distance from the point to the horizontal axis to (2) the horizontal axis coordinate of the point. Therefore, for point *A* in Figure 1.8, we draw the line *OA*; from point *A* we drop the perpendicular *AD*; and average cost is then measured as

$$AC = \frac{AD}{OD} = \frac{\$300}{10 \text{ units}} = \$30 \text{ per unit}^5 \qquad (1.29)$$

A similar computation for point *B* on the total cost curve gives us

$$AC = \frac{EB}{OE} = \frac{\$500}{20 \text{ units}} = \$25 \text{ per unit}^6 \qquad (1.30)$$

[5]The ratio *AD /OD* is the tangent of the angle ϕ_1.
[6]The ratio *EB /OE* is the tangent of the angle ϕ_2.

If we have the average cost for any output, it is possible to derive the total cost of that output by multiplying average cost by output; that is, $AC = TC/q$ and, therefore,

$$AC \cdot q = \frac{TC}{q} \cdot q = TC \tag{1.31}$$

On Figure 1.9 we can determine the total cost that corresponds to any output by multiplying the vertical distance up to the average cost curve at the given output by the horizontal distance representing the level of output. Thus, for an output of 20 units, we multiply the distance FB ($25/unit), representing average cost, by OF (20 units), representing output, and we have a measure of total cost given by the area of the rectangle $OFBG$ ($25/unit $\times$ 20 units = $500).

RELATIONSHIP BETWEEN THE MARGINAL AND TOTAL CONCEPTS

In column 4 of Table 1.6 we present the marginal costs that correspond to the total costs given in column 2. It will be recalled that a marginal quantity is the rate of change of one variable in relation to another. In this case, marginal cost measures the rate of change of cost with respect to output. It will also be recalled that marginal cost can be measured either as (1) the slope of the total cost curve in the continuous case or as (2) the ratio of the change in total cost to the change in output in the discrete case. The discrete computations are shown in column 5 and are based upon total costs in column 2.

The figures for marginal cost in column 4 can be derived graphically from the total cost curve in Figure 1.8. To determine MC at point A, construct a tangent to the curve at that point and measure its slope. This is done by taking the ratio of (1) the vertical distance of point A from the horizontal axis to (2) the distance (disregarding sign) between the horizontal axis coordinate of point A and the horizontal axis intercept of the tangent line.

Thus we have for point A (at 10 units)

$$MC = \frac{AD}{CD} = \frac{\$300}{30 \text{ units}} = \$10 \text{ per unit}[7] \tag{1.32}$$

And for point B (at 20 units)

$$MC = \frac{BE}{FE} = \frac{\$500}{12\frac{1}{2} \text{ units}} = \$40 \text{ per unit}[8] \tag{1.33}$$

The slope of the TC-curve (MC) over the range of considered outputs is plotted in Figure 1.9. At an output of 10, which corresponds to

[7]The ratio AD/CD is the tangent of the angle θ_1.
[8]The ratio BE/FE is the tangent of the angle θ_2.

point H on the MC-curve, we read the value of MC on the vertical axis as \$10. Point $\mathcal{J}$ on Figure 1.9 analogously gives the MC corresponding to an output of 20 units.

We now desire to show the relationship between marginal and average concepts: this is done with reference to Figure 1.9. We take any two points, K and L, along the AC-curve. At point K total cost may be expressed as $AC_1 \times q_1$; at point L total cost may be expressed as $AC_2 q_2$.

We can determine the discrete MC between outputs q_1 and q_2 as follows: Let

$$\Delta q = q_2 - q_1$$
$$\Delta AC = AC_2 - AC_1$$
$$\Delta TC = AC_2 q_2 - AC_1 q_1$$

$AC_2 q_2$ can be written as

$$AC_2 q_1 + AC_2(q_2 - q_1) = AC_2 q_1 + AC_2 \Delta q$$

$AC_1 q_1$ can be written as

$$AC_2 q_1 + q_1(AC_1 - AC_2) = AC_2 q_1 - q_1(AC_2 - AC_1) = AC_2 q_1 - q_1 \Delta AC$$

Substituting, we get

$$\Delta TC = (AC_2 q_1 + AC_2 \Delta q) - (AC_2 q_1 - q_1 \Delta AC)$$
$$\Delta TC = AC_2 q_1 + AC_2 \Delta q - AC_2 q_1 + q_1 \Delta AC$$
$$\Delta TC = AC_2 \Delta q + q_1 \Delta AC$$
$$MC = \frac{\Delta TC}{\Delta q} = AC_2 + \frac{\Delta AC}{\Delta q} q_1 \tag{1.34}$$

Note that when AC is falling, so that its slope $\Delta AC/\Delta q$ is negative, MC will be less than the new average cost, AC_2. If AC is rising, its slope is positive and MC is greater than the new AC. Finally, when AC is neither rising nor falling, so that $\Delta AC/\Delta q = 0$, MC and AC are equal.

Let us now suppose that point L is made to approach point K and, therefore, that Δq approaches 0 or q_2 approaches q_1. We may now rewrite our expression as

$$MC = \frac{dTC}{dq} = AC + \frac{dAC}{dq} q^* \tag{1.35}$$

*Note that we have dropped the subscripts since AC_1 and AC_2 and q_1 and q_2 approach each other as AC and q approach zero. This result can be obtained directly with calculus by using the rule for obtaining the derivative of a product:

$$TC = AC \cdot q$$

and since MC is defined as the rate of change of TC,

$$MC = \frac{dTC}{dq} = AC + \frac{dAC}{dq} q$$

For the continuous case we see that when AC is falling so that $dAC/dq < 0,$† $MC < AC$. When AC is rising so that $dAC/dq > 0,$‡ then $MC > AC$. And finally, when AC is at its minimum point and is neither rising nor falling and its slope is zero, $MC = AC$. These relationships between AC and MC can be seen in Figure 1.9.

For students who are now yearning for a down-to-earth example, we present the following:

Four men in a room have the following heights:

Man	Height in Inches
1	68
2	72
3	74
4	66
Total	280

$$\text{Average} = \frac{280}{4} = 70 \text{ inches}$$

An additional man (the marginal man) enters the room. If the average of 70 inches is to fall, his height must be less than 70 inches; if it is to rise, his height must be greater than 70 inches; and if it is to remain the same, his height must be equal to 70 inches. Further, as long as his height is a positive number (as it must be by the nature of the case), the total would rise; it could fall only if the fifth man's height were negative.

We have shown how MC can be derived from TC. It is also true that TC can be derived from MC. We shall demonstrate this first with reference to discrete marginal cost and then with reference to continuous marginal cost.

Column 5 of Table 1.6 lists MC for finite (discrete) changes in output.[9] Provided that we know what TC is at zero level of output, total cost can be computed for any other level of output in the following manner (which we shall demonstrate with reference to total cost at 3 units of output): We can get TC for one unit of output by adding to the fixed cost the addition to total cost (MC) due to producing the first unit of output ($\$100 + \$37.10 = \$137.10$). Analogously, we can get total cost for two units of output by adding to $\$137.10$ the MC of the second unit of output $[(\$100 + \$37.10) + \$31.70 = \$168.80]$. Finally, we can compute TC for three units by adding the MC of the third unit to $\$168.80$

†This is to be read dAC/dq *is less than* zero.
‡This is to be read dAC/dq *is greater than* zero.
[9]Since discrete MC is actually the average MC over the interval, it is plotted at the mid-point of the interval.

[(\$100 + \$37.10 + \$31.70) + \$26.90 = \$195.70]. Note that we are adding to the fixed cost the *MC* of every unit of output up to and including the level of output for which we are computing total cost.

Total cost can be derived graphically from marginal cost and this is done in Figure 1.10, where the discrete *MC* from column 5 in Table

FIGURE 1.10

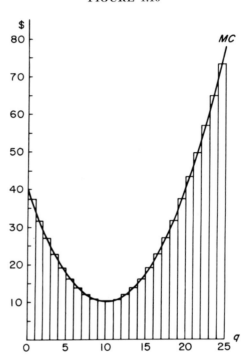

1.6 is plotted. The procedure of adding the marginal costs up to and including that for an output of 3 is equivalent to adding the first three vertical bars on the diagram; and one can obtain total cost for *n* units of output by simply adding the bars up to and including the nth. (And, of course, adding the fixed costs at zero to that.)

If we wish to obtain total cost from continuous *MC*, we no longer can rely on the tabular technique. The reason for this is that we have the continuous *MC* at specific points only but we need it for all possible levels of output. Imagine that the changes to be made in output are very small, so that our vertical bars become very narrow and extremely numerous. Then, as we add these numerous bars together, we are approximating the area under the continuous MC-curve.

Thus, finding total cost for a particular level of output from continuous MC involves finding the area under the MC-curve up to that level of output and adding to it the fixed cost. This will seem reasonable to the student if he notices that the MC-curve cuts off from each of the vertical

FIGURE 1.11

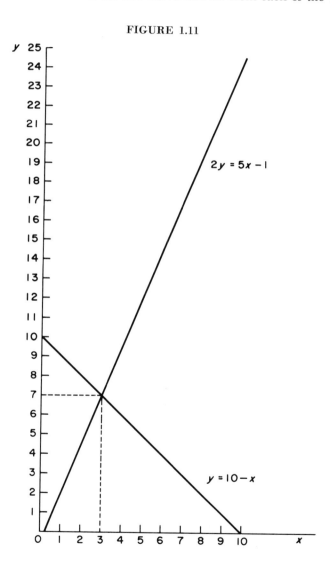

bars a triangle roughly equal in area to a newly included triangle under the *MC*-curve.[10]

Solutions of Simultaneous Equations

Consider once again the function

$$y = 10 - x \tag{1.8}$$

For such an equation we may choose a value of x and this will determine a value of y. If we choose a value of y, this uniquely determines a value of x. But notice that one of our variables is free to take on any value and

FIGURE 1.12

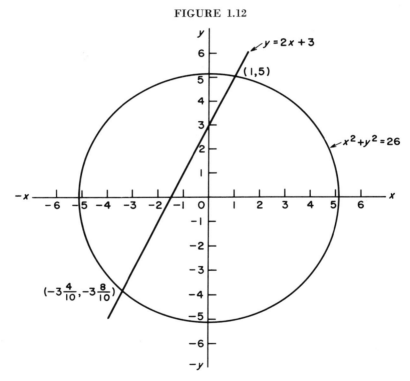

[10]The student familiar with integral calculus will realize that this amounts to taking the definite integral from 0 to 3 units of output as follows:

$$\int_0^3 \frac{3}{10} q^2 - 6q + 40\, dq = \left[\frac{1}{10} q^3 - 3q^2 + 40q \right]_0^3 = \$95.70$$

and to this we must add the fixed cost of $100.

then the value of the other variable is determined. Therefore, there are an infinite number of pairs of x and y that satisfy this equation. This can be seen graphically in Figure 1.4: given any value on either axis, the curve gives us the value of the variable on the other axis.

Now suppose that we have another functional relationship between y and x that reads

$$2y = 5x - 1 \qquad (1.36)$$

and we desire to know the value (or values) of y and x that satisfy both our equations; how many such values are there? We can get a clue in Figure 1.11, where we have plotted both equations. An x-y pair that satisfies an equation (a solution) must lie on the graph representing that equation. If we are to have such a solution that satisfies both equations, the point representing it must lie on both lines. Clearly, the only point that lies on both lines is the point of intersection.

Thus, a system of two linear equations in two unknowns can be solved by plotting the two curves and reading the solution from their point of intersection (if there is a point of intersection). In algebraic terms, this means that we set the equations equal to each other and solve for x:

$$y = 10 - x$$
$$2y = 5x - 1$$
$$10 - x = \frac{5}{2}x - \frac{1}{2}$$
$$-x = \frac{5}{2}x - \frac{21}{2}$$
$$\frac{7}{2}x = \frac{21}{2}$$
$$x = -\frac{2}{7}\left(\frac{21}{2}\right) = 3$$

Substituting, $y = 10 - 3 = 7$.

If all our equations are not linear, we may obtain multiple solutions. Consider, in the simple two-variable case, the following two equations:

$$y = 2x + 3 \qquad (1.37)$$
$$x^2 + y^2 = 26 \qquad (1.38)$$

These are the two equations plotted in Figure 1.12. The first equation represents a straight line and the second a circle. There are two points of intersection and, therefore, two solutions to the set of equations; these are $(x = 1, y = 5)$ and $(x = -3\frac{4}{10}, y = -3\frac{8}{10})$. For similar systems of equations, there could be only one solution, which would be represented geometrically by the line being tangent to the circle at a point; or there could be no solution, which would be true if the equations were inconsistent; that is, there would be no points of intersection between the circle and line.

DEMAND, SUPPLY, AND PRICE UNDER PERFECT COMPETITION

2

Demand

An individual's demand for a good is the alternative quantities per time period he would be willing to purchase at all relevant prices. His demand for the good is a function of the following variables: the price of the good, the prices of other goods — especially substitutes and complements, his income, and his tastes, this latter being a catchall category that includes psychological, sociological, and culturally conditioned attitudes. We may wish to isolate the relationship between the quantity demanded and the price of the commodity. To do this, we must regard the other variables as being constant at some given level — the *ceteris paribus* assumption. In functional notation, this demand relationship can be written as

$$q_d = D(P_x, P_s, P_c, Y, T) \tag{2.1}$$

where q_d = quantity demanded
P_x = price of the good
P_s = prices of substitute goods
P_c = prices of complementary goods
Y = individual's income per time period
T = his tastes

With the *ceteris paribus* assumption, we can write

$$q_d = D(P_x, \overbrace{P_s, P_c, Y, T}^{\text{held constant}}) \tag{2.2}$$

which is usually abbreviated as

$$q_d = D(P) \ cet. \ par. \tag{2.3}$$

The individual's demand schedule presents his demand for a good in tabular form. $q_d = 10 - P$ can be presented in tabular form for a relevant range of prices as follows:

TABLE 2.1

$$q_d = 10 - P$$

P ($ per unit)	q (units per time period)
10	0
9	1
8	2
7	3
6	4
5	5
4	6
3	7
2	8
1	9
0	10

The individual's demand curve for a good is a graphical representation of his schedule and is plotted from the schedule. This is done in Figure 2.1.[1]

The aggregate demand for a good is the total alternative quantities per time period that all individuals in the market would be willing to purchase at all relevant prices. Aggregate demand is a function of the same variables that determine an individual's demand; but in addition it obviously depends on the number of potential buyers in the market.

If we are given the demand schedule for individuals in a market, we can derive the total demand schedule by adding, at each alternative price, the quantities that each of the buyers will be willing to take. We shall demonstrate this for a market that consists of two buyers:

TABLE 2.2

(1) P	(2) q_{d1}	(3) q_{d2}	(4) = (2) + (3) Q_d
1	8	4	12
2	6	3	9
3	4	2	6

[1]In Chapter 1 we stated that the usual procedure is to plot the independent variable on the horizontal axis and the dependent variable on the vertical axis. In economics, price — which is usually the independent variable — is plotted on the vertical axis. This convention is due to Alfred Marshall, the great British economist, who in his discussion of supply envisioned the quantity as being the variable adjusted by the firm in response to given market prices. He then defined demand in terms of the demand price (the price people were willing to pay for a given quantity as a dependent variable), partly for consistency with his treatment of supply and partly because he identified price with the subjective satisfaction (utility) the consumer derives from a given quantity.

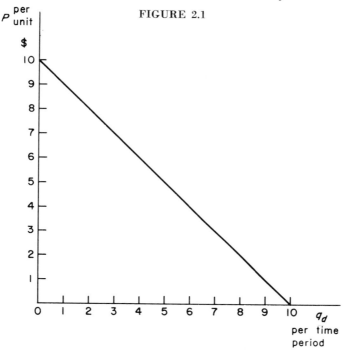

FIGURE 2.1

The aggregate demand curve can be derived in two ways: first, by simply plotting the aggregate demand schedule; second, by a horizontal aggregation of the individual demand curves. The latter method is demonstrated in Figure 2.2.

SHIFTS IN DEMAND

When the price of a good changes, resulting in a change in the quantity purchased, this is referred to as a change in quantity demanded. When there is a change in one of the variables impounded in the *ceteris paribus* assumption, a new price-quantity relationship results. This is referred to as a change (or shift) in demand and is represented graphically as an up-ward-to-the-right movement for an increase in demand and a downward-to-the-left movement for a decrease.

In Figure 2.3 we show the original demand curve as DD, and we assume an increase in demand due to, say, an increase in income. The shifted demand curve is $D'D'$. Thus, an increase in demand can be looked at in two different ways: first, at the level OP_1, consumers used to be willing to purchase OQ_1 units; after the increase they are willing to purchase OQ' units. Second, before the increase consumers were willing to pay a price

FIGURE 2.2

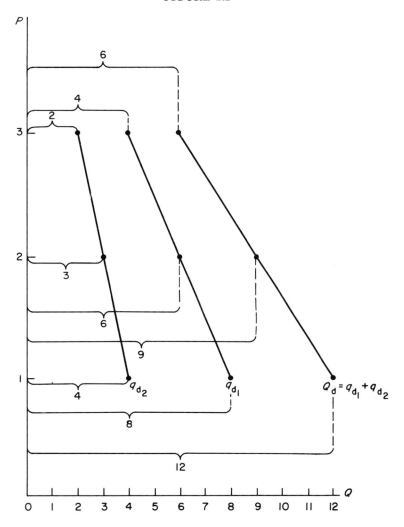

of OP_1 for OQ_1 units; after the increase they are willing to pay a price of OP' for OQ_1 units.

We also show in Figure 2.3 a change in quantity demanded. Suppose price changes from OP_1 to OP_2 when DD is the relevant schedule. (We shall discuss some possible reasons for this later.) This causes the quantity purchased to change from OQ_1 to OQ_2.

FIGURE 2.3

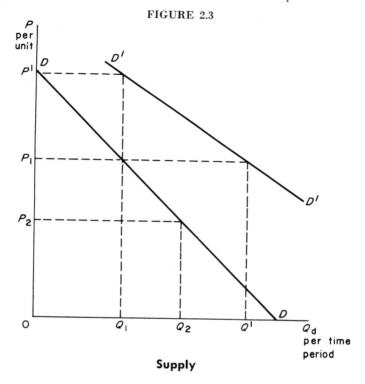

Supply

An individual producer's supply of a good is the alternative quantities per time period he would be willing to put on the market at all relevant prices. His supply of the good is a function of the following variables: the price of the good and costs of production.[2] If we wish to isolate the relationship between the quantity supplied and price of the good, we make the *ceteris paribus* assumption; that is, we assume the other factors are held constant at some given level.

In functional notation, the supply relationship can be written as

$$q_s = S(P_x, C) \tag{2.4}$$

where q_s = quantity supplied

P_x = price of the good

C = a catchall variable representing all those factors influencing costs of production

[2]The relationship between costs of production and supply will be explained in more detail in Chapter 6.

With the *ceteris paribus* assumption, we can write

$$q_s = S(P) \; cet. \; par. \tag{2.5}$$

The individual producer's supply schedule presents his supply of the good in tabular form. If the relationship between price and quantity supplied is the following:

$$q_s = -2 + 2P \tag{2.6}$$

the supply schedule will be the one presented in Table 2.3.

TABLE 2.3

$q_s = -2 + 2P$

P ($ per unit)	q_s (units per time period)
10	18
9	16
8	14
7	12
6	10
5	8
4	6
3	4
2	2
1	0
0	0

FIGURE 2.4

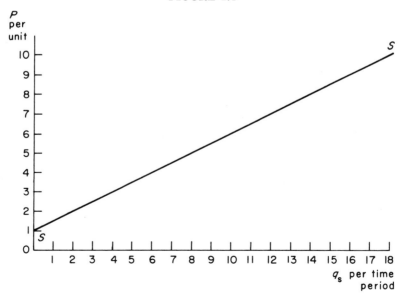

FIGURE 2.5

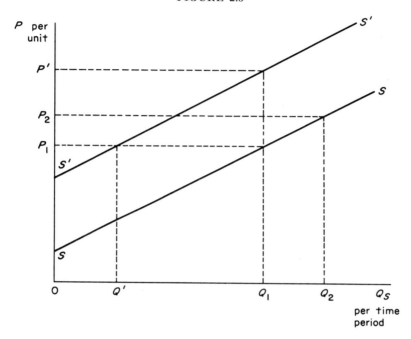

The supply curve is analogous to the demand curve. It is a graphical representation of the supply schedule and is shown in Figure 2.4.

The aggregate supply schedule of a good is the total alternative quantities per time period that all producers of this particular good would be willing to put on the market at all relevant prices. It is a function of the same variables as an individual's supply of a good, but in addition is a function of the number of producers. It can be derived by summing the supply schedules of individual firms in the same way as we derived the aggregate demand schedule by summing individual demand schedules.[3]

The aggregate supply curve is simply a graphical representation of the aggregate supply schedule. It can also be derived from the horizontal summation of the supply curves of the individual firms.

A shift in supply occurs when one of the factors held constant by the *ceteris paribus* assumption changes. An increase in supply means that for all relevant prices producers are now willing to supply more to the market; a decrease in supply means the opposite. We demonstrate a decrease in supply in Figure 2.5, where *SS* represents the original supply and *S'S'* the new one. At a price of P_1 producers originally were willing to supply

[3]Some modifications to this will be discussed in Chapter 9.

OQ_1; after the decrease they want to supply only OQ'. Looked at in another way, the decrease in supply means that for a quantity of OQ_1, producers, before the shift, were willing to accept a minimum price of OP_1 and now they must get at least OP'.

A change in quantity supplied (as distinct from a change in supply) is also shown in Figure 2.5. If price changes from OP_1 to OP_2 and the relevant supply schedule is *SS*, we have an increase in *quantity* supplied (as distinct from an increase in supply); that is, quantity increases from OQ_1 to OQ_2 as we move along the supply curve.

Determination of Price

PERFECT COMPETITION

A market is a perfectly competitive one if the following conditions exist:

1. The numbers of buyers and sellers are sufficiently numerous so that no one of them exerts a significant influence on the price of the good.

2. The good is a homogeneous one; that is, consumers are indifferent among the outputs of the firms in the market.

3. There is no interference with the free determination of price or with entry into or exit out of the market either through collusion among firms or consumers or by government intervention.

4. Producers and consumers have knowledge of prices and quantities.[4]

The presence of these conditions implies that over some time span, the price for any product or factor of production will be the same throughout the market.

PURE COMPETITION

Economists sometimes utilize the concept of pure competition that rests on assumptions 1–3 above, but does not assume either perfect knowledge or the market-locking mechanism described in footnote 4 to ensure its approximate results. This concept would appear less than useful since in the presence of *complete* ignorance the market would consist of individual buyers facing individual sellers in monopolistic isolation; hence enough

[4]It is not necessary to assume perfect knowledge in the sense that each producer and each consumer is aware of all prices and quantities in the market. It is sufficient to assume that there are enough buyers who are acquainted with more than one seller so that there is a locking together of the market by the actions of such individuals in buying from the cheapest seller and selling factor services to the highest bidders. For a more detailed discussion of this point, see George Stigler, "Perfect Competition, Historically Contemplated," *Journal of Political Economy*, Vol. LXV, no. 1 (February 1957).

knowledge must be assumed to give substance to competition in the old-fashioned sense of rivalry among sellers and buyers in the market. The absence of perfect knowledge or, at a minimum, a mechanism that approximates its results means that prices in a market need not be the same for a given commodity even over time; in fact, the concept of a market becomes vague since it is usual to say that a market exists when a uniform price prevails for a homogeneous good or factor.

THE USE OF ECONOMIC MODELS

Perfect competition is one of the "models" used in economic analysis. A model, as used in economics, is a simplified picture of some part of the economy and should capture its most significant features. Like a good caricature, it should emphasize the salient characteristics and omit the less important ones. Therefore, although we recognize that our model of perfect competition is "unrealistic" in the sense that it is not a detailed picture of the workings of actual markets, it serves to point up the crucial elements in the operation of many real markets. The validity of this model, as of any other, is in its ability to predict behavior in the real world. Thus, the degree of reality of the model is in no way a measure of its usefulness; as a matter of fact, the simpler the model — in the sense of requiring less information for its use — the more useful it will be, given its predictive power.

Although our model of perfect competition is not intended to mirror the real world, it may be helpful to bear in mind some examples of actual markets that approach this model. Some of these are organized stock markets, such as the New York and the American Stock Exchanges; organized commodity markets, such as the New York Coffee and Sugar Exchange; and auction markets, such as the kind at which rare paintings are sold.

EQUILIBRIUM PRICE

The word "equilibrium" means such a balance of forces that there is no tendency for the system to change. We can distinguish between stable and unstable equilibriums. A stable equilibrium means that should a disturbance occur to a system in equilibrium, forces will be set up that will tend to return the system to equilibrium. In an unstable equilibrium, a disturbance to equilibrium will set up forces that will cause the system to move still further away from equilibrium.

We illustrate these terms in Figure 2.6, in which we show a ball balanced on the top of an inverted bowl and resting at the bottom of the bowl. The first, shown in Figure 2.6a, represents unstable equilibrium: if we push the

FIGURE 2.6

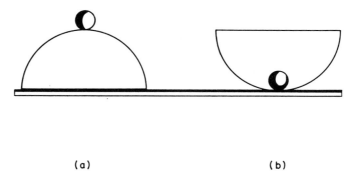

(a)   (b)

ball away from equilibrium, it will roll down the side of the bowl and
away from the initial position. In Figure 2.6b the ball, if disturbed, will
tend to return to equilibrium.

Stable equilibrium in a perfectly competitive market exists when the
prevailing market price will tend to be maintained if the underlying
supply and demand conditions remain unchanged. We illustrate this
with the following example: A market for a product X consists of 1000
consumers, all of whom have demand schedules represented by $q_d = 10$
$- P$ (see Table 2.1), and 1000 suppliers, all with supply schedules repre-

FIGURE 2.7

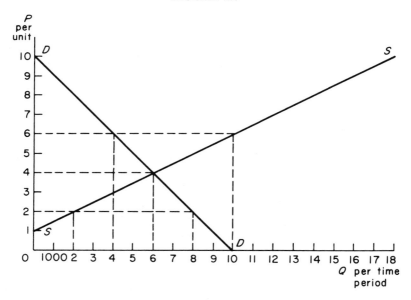

sented by $q_s = -2 + 2P$ (see Table 2.3). Thus, the aggregate demand schedule can be written as

$$Q_d = 10,000 - 1000P \qquad (2.7)$$

and the aggregate supply schedule as

$$Q_s = -2000 + 2000P \qquad (2.8)$$

These market schedules are presented in tabular form in Table 2.4 and graphically in Figure 2.7.

TABLE 2.4

P ($ per unit)	Q_d (units per time period)	Q_s (units per time period)
10	0	18,000
9	1,000	16,000
8	2,000	14,000
7	3,000	12,000
6	4,000	10,000
5	5,000	8,000
4	6,000	6,000
3	7,000	4,000
2	8,000	2,000
1	9,000	0
0	10,000	0

$$Q_d = 10,000 - 1000P$$
$$Q_s = -2000 + 2000P$$

The equilibrium price is at the level at which the demand and supply curves cross; that is, when demand and supply are equal. Recall that, in algebraic terms, this amounts to the simultaneous solution of the demand and supply equations. Since

$$Q_d = 10,000 - 1000P$$

and

$$Q_s = -2000 + 2000P$$

at the intersection of the demand and supply curves

$$Q_d = Q_s$$

Therefore, $10,000 - 1000P = -2000 + 2000P$

$$3000P = 12,000$$

$$P = \$4 \text{ per unit}$$

Through substitution in either the Q_d or the Q_s equation, we can determine the corresponding value of Q:

$Q_d = 10,000 - 1000$ (4)
$Q_d = 6000$ units per time period

or

$Q_s = -2000 + 2000$ (4)
$Q_s = 6000$ units per time period

It is not sufficient merely to state that the equilibrium price is determined by the algebraic or graphical solution of the supply and demand equations. We must specify how, in an actual market, price would be forced to this equilibrium level. We shall describe the mechanism for the attainment of equilibrium by selecting a market as close to perfect competition as is known in the real world — an auction at which potential buyers and sellers are in close contact.

This kind of market can operate in the following fashion: The suppliers make known to the auctioneer the quantities they are willing to supply at a specific price. The auctioneer then relates this information to the demanders. The demanders, in turn, inform the auctioneer of the quantities they are willing to purchase at that price. No sales, we shall see, take place until a price is reached at which the total quantity that suppliers are willing to sell is just equal to the total quantity that demanders wish to buy. By referring to Table 2.4 and Figure 2.7, we can see how this equilibrium price is reached.

Assume that when the auction convenes, the suppliers inform the auctioneer that they are willing to supply 10,000 units at a price of $6 per unit. Consumers, upon receipt of this information, respond to the auctioneer that at $6 per unit, they are willing to purchase 4000 units. Thus, there is an excess of supply over demand of 6000 units at $6 per unit. If sales were allocated by the auctioneer on the basis of order of bids of the suppliers or on a prorated basis, it would become obvious to the sellers that not all of them would be able to sell all they want to at $6. Each supplier, acting individually, thinks that by decreasing price by just a little he will be able to dispose of all he wants to.[5] Thus, a process of competitive price reduction ensues. Each time one supplier reduces price slightly there are two effects: first, the total quantity consumers are willing to buy increases as some increase the amounts

[5]The student is reminded that perfect competition assumes a homogeneous good and that each seller supplies only a small part of the total market — in our case, only 1/1000. Thus, a very slight price decrease is sufficient to ensure to any individual supplier that he will be able to increase his sales. We shall further explore this point in Chapter 6.

they are willing to buy at the now lower price, and others enter the bidding for the first time; in other words, there is a movement down the aggregate demand curve away from the $6 level. Second, after each shading in price, suppliers are willing to offer less to the market, and there is a downward movement along the total supply curve.

Therefore, as the price shading continues, the excess of demand over supply gets smaller. Finally, when the suppliers inform the auctioneer that they are willing to sell 6000 units at $4 per unit, equilibrium will be attained, since there is no motive for further price cutting as the demanders are willing also to buy 6000 units at $4. In order to test his understanding of this market mechanism, the student should be able to describe how the equilibrium price of $4 would be reached if suppliers started their offers at $2 per unit.

TOTAL, AVERAGE, MARGINAL, AND ELASTICITY CONCEPTS AS APPLIED TO DEMAND

3

Review of Concepts

In Chapter 1 we defined total, average, and marginal concepts and discussed the relationships among them. We now apply these concepts to demand.

Total revenue is equal to price times quantity:

$$TR = PQ \tag{3.1}$$

FIGURE 3.1

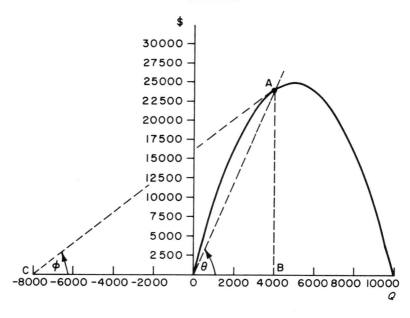

Average revenue is equal to total revenue divided by quantity:

$$AR = \frac{TR}{Q} = \frac{PQ}{Q} = P \tag{3.2}$$

Discrete marginal revenue is defined as

$$MR = \frac{\Delta TR}{\Delta Q} \tag{3.3}$$

FIGURE 3.2

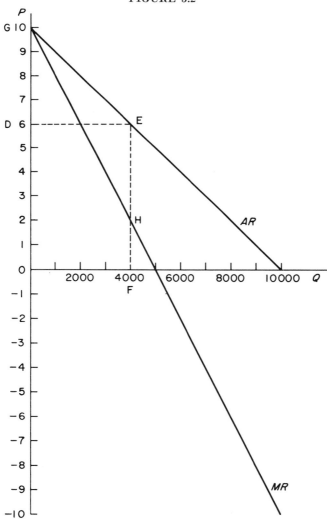

Continuous marginal revenue is defined as

$$MR = \frac{dTR}{dQ} \qquad (3.4)$$

In Table 3.1 are *TR*, *AR*, discrete and continuous *MR* for the demand function:

$$Q_d = 10,000 - 1000P \qquad (2.7)$$

Total revenue is shown graphically in Figure 3.1 and average revenue and continuous marginal revenue are shown in Figure 3.2.

As was shown in Chapter 1 with reference to costs, *AR* at 4000 units of output can be measured graphically as the slope of the line *OA* — that is, *AB/OB* or $\measuredangle \theta$ in Figure 3.1: $24,000/4000 units = $6/unit. Continuous *MR* at 4000 units can be measured as the slope of line *AC*, that is, *AB/BC* or $\measuredangle \phi$: $24,000/12,000 units = $2/unit.

In Figure 3.2, *TR* for 4000 units can be derived from the *AR*-curve by measuring the area *ODEF* ($6 per unit × 4000 units = $24,000), or it can be determined by finding the area under the *MR*-curve up to 4000 units, *OGHF*.*

We shall now apply the elasticity concept to the specific case of demand. *Demand elasticity* measures the responsiveness of quantity demanded to a change in price. There are five important determinants of elasticity:

1. The availability of substitutes for the good. If a commodity has substitutes, when there is an increase in its price, consumers will shift to the substitutes. The greater the number of substitutes and the closer they are, the more elastic will be the demand.

2. The proportion of income spent on the good. If expenditure on a good represents a large percentage of income, an increase in the price of the good will lower the consumer's real income substantially and cause him to react sharply in readusting his expenditures.

3. If a commodity is complementary to another considerably more expensive one, then the responsiveness of its demand to a change in price will be less than it would otherwise be. For example, if a tape recorder costing $400 has been purchased in the recent past and now the price of a roll of tape goes from $5 to $6, this represents a 20% in-

---

*In Table 3.1 we have $MR = 10 - (Q/500)$. We may find the area under this curve by integration as follows:

$$\int_0^{4000} 10 - \frac{Q}{500}\, dQ = \left[10Q - \frac{Q^2}{1000} \right]_0^{4000} = 24,000$$

TABLE 3.1

(1) P	(2) Q_d	(3) TR	(4) AR	(5) Continuous MR	(6) Discrete MR
$10	0	$ 0	$10	$10	
					$9
9	1,000	9,000	9	8	
					7
8	2,000	16,000	8	6	
					5
7	3,000	21,000	7	4	
					3
6	4,000	24,000	6	2	
					1
5	5,000	25,000	5	0	
					−1
4	6,000	24,000	4	−2	
					−3
3	7,000	21,000	3	−4	
					−5
2	8,000	16,000	2	−6	
					−7
1	9,000	9,000	1	−8	
					−9
0	10,000	0	0	−10	

(1) and (2) fit the equation $Q_d = 10{,}000 - 1000P$

(3) = (1) × (2); $TR = P \times Q_d$

(4) = (3) ÷ (2); $AR = \dfrac{TR}{Q_d} = \dfrac{P \times Q_d}{Q_d} = P$

(5) is derived as follows:

$$Q_d = 10{,}000 - 1000P$$
$$P = 10 - \frac{1}{1000} Q_d$$
$$TR = Q_d P = 10Q - \frac{1}{1000} Q_d^2$$
$$MR = \frac{dTR}{dQ} = 10 - \frac{Q_d}{500}$$

(6) is derived as $MR = \dfrac{\Delta TR}{\Delta Q}$

crease in tape cost. But as a proportion of the combined cost per re-
cording of the machine time and tape, this increase is much less significant.

4. Durable commodities will tend to be more elastic than nondurable
commodities for the reason that they are usually replaced before they
have completely worn out in the physical sense. A car or a TV set can
usually be made to do a bit more service with appropriate maintenance.

Further, durable commodities are storable and can be purchased for future use when the price is propitious.

5. Demand tends to be more elastic over a longer than a shorter time period because consumers have the opportunity to become aware of existing alternatives and to adjust their purchases to a price change. This is particularly true when some complementary product is involved that also needs to be replaced for the adjustment to be made; for example, if electricity were to decline in price relative to gas, in the long run when gas ranges had worn out and people could buy electric ranges, the response to the change in the price of electricity would be much greater than in the short run when gas ranges were not yet depreciated.

The coefficient of elasticity at a point on the demand schedule is computed as

$$E_d = \frac{dQ/Q}{dP/P} = \frac{dQ}{dP} \cdot \frac{P^*}{Q} \qquad (3.5)$$

Arc elasticity between two points on a demand curve is measured as

$$E_d = \frac{\Delta Q/(Q_1 + Q_2)}{\Delta P/(P_1 + P_2)} = \frac{\Delta Q}{\Delta P} \cdot \frac{P_1 + P_2}{Q_1 + Q_2} \qquad (3.6)$$

To show the *relationship between TR and elasticity*, we start with the definition of total revenue:

$$TR_1 = PQ$$

*The student should note that, because of the convention of placing the independent variable, P, on the vertical axis, the first term, dQ/dP, in the elasticity formula is the reciprocal of the slope of the demand curve, dP/dQ. The tangent $\measuredangle \phi = dP/dQ$ but E requires $dQ/dP = 1/dP/dQ$. There is, of course, no reason why we could not compute a measure of the responsiveness of P to a change in Q. This measure would

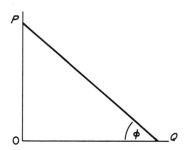

be written as $(dP/dQ)(Q/P)$; which variable is considered dependent is determined by the context of the particular problem. In a later chapter we shall find it convenient to define the elasticity of average cost as $(dQ/dAC)(AC/Q)$, even though it would be more usual to consider Q the independent variable.

Assume a change in price, ΔP, and a resulting change in quantity demanded equal to ΔQ.

$$TR_2 = (P + \Delta P)(Q + \Delta Q)$$

Multiplying out, we have

$$TR_2 = PQ + \Delta P \Delta Q + \Delta PQ + \Delta QP$$

The change in TR is

$$\Delta TR = TR_2 - TR_1 = \Delta P \Delta Q + \Delta PQ + \Delta QP$$

Now let ΔP and ΔQ approach zero and we have

$$dTR = dPdQ + dPQ + dQP$$

Now note that dP and dQ are extremely small quantities, say $1/100,000$ and $1/500,000$. If we multiply them, we get a very much smaller quantity. In the example above it is $1/50,000,000,000$ which is close enough to zero so that we can ignore it. We therefore write

$$dTR = dPQ + dQP \tag{3.7}$$

The point elasticity formula may be written as

$$E_d = \frac{dQ \times P}{dP \times Q} \tag{3.8}$$

and the numerator and denominator are always of opposite signs; that is, when $dP > 0$, $dQ < 0$ and when $dP < 0$, $dQ > 0$. Thus,

$$
\begin{array}{ccc}
 & A & B \\
\text{if } E > 1, & (dQ \times P) > & (dP \times Q) \\
\text{if } E = 1, & (dQ \times P) = & (dP \times Q) \\
\text{if } E < 1, & (dQ \times P) < & (dP \times Q)
\end{array}
$$

If we consider a price rise, the "B" term above is positive and the "A" term negative and since dTR is the sum of the "A" and "B" terms, TR will fall when $E > 1$, remain constant when $E = 1$, and rise when $E < 1$. If we consider a price fall, the "B" term is negative and the "A" term positive. Again, since dTR is equal to the sum of these terms, TR will rise when $E > 1$, remain constant when $E = 1$, and fall when $E < 1$. When demand is inelastic the direction of change of TR is always the same as that of price, and when demand is elastic the direction of change of TR is always opposite to the change in price.

We may return to equation (3.7) and derive an extremely useful *relationship among MR, AR, and E.*

$$dTR = dPQ + dQP \tag{3.7}$$

We divide both sides by dQ:

$$\frac{dTR}{dQ} = \frac{dPQ}{dQ} + P$$

Since dTR/dQ is MR, we can rewrite

$$MR = \left(\frac{dP}{dQ}\right)Q + P* \tag{3.9}$$

Since

$$E_d = \frac{dQ \times P}{dP \times Q} \quad \text{and} \quad \frac{1}{E_d} = \frac{dP \times Q}{dQ \times P}, \quad P\left(\frac{1}{E_d}\right) = \left(\frac{dP}{dQ}\right)Q$$

We may now rewrite equation (3.8) as

$$MR = P\left(\frac{1}{E_d}\right) + P \quad \text{or} \quad P\left(1 + \frac{1}{E_d}\right) \tag{3.9a}$$

where it is to be remembered that $E < 0$.

FIGURE 3.3

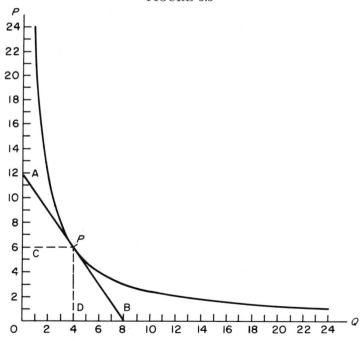

*This, it should be noted, is a relationship already obtained in Chapter 1, equation 1.36.

A Geometrical Interpretation of Point Elasticity

If a function is presented graphically, there is a time-saving method of obtaining graphically the elasticity at a point on the function. We can demonstrate this technique with the use of Figure 3.3, ignoring the numbers on it for the present. We know that the formula for point elasticity of demand is

$$E_d = \frac{dQ}{dP} \cdot \frac{P}{Q} \tag{3.5}$$

If we want to find the elasticity of the curve at point P, we can substitute in this formula as follows:

$$E_d = \frac{CP}{AC} \cdot \frac{OC}{OD}$$

Since $CP = OD$, we can write

$$E_d = \frac{CP}{AC} \cdot \frac{OC}{CP}$$

The CP's cancel out and we are left with

$$E_d = \frac{OC}{AC} \tag{3.10}$$

In words, this is the ratio of (1) the price to (2) the difference between the vertical axis intercept of the tangent at P and the price.[1]

We can use this ratio to compute the value of the elasticity coefficient at point P, whose coordinates are $Q = 4$ and $P = 6$. (The function graphed in Figure 3.3 is $PQ = 24$; the same one as Figure 1.5.) Substituting, we get

$$E_d = \frac{6}{6} = 1 \tag{3.11}$$

Notice that this interpretation does not explicitly take into consideration the sign of the coefficient, but gives us the absolute value of elasticity. Thus, it must be kept in mind that if the function is downward sloping, the coefficient will be negative. At point P, then, the elasticity is -1.

The elasticity at a point on a straight-line function can be obtained graphically, too. Assume the linear demand relationship

$$Q_d = 8 - \left(\frac{2}{3}\right)P \tag{3.12}$$

[1]Elasticity at point P can also be derived as $E_d = (dQ/dP)(P/Q) = (DB/DP)(OC/OD)$. Since $DP = OC$, $E_d = DB/OD = 4/4 = 1$.

This is the function shown in Figure 3.3 as the line AB. The elasticity at P would simply be

$$E_d = \frac{OC}{CA} \tag{3.13}$$

where OC is the price at point P and CA is the price-axis intercept of the function. Therefore, the elasticity of a downward-sloping linear demand function is equal to -1 at the mid-point of the line (as at P); $|E| > 1$ and increases as C moves closer toward A, and $|E| < 1$ and decreases as C approaches O.

Other Elasticities

Supply elasticity is defined as the responsiveness of quantity supplied to a change in price and is measured as

$$E_s = \frac{dQ_s/Q_s}{dP/P} = \frac{dQ_s}{dP} \cdot \frac{P}{Q_s} \tag{3.14}$$

for point elasticity, and

$$E_s = \frac{\Delta Q_s/(Q_{s1} + Q_{s2})}{\Delta P/(P_1 + P_2)} = \frac{\Delta Q_s}{\Delta P} \cdot \frac{P_1 + P_2}{Q_{s1} + Q_{s2}} \tag{3.15}$$

for arc elasticity.

Cross elasticity relates the responsiveness of quantity demanded of commodity A to a change in the price of another commodity B. It is measured as

$$E_{AB} = \frac{dQ_A/Q_A}{dP_B/P_B} = \frac{dQ_A}{dP_B} \cdot \frac{P_B}{Q_A} \tag{3.16}$$

for point elasticity. For arc elasticity it is measured as

$$E_{AB} = \frac{\Delta Q_A/(Q_{A1} + Q_{A2})}{\Delta P_B/(P_{B1} + P_{B2})} = \frac{\Delta Q_A}{\Delta P_B} \cdot \frac{P_{B1} + P_{B2}}{Q_{A1} + Q_{A2}} \tag{3.17}$$

The concept of cross elasticity permits us to give a precise definition to substitutes and complements. Goods that are substitutes for one another will have a coefficient of cross elasticity between them that is positive. Analogously, complementary goods will have a negative coefficient.

Some Special Cases of Elasticity

There are several unique elasticity cases that will be used in later chapters. If a function is of the form $P = a$, where a is a constant, the graphical picture of the function will be a horizontal line, parallel to the quantity-axis, at the level of a. In Figure 3.4, we have drawn the function $P = 7$. The elasticity at any point or between any two points on this function, or

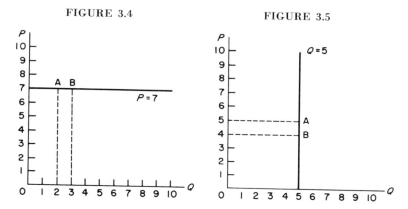

FIGURE 3.4   FIGURE 3.5

any function of the type $P = a$ approaches infinity. Demonstrating this first with the arc formula between points A and B,

$$E = \frac{Q}{P} \cdot \frac{P_1 + P_2}{Q_1 + Q_2} = \frac{1}{0} \cdot \frac{7+7}{2+3} \rightarrow \infty \tag{3.18}$$

To get the point elasticity at point A, we have

$$E = \frac{dQ}{dP} \cdot \frac{P}{Q} = \rightarrow \infty \cdot \frac{2}{7} \rightarrow \infty \tag{3.19}$$

Whenever the denominator of a quotient approaches zero, the quotient approaches infinity. It is obvious that, since the slope of a horizontal demand or supply curve is zero, the reciprocal of the slope approaches infinity and the elasticity of such a line will approach infinity.[2]

A second special case is elasticity along a vertical line that is parallel to the price-axis; that is, a function of the form $Q = a$, where a is a constant. Such a function is pictured in Figure 3.5, where it is assumed $Q = 5$. If we compute elasticity between points A and B, we get

$$E = \frac{\Delta Q}{\Delta P} \cdot \frac{P_1 + P_2}{Q_1 + Q_2} = \frac{0}{1} \cdot \frac{5+5}{5+4} = 0 \tag{3.20}$$

Thus, the elasticity all along a vertical demand or supply curve will be zero.

[2]For the sake of brevity, we shall state in the future that the elasticity of such a function is infinity, instead of approaching infinity.

The last special case we shall consider is the elasticity of a function of the form $PQ = a$, where a is a constant. We have already considered such a case in the function $PQ = 24$, presented in Table 1.4, Figure 1.5, and Figure 3.3. If we compute the elasticity between any two points or at any point on this curve, the coefficient is equal to -1, and this would be true for all functions of this type. (The graph of this kind of function is a rectangular hyperbola.)

The reason for the constant elasticity of -1 is quite simple. Remember that the basic purpose of the coefficient of demand or supply elasticity is to compare the percentage change in quantity with the initiating percentage change in price, $\dfrac{\% \text{ change in } Q}{\% \text{ change in } P}$. Since the product of P and Q must stay the same, any percentage change in P must be offset by an equal percentage change in Q in the opposite direction.[3]

Some Applications of the Elasticity Concept

AGRICULTURAL PRICE SUPPORTS

Two important methods by which a government can guarantee a price to farmers are purchase and subsidy programs. The purchase program can operate in the following manner, which is explained in Figure 3.6a. We assume the equilibrium market price to be OP_1 and the corresponding quantity OQ_1, while the government agrees to support the higher-than-equilibrium price of OP_2. Farmers sell to consumers all they can at OP_2; the government purchases at OP_2 whatever consumers do not buy. Notice that under typical supply conditions, farmers wish to sell more at OP_2 than at OP_1.

[3]This is demonstrated rigorously on page 49. The student familiar with double-log paper will realize that when the function $PQ = 24$ is plotted on such paper, it will be a straight line with a slope of -1. Furthermore, there is a family of constant elastic functions, of which $PQ = a$ is only one member. The basic function for this family of curves is $x^n y = a$, and $E = -n$. Therefore, in our example above, we have $P^1 Q = 24$ and $E = -1$.

We can prove this as follows:

$$x^n y = a$$
$$y = ax^{-n}$$
$$\frac{dy}{dx} = -nax^{-n-1}$$
$$E = \frac{dy}{dx} \cdot \frac{x}{y} = (-nax^{-n-1})\frac{x}{y}$$
$$E = \frac{-n(ax^{-n})}{y} = -n\frac{y}{y} = -n$$

FIGURE 3.6

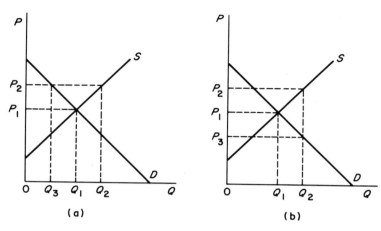

(a)   (b)

The subsidy program is demonstrated in Figure 3.6b. Once again, the initial equilibrium is OP_1 and OQ_1 and the support price is OP_2. Farmers sell at the market price; then the government pays a subsidy to the farmers on each unit sold equal to the difference between the support price and the market price. OQ_2 represents the amount that farmers wish to sell at OP_2; but consumers are willing to pay only OP_3 per unit for OQ_2 units. Therefore, the new market price is OP_3 and the subsidy per unit is P_2P_3.

With the use of the elasticity concept, we can compare the costs of these two programs to the consumer and to the government.

	Purchase Program	Subsidy Program
In the absence of price supports	$TR_1 = OP_1 \cdot OQ_1$	$TR_1 = OP_1 \cdot OQ_1$
With supports		
Expenditure by consumers	$TR_c = OP_2 \cdot OQ_3$	$TR_c = OP_3 \cdot OQ_2$
Expenditure by government	$TR_g = OP_2 \cdot Q_2Q_3$	$TR_g = OQ_2 \cdot P_2P_3$
Total	$TR_2 = OP_2 \cdot OQ_2$	$TR_2 = OP_2 \cdot OQ_2$

If $E_d > 1$,* $OP_2 \cdot OQ_3 < OP_1 \cdot OQ_1$ and $OP_3 \cdot OQ_2 > OP_1 \cdot OQ_1$; or $OP_3 \cdot OQ_2 > OP_1 \cdot OQ_1 > OP_2 \cdot OQ_3$. Therefore, $OP_3 \cdot OQ_2$ (expenditure by consumers under the subsidy program) is greater than $OP_2 \cdot OQ_3$ (expenditure by consumers under the purchase program). We have shown that combined expenditures of consumers and the government will be the same under both programs; thus since consumer expenditure

*We assume that $E_d > 1$ both above and below P_1.

is greater under the subsidy program, the cost to the government is less.

If $E_d < 1$,† $OP_2 \cdot OQ_3 > OP_1 \cdot OQ_1$ and $OP_3 \cdot OQ_2 < OP_1 \cdot OQ_1$ or $OP_2 \cdot OQ_3 > OP_1 \cdot OQ_1 > OP_3 \cdot OQ_2$. Therefore, $OP_2 \cdot OQ_3 > OP_3 \cdot OQ_2$; the consumer expenditure is greater with the purchase program and the cost to the government is less.[4]

EFFECTS OF AN EXCISE TAX

Elasticities of demand and supply are important in determining the effects of an excise tax. This is illustrated with reference to Figure 3.7, where SS and DD represent the initial supply and demand schedules and OP_1 and OQ_1 the equilibrium price and quantity. We assume the tax levied to be equal to P_2P_3, and we can show the effects of the tax by shifting the supply curve vertically upward by the amount of the tax.

FIGURE 3.7

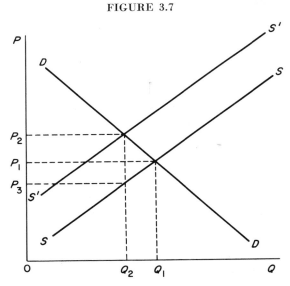

This new supply curve, $S'S'$, shows the prices suppliers must receive for selling various alternative quantities. Thus, after the imposition of the tax, OP_2 is the price paid by consumers and OQ_2 the quantity purchased. OP_3 is the price kept by producers — OP_2 minus the tax of P_2P_3. Whether consumers or producers physically pay the tax makes no

†We assume that $E_d < 1$ both above and below P_1.
[4]The storage costs incurred by the government are ignored; if they are taken into consideration, even if $E_d < 1$, the purchase program may cost the government more than the subsidy program.

difference; this graphical technique — which seems to indicate it is the producers who pay the tax — will show the effect of the tax.[5]

No matter who actually pays the tax, we are interested in its *incidence*. The concept of incidence simply asks: If a tax of t per unit is imposed upon a commodity, when all adjustments have been made and the market is once again in equilibrium, how will the price paid by the consumer (including the tax if it is imposed on the consumer) compare with the price before the tax was imposed? Analogously, how does the price per unit (after tax if the tax is imposed upon the producer) compare with the price received before the tax was imposed?

The incidence concept does not take into account the loss to consumers who now buy less of the commodity because of its higher price, nor the possible loss in revenue to the producer.

The entire burden of the tax is borne by consumers if the price increases by the amount of the tax; analogously, producers bear the entire burden if price, inclusive of the tax, remains the same, for the price then kept by the producers is equal to the original price less the tax.[6] Usually, the tax burden is shared in some degree by producers and

[5]There is another graphical technique that will give the same results; the demand curve is shifted vertically downward by the amount of the tax. Thus, OP_2 is the price paid by consumers including the tax; OP_3 is the price paid by consumers exclusive of the tax; and OQ_2 is the quantity purchased after the tax is levied. This technique indicates it is

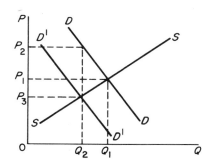

the consumer who actually makes the tax payment. The consumer pays OP_3 per unit to the producer, but his total cost per unit is OP_3 + the tax = $OP_3 + P_2P_3 = OP_2$. Note that in both cases quantity goes to Q_2. We see, therefore, that the result is identical in the case where we impose the tax on producers or on consumers.

[6]An example will help to clarify this concept. If a $1.00 tax were imposed upon consumers and as a result of the change in their demand the equilibrium price went from $5.00 to $4.50, the price to consumers, including the tax, would now be $5.50. Clearly, 50¢ or 50% of the tax is borne by consumers. Also producers were getting $5.00 per unit and are now getting $4.50; hence, they bear 50¢ or 50% of the tax.

consumers together; this is the situation in Figure 3.7. We now investigate the determinants of the share of the tax borne by each group.

Let $T = \text{tax} = P_2P_3 = \Delta P + \Delta P'$
$\Delta P = OP_2 - OP_1$
$\Delta P' = OP_1 - OP_3$
$\Delta Q = OQ_2 - OQ_1$
$a = $ slope of DD (in absolute terms)
$b = $ slope of $SS = $ slope of $S'S'$ (in absolute terms)

Therefore,

$$a = \frac{OP_2 - OP_1}{OQ_1 - OQ_2} = \frac{\Delta P}{-\Delta Q}$$

$$b = \frac{OP_1 - OP_3}{OQ_1 - OQ_2} = \frac{\Delta P'}{-\Delta Q}$$

$$\Delta P = a(-\Delta Q)$$

$$\Delta P' = b(-\Delta Q)$$

$$T = \Delta P + \Delta P' = a(-\Delta Q) + b(-\Delta Q)$$

$$\frac{\Delta P}{\Delta P + \Delta P'} = \text{the proportion of the tax borne by consumers}$$

$$= \frac{a(-\Delta Q)}{a(-\Delta Q) + b(-\Delta Q)} = \frac{a}{a + b} \tag{3.21}$$

We see the share of the tax borne by consumers is based on the relative slopes of the demand and supply schedules. We now wish to translate this into terms of elasticities of demand and supply:

$$E_d = \frac{1}{a} \cdot \frac{OP_1{}^*}{OQ_1} \quad \text{and} \quad E_s = \frac{1}{b} \cdot \frac{OP_1}{OQ_1} \text{ (where } E_d \text{ and } E_s \text{ are in absolute terms)}$$

These can be rewritten as

$$E_d a = \frac{OP_1}{OQ_1} \quad \text{and} \quad E_s b = \frac{OP_1}{OQ_1}$$

or

$$a = \frac{OP_1}{E_d OQ_1} \quad \text{and} \quad b = \frac{OP_1}{E_s OQ_1}$$

We can substitute as follows:

$$\frac{a}{a + b} = \text{percentage of tax paid by consumers}$$

$$= \frac{OP_1/E_d OQ_1}{OP_1/E_d OQ_1 + OP_1/E_s OQ_1}$$

*This is the point elasticity formula and means we assume a small tax.

This expression can be rewritten in simplified form. First we simplify the denominator; then we invert it and multiply it by the numerator:

$$\frac{OP_1}{E_dOQ_1} + \frac{OP_1}{E_sOQ_1} = \frac{OP_1(E_sOQ_1) + OP_1(E_dOQ_1)}{E_dE_s(OQ_1)^2} = \frac{OP_1(E_dOQ_1 + E_sOQ_1)}{E_dE_s(OQ_1)^2}$$

$$\frac{a}{a+b} = \frac{OP_1}{E_dOQ_1} \cdot \frac{E_dE_s(OQ_1)^2}{OP_1(E_dOQ_1 + E_sOQ_1)} = \frac{E_sOQ_1}{E_dOQ_1 + E_sOQ_1} = \frac{E_s}{E_d + E_s}$$

(3.22)

Therefore, the share borne by consumers will tend to be greater the higher is E_s or the smaller is E_d.

The student should be able to determine the relationship between the share of the tax paid by producers and the elasticities of supply and demand.

EXCHANGE-RATE DEPRECIATION

The field of international trade provides another interesting example of the application of the elasticity concept. When a country has a deficit in its balance of trade (when the value of its imports exceeds the value of its exports), it may decide to try to reduce this deficit by depreciation; that is, reducing the value of its currency in terms of the currencies of other countries. A hypothetical example will show the rationale. Let us assume a two-country world consisting of the United States and Great Britain and an exchange rate between the dollar and pound of $4.00 = £1. We further assume that the British have a deficit in their balance of trade that they hope to reduce by depreciating the pound to $3.00 = £1. What will be the probable initial effects? First, American importers will be able to buy British goods at lower prices, since £1's worth of British goods will now cost $3.00 rather than $4.00. Second, British importers will find that American goods are higher priced; before the depreciation it cost them £1 to buy $4.00's worth of American goods and now the same goods will cost them £1⅓.

The success of the depreciation in correcting the balance of trade deficit depends on the elasticity conditions. If the elasticity of demand of Americans for British goods is greater than 1, then at the lower prices for British goods, Americans will spend more on British goods; and if the elasticity of British demand for American goods is also greater than 1, at the higher prices for American goods, British importers will spend less on these goods. Therefore, the value of British exports will increase, the value of their imports will decrease, and the trade balance will be narrowed.

However, if the two demand elasticities are both less than 1, the deficit can be enlarged by the depreciation. At the lower prices for

British goods, Americans will buy more, but their total expenditure for them will be less; and at the higher prices for American goods, Britons will buy less, but their total expenditure for them will increase. If this type of situation exists, appreciation — rather than depreciation — may be needed to reduce a trade deficit.[7]

COBWEB THEOREM

In our usual supply-demand analysis we assume that suppliers and demanders react to changes in price instantaneously. It is interesting, however, to investigate the process by which equilibrium is achieved in a market in which there is a lag in adjustment of supply to demand. Specifically in markets for agricultural commodities, once the crop has been planted, the supply is, in effect, fixed for the year or some other time period (ignoring weather and other natural phenomena). A change in price of the commodity can be reacted to only after a one-year lag — at the next planting season.

Let us assume an agricultural market in which an equilibrium price and quantity have been established at OP_1 and OQ_1. (See Figure 3.8a.) Farmers plant an amount OQ_1 but during the growing season the demand curve shifts to $D'D'$ and the amount OQ_1 sells at a price per unit of OP_2. Now based upon a price of OP_2, farmers plant OQ_2, which fetches a price of OP_3; this induces farmers to plant OQ_3; and so on.

Notice that price and quantity fluctuate around their new equilibrium values of OP_1' and OQ_1' and that the fluctuations diminish over time so that equilibrium is finally reached. Figure 3.8b shows a case in which the fluctuations around equilibrium are divergent: they increase in magnitude over time and so equilibrium is never reached. Figure 3.8c shows a case in which the fluctuations are of constant magnitude, but again equilibrium is not reached.

It is important to investigate the conditions under which such a lagged system will approach equilibrium — that is, of the type shown in Figure 3.8a. If the movement is to converge, the decrease in price, AB, which gives rise to the quantity change, CB, must be greater than the change in price, CE, that results from the quantity change. In other words, $AB/CB > EC/CB$. Since AB/CB is the slope of the supply curve and

---

[7]If the supply elasticities in the two countries are infinite (the prices of the goods in the two countries remain constant), depreciation will improve the deficit if the sum of the two demand elasticities is greater than 1; this is known as the Marshall-Lerner condition. If the supply elasticities are less than infinity, the condition is a more complicated one. For a proof of the Marshall-Lerner condition and for a statement of the more general condition, see Charles P. Kindleberger, *International Economics* (3d ed.; Homewood, Ill.: Irwin, 1963), Appendix D.

EC/CB is the slope (disregarding sign) of the demand curve, we can see that for convergence the slope of the supply curve must be greater than the slope of the demand curve (disregarding sign).

FIGURE 3.8

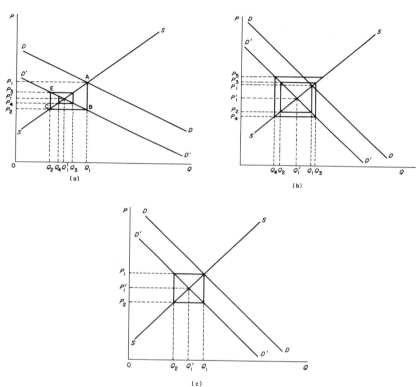

This condition can be stated in terms of elasticities of demand and supply.[8]

$$| E_d | = \frac{CB}{EC} \cdot \frac{OP_1}{OQ_1} * \quad \text{and} \quad | E_s | = \frac{CB}{AB} \cdot \frac{OP_1}{OQ_1}$$

[8]Note that we are using the absolute values of the elasticity coefficients.
*See note 6 above. Further, with straight-line demand and supply curves, the slopes are the same along the curves. This permits us to state our conditions for divergence and convergence at the point of intersection of the curves where the point is the same for both curves and the elasticity measures will have a common term.

Therefore, $\dfrac{OP_1}{OQ_1} = |E_d| \cdot \dfrac{EC}{CB}$ and $\dfrac{OP_1}{OQ_1} = |E_s| \cdot \dfrac{AB}{CB}$

Since $\dfrac{OP_1}{OQ_1} = \dfrac{OP_1}{OQ_1}$, $|E_d| \cdot \dfrac{EC}{CB} = |E_s| \cdot \dfrac{AB}{CB}$

We know that for convergence, $AB/CD > EC/CB$. Therefore, it must also hold that if there is to be convergence, $|E_d| > |E_s|$.

THE THEORY
OF DEMAND:
CLASSICAL UTILITY
APPROACH

4

Economists have not generally been content with noting the observable general inverse relationship between the price of a commodity and the amount purchased by consumers; nor have they been satisfied simply to postulate negative sloping demand curves based on this evidence. They have attempted, rather, to explain the observable demand phenomena through an analysis of the way in which consumers attempt in some "optimum" sense to spend their incomes on the commodities available to them.

We shall review the classical utility approach to consumer equilibrium in this chapter and the indifference curve approach in the following chapter.

Total and Marginal Utility

It is assumed that the consumer has a finite money income, I, and that he is faced by n commodities, $a, b, \ldots, n$, with prices $P_a, P_b, \ldots, P_n$. It is also assumed that the consumer will want to spend his income in such a manner as to maximize the benefit or satisfaction he receives from it.[1] We give the name "utility" to the subjective quantity the individual is assumed to maximize. Given that the individual is consuming quantity A of the commodity a per unit of time, he will then be receiving TU_a (*total utility*), which is the total satisfaction to him of consuming this amount.

We may also ask what is the change in total utility at any quantity due to changing quantity consumed by one unit — this measure is

[1]This is the rationality postulate that assumes that the consumer is aware of the alternatives facing him, that he is capable of evaluating them, and that his choices will be consistent.

called *marginal utility* (*MU*) and is defined for the discrete case as

$$MU = \frac{\Delta TU}{\Delta Q} \tag{4.1}$$

or for continuous functions as

$$MU = \frac{dTU}{dQ} \tag{4.1a}$$

TABLE 4.1

TOTAL AND MARGINAL UTILITY SCHEDULES

(1) A	(2) TU_a	(3) $MU_a = \dfrac{dTU_a}{dQ_a}$	(4) $MU_a = \dfrac{\Delta TU_a}{\Delta Q_a}$
0	0		
			100
1	100	95	
			90
2	190	85	
			80
3	270	75	
			70
4	340	65	
			60
5	400	55	
			50
6	450	45	
			40
7	490	35	
			30
8	520	25	
			20
9	540	15	
			10
10	550	5	
			0
11	550	-5	

Column 2 is derived from the equation $TU_a = 105A - 5A^2$.
Column 3 is continuous MU which can be derived from the equation $dTU_a/dA = 105 - 10A$.
Column 4 is discrete MU and is equal to $\Delta TU_a/\Delta A$.

Table 4.1 gives examples of total utility and marginal utility schedules. Total utility and continuous marginal utility are shown graphically in Figures 4.1 and 2. In graphical terms, *MU* represents the slope of the total utility schedule.

Notice that the *MU* column shows *MU* declining as quantity increases. Although this is the assumption usually made, it is conceivable that for certain goods there is increasing *MU* over an initial range. For example, if a good is more useful when used in sets, then *MU* will increase — at least at first.[2]

The so-called Law of Diminishing Marginal Utility — the proposition that as an individual consumes more units of a commodity the increments

FIGURE 4.1

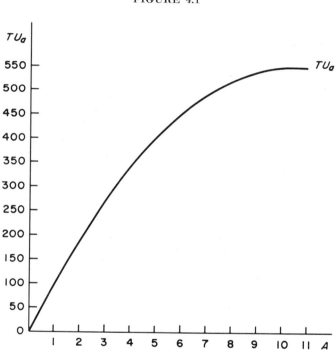

to his satisfaction due to receiving an additional unit decrease — was generally defended on subjective grounds as being intuitively obvious because the desire for a particular good will become relatively satiated.

The classical utility approach depends upon a concept of cardinal utility; that is, it is assumed that the consumer not only knows that he prefers A to B but he can give numerical expression to his desires which permits him to say he prefers A, say, twice as much as B.

[2]Of course, if a single unit of the good is useless by itself, then the correct unit of measurement would be the set — for example, shoes and gloves.

FIGURE 4.2

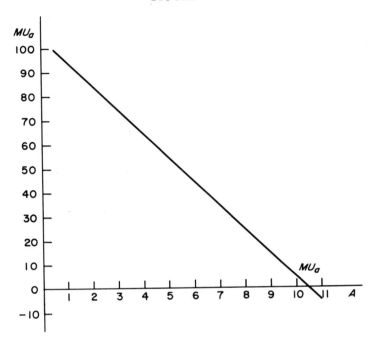

Consumer Equilibrium

Given our rationality assumption and the "law" of diminishing marginal utility, we have the following two equilibrium conditions for the consumer:

$$\text{Condition 1:} \quad I = AP_a + BP_b + CP_c + \cdots + NP_n \qquad (4.2)$$

Some of the quantities $A \ldots N$ may be zero. Further, we may include saving by having as one of our terms the present marginal utility of the future yield of earning assets as a ratio of the current price and as another the marginal utility of idle balances as a ratio of their cost in terms of the forgone rate of return. Condition 1 simply states that all income will be spent.

$$\text{Condition 2:} \quad \frac{MU_a}{P_a} = \frac{MU_b}{P_b} = \frac{MU_c}{P_c} = \cdots = \frac{MU_n}{P_n} \qquad (4.3)$$

Condition 2 states that in equilibrium the MU's must be in proportion to prices. We have said that the rational consumer will want to maximize his satisfaction, given his income and preferences. Condition 2 will be, therefore, a true equilibrium condition if it is impossible for the consumer, once having achieved this condition, to increase TU by rearranging his expenditures. The assumption of diminishing marginal utility guarantees that, when condition 2 is fulfilled, the consumer has indeed a distribution of expenditures where he is maximizing utility.[3] We can see this in an example. Suppose that an individual consumes only A and B, which are substitutes for one another, and that he is allocating his expenditures so that $MU_a/P_a = MU_b/P_b$ and that the numerical values are $50/\$2 = 100/\$4$. If the individual removes \$1 from A he will lose 25 utils, but when he increases his consumption of B, MU_b will fall and he will gain something less than 25 utils. Therefore, since the gain is less than the loss, he should not undertake this rearrangement of expenditure — he was already at a maximum.

We can show this point somewhat differently by assuming that the consumer is distributing his expenditures so that $MU_a/P_a \neq MU_b/P_b$. In numerical terms assume $60/\$2 > 80/\$4$. In this case the individual is receiving 30 marginal utils per dollar of expenditure on A and 20 utils per dollar of expenditure on B. Clearly, if he shifts a dollar of his expenditure from B to A he will lose 20 utils and gain approximately 30. Hence he will rearrange his expenditure so that $MU_a/P_a = MU_b/P_b$, and if we assume diminishing MU this guarantees he is at maximum TU.

Derivation of Demand Schedule from MU Schedule

Using the concept of marginal utility it is possible to explain the shape of a demand schedule as well as shifts in demand. We demonstrate this with the use of a numerical example. A consumer, who spends his entire income on two goods, A and B, has utility schedules for these goods as shown in Table 4.2, where the schedules for good A are the same as those in Table 4.1.[4]

If the price of good A is initially \$5 and of good B \$10, and if the consumer's income is \$130, the initial equilibrium quantities the consumer will purchase are 10 units of A and 8 units of B. To prove that this is

---

[3]See Appendix 4A for a further discussion of diminishing MU and the mathematical conditions for maximizing TU.

[4]These utility schedules are assumed to be independent of each other. If the goods were extremely good substitutes, then the level of the utility schedule of one good would depend on the quantity consumed of the other. This is also true of complementary commodities. The difficulty of handling such schedules numerically is one of the reasons for using an alternative approach — the indifference curve approach — which is discussed in the next chapter.

a true equilibrium situation, we show that conditions 1 and 2 are met:

Condition 1: $\qquad I = AP_a + BP_b$

$\qquad\qquad\quad \$130 = (10)\$5 + (8)\$10$

Condition 2: $\qquad \dfrac{MU_a}{P_a} = \dfrac{MU_b}{P_b}$

$\qquad\qquad\quad \dfrac{5}{\$5} = \dfrac{10}{\$10}$

$\qquad\qquad\qquad 1 = 1$

TABLE 4.2

TOTAL AND MARGINAL UTILITY SCHEDULES

(1)	(2)	(3)	(4)	(5)	(6)	(7)	(8)	(9)
A	TU_a	MU_a	$\dfrac{MU_a}{P_a}\ (=\$5)$	B	TU_b	MU_b	$\dfrac{MU_b}{P_b}\ (=\$10)$	$\dfrac{MU_b}{P_b}\ (=\$8)$
1	100	95	$19	1	40	38	$3.80	$4.75
2	190	85	17	2	76	34	3.40	4.25
3	270	75	15	3	108	30	3.00	3.75
4	340	65	13	4	136	26	2.60	3.25
5	400	55	11	5	160	22	2.20	2.75
6	450	45	9	6	180	18	1.80	2.25
7	490	35	7	7	196	14	1.40	1.75
8	520	25	5	8	208	10	1.00	1.25
9	540	15	3	9	216	6	0.60	0.75
10	550	5	1	10	220	2	0.20	0.25
11	550	−5	−1	11	220	−2	−0.20	−0.25

Column 2 is derived from the equation $TU_a = 105A - 5A^2$.
Column 3 is continuous MU_a derived from the equation $MU_a = 105 - 10A$.
Column 6 is derived from the equation $TU_b = 42B - 2B^2$.
Column 7 is continuous MU_b derived from the equation $MU_b = 42 - 4B$.

These results can be obtained graphically from Figure 4.3. In the left-hand portion of the graph is plotted $MU_a/\$5$ (with the horizontal axis read from right to left) and in the right-hand portion, $MU_b/\$10$. Instead of showing these as functions of the quantities of A and B, we have placed dollars on the horizontal axis. Thus, to plot the combination $A = 8$, $MU_a/\$5 = 5$ from Table 4.2, the horizontal axis coordinate is $40 as 8 units of A in dollar terms is $40 (= \$5 \times 8$ units). Since we assumed an income of $130, equilibrium exists when $MU_a/\$5 = MU_b/\$10$ and the absolute distance between the two schedules is $130 (line AB).[5]

[5]See Appendix 4B for an algebraic solution.

FIGURE 4.3

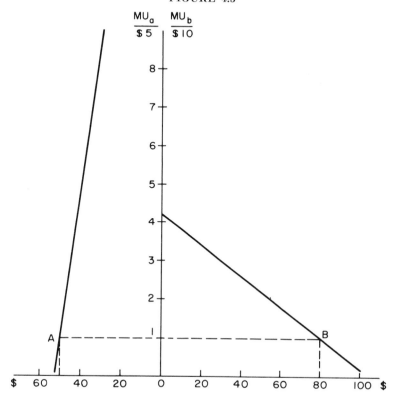

We now assume a change in P_b from \$10 per unit to \$8. If the consumer desired to continue buying the same quantities of A and B as before, he would be spending \$114:

$$AP_a + BP_b = \text{Expenditure}$$
$$(10 \cdot \$5) + (8 \cdot \$8) = \$114$$

Therefore, there has been an increase in the consumer's purchasing power of \$16. Notice that neither equilibrium condition is being fulfilled:

Condition 1: $\$130 > 10 \cdot \$5 + 8 \cdot \$8 = \$114$

Condition 2: $\dfrac{5}{\$5} < \dfrac{10}{\$8}$

As a result of both the change in relative prices and the resulting increase in purchasing power, the consumer must once again redistribute his income of $130 in such a way as to maximize his satisfaction. This new equilibrium position is achieved when the consumer buys (rounded off to 3 decimal places) 10.325 units of A and 9.797 units of B, since with these quantities both equilibrium conditions are being fulfilled:

Condition 1: $AP_a + BP_b = I$
$$(10.325)\$5 + (9.797)\$8 = \$51.625 + \$78.376 = \$130$$

Condition 2: $\dfrac{MU_a}{P_a} = \dfrac{MU_b}{P_b}$

$$\dfrac{1.75}{\$5} = \dfrac{2.812}{\$8}$$

$$0.35 = 0.35$$

These results can be obtained approximately from Figure 4.4, where the MU_a/P_a schedule is the same as in Figure 4.3, but the MU_b/P_b is

FIGURE 4.4

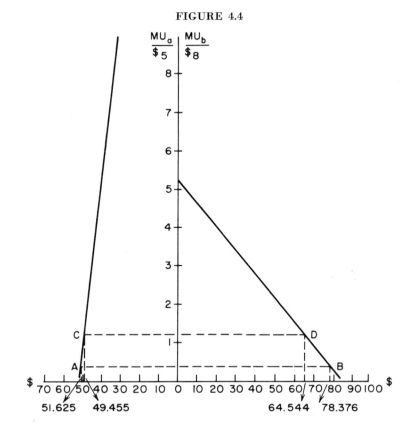

now based upon $P_b = \$8$. The line $AB = \$130$; thus equilibrium occurs when \$51.625 is spent on A (or \$51.625/\$5 = 10.325 units of A) and \$78.376 is spent on B (or \$78.376/\$8 = 9.797 units of B).[6]

It is possible to derive the demand schedule for good B by assuming a sufficient number of prices for B and then determining the equilibrium quantity of B that the consumer would buy at each of these prices.

Marginal utility analysis explains why a demand curve shifts when a change occurs in the consumer's income or tastes, or in the price of some other commodity. Thus, in our numerical example, when the price of B changed, the demand for A also changed. Analogously, if the individual's income increased, there would be an increase in the demand for both A and B provided they were not inferior goods.[7] A change in tastes would influence the level and shape of the marginal utility curve and, at any particular price, the consumer would desire a different quantity of the commodity affected.

Income and Substitution Effects

For analytical purposes it is sometimes useful to break down the effect of the price change into its two component parts:

the effect due to the change in relative prices alone — *the substitution effect* — and

the effect due to the change in purchasing power resulting from the change in the price of one good — *the income effect*.

In order to distinguish between these two, we first assume (simply as an expository device) that, after the reduction in price of good B, a tax is levied on the consumer equal to the increase in his purchasing power — \$16; and we determine the quantities of goods A and B he would purchase in response to this change in relative prices alone.

After determining these quantities, we next assume that a subsidy of \$16 is paid to the consumer. We make this assumption in order to determine what the effects of an increase in income of \$16 is on the quantities of A and B purchased if no change in relative prices occurs.

When the \$16 tax is levied on the consumer, income again becomes \$114; however, equilibrium is not achieved since the second condition is not being satisfied:

Condition 1: $\$114 = (10)\$5 + (8)\$8$

[6]See Appendix 4B for the algebraic solution.
[7]See the final section in this chapter.

Condition 2: $\dfrac{5}{\$5} < \dfrac{10}{\$8}$

$$1 < 1.25$$

The consumer, by transferring a dollar of expenditure away from A, will lose 1 util; and by spending that dollar on B will gain approximately 1.25 utils. This is a net increase of roughly 0.25 util.

The equilibrium resulting from the efforts of the consumer once again to distribute his expenditures in an optimum fashion would be 9.891 units of A and 8.068 units of B. This is demonstrated in Figure 4.4. When $114 is spent on both goods (line CD), equilibrium is achieved when $49.455 is spent on A (or $49.455/$5 = 9.891 units of A) and $64.544 on B (or $64.544/$8 = 8.068 units of B).[8]

When the $16 subsidy is paid to the consumer, a new disequilibrium situation arises, this time because the first equilibrium condition is violated:

Condition 1: $130 > (9.891)$5 + (8.068)$8 = $114

Condition 2: $\dfrac{6.090}{\$5} = \dfrac{9.728}{\$8}$

$$1.22 = 1.22$$

Clearly, if the individual is to maintain an equality between MU_a/P_a and MU_b/P_b, he must spend more on both A and B.[9] As we saw before, the final new equilibrium position is reached when the consumer buys 10.325 units of A and 9.797 units of B.

Before proceeding further, we summarize the income and substitution effects of the decrease in the price of B.

| | Quantities | |
	Good A	Good B
(1) Initial equilibrium	10.000	6.000
(2) Equilibrium after reduction in P_b to $8 and compensating decrease in income of $16	9.891	8.068
(3) Equilibrium after a subsidy of $16 (final equilibrium)	10.325	9.797
(4) Substitution effect = (2) − (1)	−0.109	+2.068
(5) Income effect = (3) − (2)	+0.434	+1.729
(6) Net effect = (3) − (1) = (4) + (5)	+0.325	+3.797

An Aside on Income Effects

For a given good the substitution effect is always negative: as P decreases, quantity increases and vice versa. The income effect, however, may be

---

[8]See Appendix 4B for the algebraic solution.
[9]This rests on our assumption of diminishing MU for both goods.

either positive or negative, depending on the consumer's tastes. For most goods, when the consumer experiences an increase in income, he will buy more of the commodity; these are called "superior" goods. There are some goods (oleo, potatoes, bread, subway rides) that are considered "inferior" by many consumers who buy less of these goods when incomes rise.

Since the net effect of a price change is the sum of the income and substitution effects[10] and since the substitution effect is always in the direction of giving negatively sloping demand curves, it is to the income effect that one must look for a positive reaction of quantity to an increase in price. This would clearly occur if a powerful negative income effect (for an inferior good) were to overpower a weaker substitution effect. Such a good, which would have a positively sloping demand curve, is called a Giffen Good and is discussed in more detail in Chapter 5.

[10]Alfred Marshall, who was responsible for the fullest development of the utility analysis of demand, avoided the complications of income effects by assuming the commodities under discussion to constitute only a small part of a consumer's budget and that one could safely disregard the consequently unimportant income effects. This was a convenient analytical simplification but it avoided the problem of income effects, instead of solving it. See Appendix 10.

Assume that there are but two commodities, A and B, with prices P_a and P_b and that the individual has an income, I, which he spends on the two commodities.

$$I = AP_a + BP_b \quad \text{Income constraint} \tag{A4A.1}$$

$$U = U(A,B) \quad \text{Utility function} \tag{A4A.2}$$

We may rewrite equation A4A.1 as

$$\frac{I - AP_a}{P_b} = B \tag{A4A.3}$$

and then rewrite equation A4A.2 as

$$U = U\left(A, \frac{I - AP_a}{P_b}\right) \tag{A4A.4}$$

Let

$$\mu_a = \frac{\partial U}{\partial A}$$

and

$$\mu_b = \frac{\partial U}{\partial B}$$

We now compute

$$\frac{dU}{dA} = \mu_a + \mu_b\left(-\frac{P_a}{P_b}\right) \tag{A4A.5}$$

Set this expression equal to zero:

$$\mu_a + \mu_b\left(-\frac{P_a}{P_b}\right) = 0 \tag{A4A.6}$$

$$\mu_a = \mu_b\left(\frac{P_a}{P_b}\right) \tag{A4A.7}$$

or

$$\frac{\mu_a}{\mu_b} = \frac{P_a}{P_b} \tag{A4A.8}$$

or

$$\frac{\mu_a}{P_a} = \frac{\mu_b}{P_b} \tag{A4A.9}$$

Expression A4A.9 which states that for utility to be maximized the marginal utility of the goods consumed must be proportional to their prices, is a necessary but not a sufficient condition for maximization of utility. This condition ensures only that an extreme — either a maximum or a minimum — has been found. To ensure a maximum a "second order" condition must be fulfilled (that is, a condition involving second partial derivatives).
Let

$$\mu_{aa} = \frac{\partial^2 U}{\partial A^2}$$

$$\mu_{bb} = \frac{\partial^2 U}{\partial B^2}$$

$$\mu_{ab} = \frac{\partial^2 U}{\partial A \partial B}$$

For a maximum to exist, the following must be true:

$$\frac{d^2 U}{dA^2} = \left[\mu_{aa} + 2\mu_{ab}\left(-\frac{P_a}{P_b}\right) + \mu_{bb}\left(-\frac{P_a}{P_b}\right)^2 \right] < 0$$

$$= \left[\mu_{aa} + 2\mu_{ab}\left(-\frac{P_a}{P_b}\right) + \mu_{bb}\left(\frac{P_a^2}{P_b^2}\right) \right] < 0 \qquad \text{(A4A.10)}$$

Multiply by $(P_b)^2$ and the inequality remains.

$$[(\mu_{aa}P_b^2) - (2\mu_{ab}P_aP_b) + (\mu_{bb}P_a^2)] < 0 \qquad \text{(A4A.11)}$$

If an additive utility function is assumed, so that the utility of each commodity is independent of the utility of the other commodities (this was generally assumed by the founders of utility theory), μ_{ab} would be 0. If then we assume diminishing marginal utility to hold for both commodities, that is, $\mu_{aa} < 0$, $\mu_{bb} < 0$, then the entire expression on the left is negative and the second condition for a maximum is fulfilled. The role of the assumption of diminishing marginal utility is therefore to ensure that the "second order" condition will be met.

It can be seen, however, that in our general utility function this condition could be fulfilled even if $\mu_{aa} > 0$ and $\mu_{bb} > 0$, provided that $\mu_{ab} > 0$ (complements) and the negative middle term were large enough to overpower the end terms. It could also be fulfilled if one commodity displayed diminishing marginal utility and the other did not if the sum of the negative terms were greater (in absolute terms) than the positive terms. On the other hand, if μ_{ab} is negative (substitutes) the entire expression may be positive even when $\mu_{aa} < 0$ and $\mu_{bb} < 0$. From these considerations it is clear that diminishing marginal utility is necessary and sufficient in order that the second order conditions for maximum total utility be fulfilled only in the case of an additive utility function (a function in which the utilities of the goods are assumed independent).

Indifference curve analysis permits a less restrictive assumption to be made. This will be discussed in Chapter 5.

The initial equilibrium levels of A and B can be determined algebraically in the following way. The equations for the MU schedules are (see Table 4.2)

$$MU_a = 105 - 10A \qquad (A4B.1)$$

$$MU_b = 42 - 4B \qquad (A4B.2)$$

Therefore

$$\frac{MU_a}{P_a} = \frac{MU_a}{\$5} = 21 - 2A \qquad (A4B.3)$$

$$\frac{MU_b}{P_b} = \frac{MU_b}{\$10} = 4.2 + 0.4B \qquad (A4B.4)$$

We assumed that the consumer spends his entire income on these goods:

$$\$5A + \$10B = \$130 \qquad (A4B.5)$$

or

$$\$5A = \$130 - \$10B$$

$$A = 26 - 2B \qquad (A4B.6)$$

Substituting in equation A4B.3, we have

$$\frac{MU_a}{P_a} = 21 - 2(26 - 2B) = 21 - 52 + 4B = -31 + 4B \qquad (A4B.7)$$

In equilibrium $MU_a/P_a = MU_b/P_b$. Therefore,

$$-31 + 4B = 4.2 + 0.4B \qquad (A4B.8)$$

Solving for B, we have

$$4.4B = 35.2$$

$$B = 8$$

Substituting in equation A4B.6, we have

$$A = 26 - 2(8)$$

$$A = 10 \qquad (A4B.9)$$

To determine the new equilibrium quantity of A and B after P_b changes from \$10 to \$8, we can follow the same procedure as above:

$$MU_a = 105 - 10A \qquad (A4B.1)$$

$$MU_b = 42 - 4B \qquad (A4B.2)$$

$$\frac{MU_a}{P_a} = \frac{MU_a}{\$5} = 21 - 2A \qquad \text{(A4B.3)}$$

$$\frac{MU_b}{P_b} = \frac{MU_b}{\$10} = 5.25 - 0.5B \qquad \text{(A4B.4)}$$

$$\$5A + \$8B = \$130 \qquad \text{(A4B.5)}$$

or

$$\$5A = \$130 - \$8B$$

$$A = 26 - 1.6B \qquad \text{(A4B.6)}$$

$$\frac{MU_a}{P_a} = 21 - 2(26 - 1.6B) = 21 - 52 + 3.2B = -31 + 3.2B \qquad \text{(A4B.7)}$$

$$-31 + 3.2B = 5.25 - 0.5B$$

$$3.7B = 36.25$$

$$B = 9.797 \qquad \text{(A4B.8)}$$

$$A = 26 - 1.6(9.797) = 26 - 15.675$$

$$A = 10.325 \qquad \text{(A4B.9)}$$

Once again the same method can be used to determine the substitution effect of the decrease in P_b from \$10 to \$8:

$$MU_a = 105 - 10A \qquad \text{(A4B.1)}$$

$$MU_b = 42 - 4B \qquad \text{(A4B.2)}$$

$$\frac{MU_a}{P_a} = \frac{MU_a}{\$5} = 21 - 2A \qquad \text{(A4B.3)}$$

$$\frac{MU_b}{P_b} = \frac{MU_b}{\$8} = 5.25 - 0.5B \qquad \text{(A4B.4)}$$

$$\$5A + \$8B = \$114 \qquad \text{(A4B.5)}$$

or

$$\$5A = \$114 - \$8B$$

$$A = 22.8 - 1.6B \qquad \text{(A4B.6)}$$

$$\frac{MU_a}{P_a} = 21 - 2(22.8 - 1.6B) = 21 - 45.6 + 3.2B = -24.6 + 3.2B \qquad \text{(A4B.7)}$$

$$-24.6 + 3.2B = 5.25 - 0.5B$$

$$3.7B = 29.85$$

$$B = 8.068 \qquad \text{(A4B.8)}$$

$$A = 22.8 - 1.6(8.068) = 22.8 - 12.909$$

$$A = 9.891 \qquad \text{(A4B.9)}$$

THE THEORY OF
DEMAND:
INDIFFERENCE
CURVE APPROACH

5

Indifference Curves

The indifference curve approach enables us to derive all the theorems concerning consumer behavior that we deduced from utility analysis, using less restrictive assumptions. Furthermore, indifference curve analysis simplifies the solution of certain problems. This analysis depends on the concept of ordinal rather than cardinal utility. *Ordinal utility* is based on the idea that the consumer is capable of ranking quantities according to his preferences without assigning specific preference values to the quantities. In other words, with ordinal utility, the consumer is able to decide whether he prefers combination A to combination B, but not by how much. Because of this virtue, economists prefer the indifference curve approach over the utility approach.

Visualize the following experiment: We endow a consumer with a combination of two goods, X and Y, and ask him a series of questions concerning his preference for alternative combinations of X and Y. For each of the alternative combinations presented to the consumer, he is to decide whether he prefers it to his endowment or if he prefers the endowment to it. We get the results shown in Table 5.1.

If we start with the assumption that X and Y are both commodities (as contrasted with discommodities such as garbage), then clearly the consumer will always prefer a combination that consists of more of both goods to his endowment. Therefore, this particular consumer prefers combinations B, C, D, I, and N to A. Analogously, the consumer will prefer his endowment to all combinations that consist of less of both goods, such as combinations E, F, G, and K.

The consumer's ranking of those combinations containing more of one good and less of the other depends on his individual tastes. Thus, the consumer ranks combinations H, J, L, O, and P equally with his endow-

TABLE 5.1

Combination	X	Y	Ranking (Compared to A)
A (Endowment)	30	15	
B	35	20	+
C	40	16	+
D	56	25	+
E	27	13	−
F	15	14	−
G	10	13	−
H	25	18	=
I	50	17	+
J	10	45	=
K	10	5	−
L	6	75	=
M	25	16	−
N	40	20	+
O	50	9	=
P	15	30	=
Q	45	14	+

ment; he prefers the endowment to combination M, while combination Q is ranked as preferable to the endowment.

In Figure 5.1 we plot and label the different combinations of goods X and Y. Notice that all those combinations that are preferable to the endowment appear to the right and above — that is, northeast of — the endowment combination. Those combinations less preferred are to the left and below — southwest of — point A. And those combinations that yield the same benefit as the endowment may be connected by a smooth curve if we assume that we have presented to the consumer a sufficient number of combinations to sketch in intermediate points. This curve is called an indifference curve and represents all those combinations of X and Y equally preferred by the consumer — that is, the consumer is indifferent among them. If we had started with a different initial endowment, we would have derived a different indifference curve. An infinite number of these curves could be sketched.

With reference to Figure 5.1, we can define the *marginal rate of substitution* between X and Y. MRS_{xy} — which is read "the marginal rate of substitution of X for Y" — is the number of units of Y the consumer would be willing to give up for an additional unit of X to maintain the same level of satisfaction. Therefore,

$$MRS_{xy} = \frac{\Delta Y^*}{\Delta X} \tag{5.1}$$

*We can also define $MRSyx$ as the number of units of X the consumer would be willing to give up for one extra unit of Y; this is equal to $\Delta X/\Delta Y$.

FIGURE 5.1

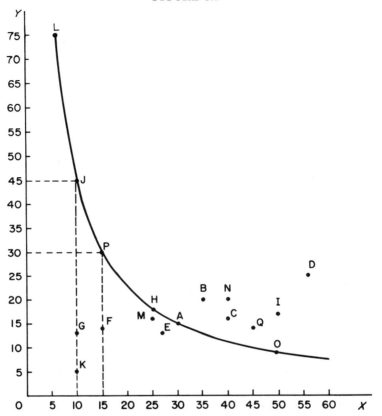

and we see that this is the slope of the indifference curve.[1] Between points J and P,

$$MRS_{xy} = \frac{-15}{5} = -3 \qquad (5.2)$$

When a consumer makes comparisons among combinations of X and Y, he must compare a comparable attribute of the commodities. We call this attribute utility; and we may express it as a function of the quantities of X and Y consumed:

$$U = f(X,Y) \qquad (5.3)$$

[1]Discrete MRS measures the slope between 2 points on an indifference curve, and continuous MRS measures it in the vicinity of a point.

Specifically, we assume the following utility function:

$$U = XY \tag{5.4}$$

A sketch of this function is shown in Figure 5.2. As we showed in Chapter 1, it is possible to draw a contour map reducing such a three-dimensional relationship to two dimensions. The indifference curve of Figure 5.1 is one of the contour lines of the utility surface shown in Figure 5.2. The concept of ordinal utility implies that the consumer is able to tell whether he is higher or lower on the utility hill, but does not require that he know the altitude. In Figure 5.3 we present an *indifference map* that shows some of the infinite number of indifference curves corresponding to this utility hill.[2]

PROPERTIES OF INDIFFERENCE CURVES

1. Indifference curves are nonintersecting.[3]
2. They must be negatively sloping; that is, $\Delta Y/\Delta X < 0$. A positively sloped indifference curve would imply that as a consumer received more of both commodities, his satisfaction would remain the same. This contradicts our assumption of two utility-yielding goods.
3. In the normal case, we assume the (absolute) MRS_{xy} to be declining; that is, moving along an indifference curve from left to right results in

[2] These curves could all be derived from the kind of empirical experiment we have described. We have, however, assumed a function — $U = XY$ — and can, therefore, derive the indifference curves by setting utility equal to different given levels and finding the corresponding combinations of X and Y that yield the given level of utility.
[3] On U_1, satisfaction yielded by $Y_1 + X_1$ = satisfaction yielded by $Y_2 + X_2$.
On U_2, satisfaction yielded by $Y_1 + X_1$ = satisfaction yielded by $Y_2 + X_3$.
Therefore, satisfaction yielded by $Y_2 + X_2$ = satisfaction yielded by $Y_2 + X_3$.

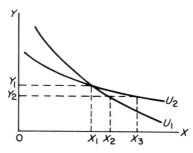

And so the satisfaction yielded by X_2 is equal to that yielded by X_3; hence it is concluded that the individual receives equal satisfaction from more and less of commodity X, which is impossible (if X is satisfaction-yielding).

$| \Delta Y / \Delta X |$ decreasing.[4] As we observe the world around us, we note that people do not practice monomania (the consumption of merely one commodity); and if we assumed an increasing MRS_{xy}, we would be implying

FIGURE 5.2

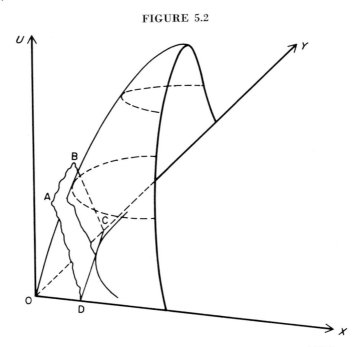

that people acted in this fashion. If we assume a constant MRS_{xy}, we get results that imply consumers acting as monomaniacs or else vacillating between the two goods.

The Budget Line[5]

It is obvious that the consumer would like to reach the highest possible indifference curve. Unfortunately, however, he is prevented from doing this because of his limited resources and the positive prices he must pay for the commodities he consumes. In general terms, the budget con-

[4] $| MRS_{xy} | = | \Delta x / \Delta y |$ would increase moving from left to right and decrease moving from right to left. (See Appendix 5.) In the literature it is customary to talk of declining MRS_{xy} along an indifference curve, where it is understood that this refers to absolute MRS_{xy}.

[5] The budget line is also called the consumption possibility schedule, the line of attainable combinations, and the price line.

FIGURE 5.3

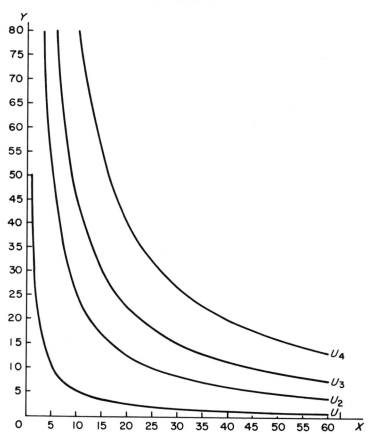

straint can be expressed as

$$I = AP_a + BP_b + \cdots + NP_n \qquad (5.5)$$

In three dimensions, the budget constraint is shown as a plane cutting the utility hill, $ABCD$ in Figure 5.2. In his effort to achieve the highest possible altitude on the utility hill, the consumer may be pictured as moving up the hill until he hits the wall (plane) that represents the budget constraint.

In two dimensions the budget constraint is a straight line of the form

$$Y = \frac{I}{P_y} - \frac{P_x}{P_y} X \qquad (5.6)$$

and is presented in Table 5.2 and Figure 5.4 for an income of $300, $P_x = \$5$ and $P_y = \$10$. In general terms, the slope of the budget line, $\Delta Y/\Delta X$, is $-P_x/P_y$. Thus, for this specific one, the slope is $-\$5/\$10$ or $-1/2$.*

Consumer Equilibrium in Terms of Indifference Curves

We have said that the consumer desires to move up as high as possible on the utility hill but that he is prevented from doing this by the budget wall. Therefore, in these terms, equilibrium will be achieved when the consumer arrives at the highest possible level on his utility hill permitted by the budget constraint (wall).

In terms of a two-dimensional diagram, since the utility hill is represented by the indifference contours and the budget wall by the budget line, equilibrium will be achieved at the point where the consumer has moved to his highest possible indifference curve within the attainable area

*One can derive the slope of the budget line directly from the graph. If a consumer is initially purchasing the combination represented by A and then switches to B, he buys more X and less Y at B than at A. But since total expenditure at A is equal to total expenditure at B, we can write

$$-\Delta Y P_y = \Delta X P_x$$

Therefore,

$$\frac{\Delta Y}{\Delta X} = -P_x/P_y$$

The equation for the budget line can also be derived graphically. OY represents the amount of Y purchased if the consumer spends his entire income on Y. Therefore,

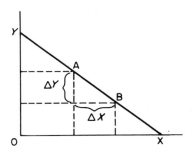

$OY = I/P_y$ and since the formula for a straight line is $y = a + bx$ (the vertical-axis intercept plus the slope times the x-coordinate) we can write

$$Y = \frac{I}{P_y} - \frac{P_x}{P_y}X$$

TABLE 5.2

X	Y
0	30
2	29
4	28
6	27
8	26
10	25
12	24
14	23
16	22
18	21
20	20
22	19
24	18
26	17
28	16
30	15
32	14
34	13
36	12
38	11
40	10
42	9
44	8
46	7
48	6
50	5
52	4
54	3
56	2
58	1
60	0

The X and Y values were obtained from the equation

$$Y = \frac{\$300}{\$10} - \frac{\$5}{\$10} X = 30 - \frac{1}{2} X$$

delimited by the budget line. We show this in Figure 5.5, in which we have redrawn the indifference map of Figure 5.3 and superimposed upon it the budget line of Figure 5.4. The consumer will be in equilibrium when he purchases 30 units of X and 15 of Y. These are the coordinates of the point of tangency between the budget line and U_3 — the highest possible indifference curve the consumer can reach. Although there is only one budget line at any given time, there are an infinite number of indifference curves; thus, with normally shaped curves, there will always be such a tangency point.

Outline of Price Theory

FIGURE 5.4

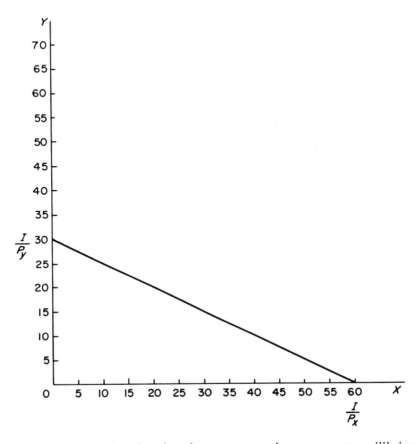

Another way of showing that the tangency point represents equilibrium is to picture first the consumer being somewhere to the left, then somewhere to the right of equilibrium, and then to show how he would always necessarily move toward the tangency point. We may think of the slope of the budget line as being the rate at which the individual can exchange Y for X in the market place. In our example, the slope is $-\$5/\$10$ $(= -P_x/P_y)$ and that means the consumer can exchange $\frac{1}{2}$ unit of Y for 1 unit of X in the market place. The slope of the indifference curve indicates the amount of Y that the consumer would be willing to give up for an additional unit of X. Suppose the consumer is initially at point A and we ask him how much more X he would need in order to be compensated for a loss in Y of 10 units (a change in Y from 25 to 15 units). We find that we would have to give him $6\frac{2}{3}$ units of X to compensate him for this loss of Y.

FIGURE 5.5

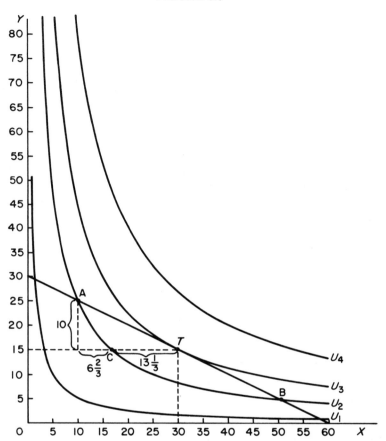

This would bring him from point A to point C along indifference curve U_2. At the prevailing market prices, if the individual were to exchange 10 units of Y, he would be able to receive 20 units of X, which would bring him to point T on the higher indifference curve, U_3. Under these conditions, the consumer will go to the market and move along his budget line to point T, where his subjective valuation of the two goods is the same as the market rate of exchange.

To test your understanding of the equilibrium condition, show that if the consumer is initially at point B, he will necessarily move up the budget line to point T.

Similarity between the Indifference Curve and Utility Approaches. We can now show that the equilibrium condition derived from indifference curve analysis is identical with that derived from utility analysis. Moving from left to right between any two points on an indifference curve, the following is true:

$$-\Delta Y \cdot MU_y = +\Delta X \cdot MU_x \qquad (5.7)$$

That is, the loss in utility from consuming fewer units of one good is just matched by the gain from consuming more of the other good. We can rewrite equation 5.7 as

$$\frac{\Delta Y}{\Delta X} = -\frac{MU_x}{MU_y} \qquad (5.8)$$

In words, this states that the slope of the indifference curve is equal to the ratio of the marginal utility of X to the marginal utility of Y. At the point of equilibrium, the slope of the budget line is equal to the slope of the indifference curve.[6]

Slope of budget line

$$\frac{\Delta Y}{\Delta X} = -\frac{P_x}{P_y}$$

Slope of indifference curve

$$\frac{\Delta Y}{\Delta X} = -\frac{MU_x}{MU_y}^*$$

or

$$\frac{P_x}{P_y} = \frac{MU_x}{MU_y} \qquad (5.9)$$

which can be rewritten as

$$\frac{MU_x}{P_x} = \frac{MU_y}{P_y} \qquad (5.10)$$

And this is the result we obtained from the utility approach.

Cases of Nonnormal Indifference Curves. If two goods are perfect substitutes for one another, an indifference curve for the goods would be of the kind shown in Figure 5.6a. The exact nature of the substitutability is reflected in the slope (MRS_{xy}) of the straight-line indifference curve.[7] If the budget-line slope is equal to the constant MRS_{xy}, then the consumer will

[6]For a proof that the consumer is indeed in equilibrium when the price line and the indifference curve are tangent, see Appendix 4A.

*The indifference map of Figure 5.5 was derived from the function $U = XY$. The student familiar with calculus will see that the slope of an indifference curve *at* a point could be determined from $dY/dX = -UX^{-2}$. Thus, at point A (whose coordinates are $X = 10$ and $Y = 25$), $dY/dX = -250/100 = -2.5$. At B ($X = 50$, $Y = 5$), the slope is $-250/2500 = -.10$. And at T ($X = 30$, $Y = 15$), $dY/dX = -450/900 = -.50$, which is also the slope of the budget line.

[7]If $MRS_{xy} = 1$, then the cross elasticity between these two goods is infinite and we have the uninteresting case of analyzing the substitution between a good and itself.

be satisfied with any combination of X and Y along the budget line. If the slope of the budget line is not equal to MRS_{xy}, the model predicts monomania. The highest possible indifference curve the consumer can

FIGURE 5.6

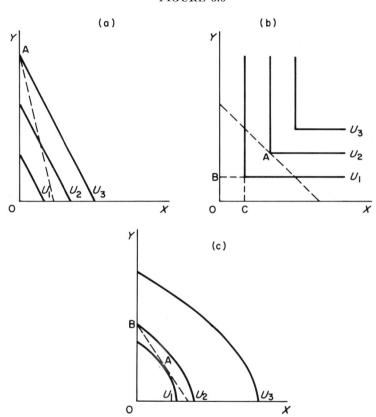

reach will always be on one of the axes, where the consumer is consuming one good to the exclusion of the other; this is indicated by point A in Figure 5.6a.[8]

Figure 5.6b represents a case in which substitution is impossible. The two goods must be used in some fixed proportion indicated by the ratio OB/OC. Equilibrium will always be at a corner of an indifference curve,

[8]The condition for equilibrium is the same as in the normal case, if we restate the equilibrium condition in more general terms:

Immediately to the left of equilibrium: $MU_x/MU_y > P_x/P_y$

Immediately to the right of equilibrium: $MU_x/MU_y < P_x/P_y$

FIGURE 5.7(a)

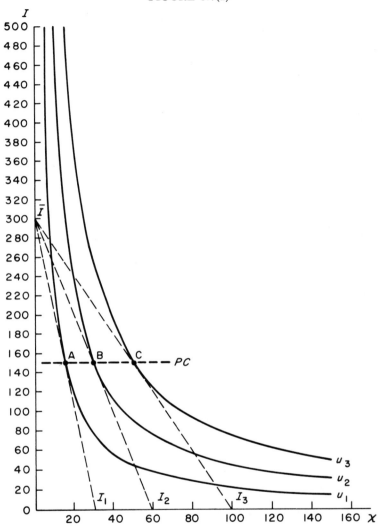

such as *A*. The equilibrium condition is being fulfilled at *A* since the
slope of the vertical segment of the indifference curve is equal to infinity
and, therefore, is greater than the slope of the budget line; and the slope
of the horizontal segment is zero and, therefore, less than the slope of the
budget line.

In Figure 5.6c we show a case of concave indifference curves. A point
of tangency, such as *A*, that shows the consumer buying some of each com-

FIGURE 5.7(b)

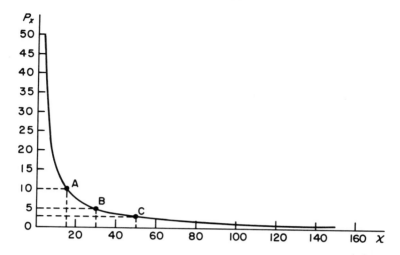

modity is not an equilibrium; it is actually a point of minimum satisfaction.[9] The consumer can always increase satisfaction by moving toward one of the axes to the point, such as B, where he will consume only one commodity and where he will be on the highest possible indifference curve.

Price-Consumption Curve

The ordinal utility approach is completely general and can be expanded to include any number of goods. We can still make use of two-dimensional representation, but the indifference curve technique as developed so far necessitates using only two commodities. We may, however, conceive of the consumer choosing between a particular good and purchasing power — income — which represents command over all other commodities. Thus, in Figure 5.7a, we show good X in the usual fashion on the horizontal axis, and on the vertical axis we plot income, I. The indifference curves drawn show the consumer's preference between good X and I. The vertical axis intercept of the various budget lines is I, which is the consumer's money income — assumed to be constant.

[9]Another way of seeing this is to refer to Appendix 5. For a concave indifference curve, expression A5.4 must be positive, but if this term is positive then the second term on the left must be positive; and Appendix 4A shows that when this is true we have a minimum, not a maximum.

FIGURE 5.8(a)

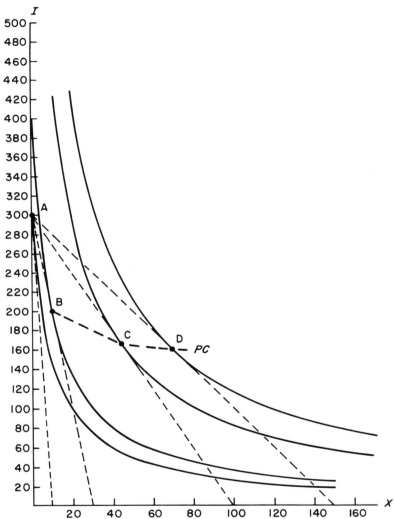

In general terms, the equation for such budget lines is

$$I = \bar{I} - P_x X \qquad (5.11)$$

where I = income spent on all goods excluding X

$\bar{I}$ = total money income, assumed to be constant

P_x = price of good X

X = quantity of good X purchased

FIGURE 5.8(b)

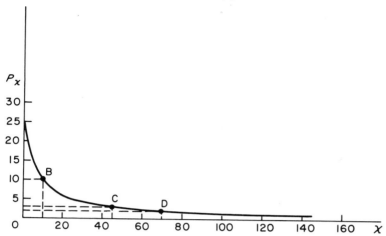

And the slope is simply $-P_x$.

The three budget lines shown in Figure 5.7a are all based on a constant income, $\bar{I}$, of \$300. That is why they have a common vertical-axis intercept. A different price for X was assumed in each case, accounting for the different slopes and the different horizontal-axis intercepts. The horizontal-axis intercept shows the quantity of X that the consumer can buy at a given P_x, when he spends his entire income on X. For budget line I_1, the X-axis intercept is 30 units of X — which means P_x is \$10 (that is, \$300/30). Similarly, budget line I_2 is drawn on the assumption of $P_x = \$5$ and budget line I_3 is based on $P_x = \$3$.

A point of tangency, such as B, represents consumer equilibrium; that is, when the consumer's income is \$300 and $P_x = \$5$, he maximizes his satisfaction by consuming 30 units of X and spending \$150 of his income on all other goods.[10] Notice that total expenditures on X (\$5 × 30 units = \$150) can be obtained from the graph as the difference between the vertical-axis intercept of the budget line, I, and the amount spent on all other goods. Thus, \$300 − \$150 = \$150. Analogously, points A and C represent consumer equilibrium at the respective prices for X of \$10 and \$3.

[10]It is assumed that the consumer is maximizing his satisfaction not only between X and I but with regard to the various goods he purchases with I. In other words, $MU_x/MU_I = P_x$ implies

$$\frac{MU_a}{P_a} = \frac{MU_b}{P_b} = \cdots = \frac{MU_x}{P_x}$$

FIGURE 5.9(a)

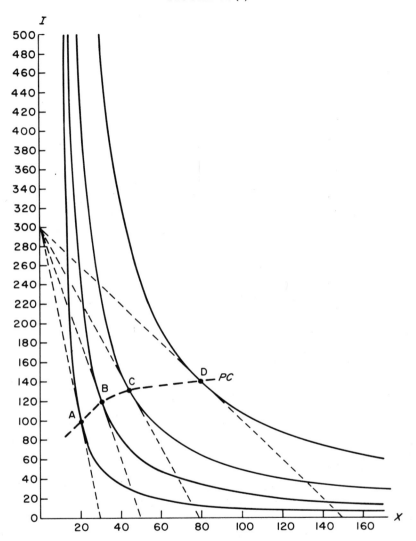

With the use of this technique, it is a fairly simple matter to derive the demand schedule for good X. Recall that the demand schedule for good X shows the $P_x - X$ relationship with tastes (which here is expressed as a constant indifference map), income, and the prices of all other goods held constant. By assuming different levels for P_x, we can find the equilibrium quantities of X corresponding to the various budget

FIGURE 5.9(b)

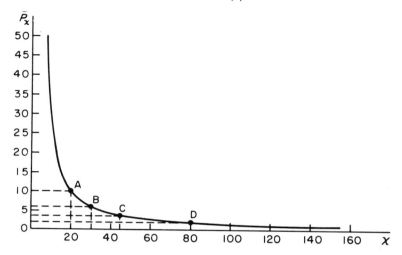

lines (which, of course, are all anchored at the same point on the vertical axis). In Figure 5.7a we have assumed only three different levels of P_x, but there are an infinite number of budget lines that can be drawn.

In this manner we generate a series of tangency points that, when connected, result in a price-consumption line. Each point on the price-consumption line represents a point of tangency between an indifference curve and a budget line.

In Figure 5.7b we show the demand curve corresponding to the price-consumption line of Figure 5.7a. The demand curve is derived in the following way: Each point of tangency between a budget line and an indifference curve gives an equilibrium quantity on the horizontal axis. All that we need to have for a demand curve is the price that corresponds to each of these equilibrium quantities. The slope of each budget line, we have seen, gives us the price of X. So it is an easy matter to read from the price-consumption curve the data needed for the construction of a demand curve. For example, at point A in Figure 5.7a, the equilibrium quantity is 15 units of X. The budget line tangent at A has a slope equal to $300/30 = $10. Therefore, in Figure 5.7b we have plotted the quantity of 15 units of X against a P_x of $10.

Note the following: The fact that the price-consumption line is horizontal means that the demand schedule will be a rectangular hyperbole with a constant elasticity coefficient of -1; i.e., Figure 5.7a shows the consumer spending a constant amount of $150 on X at all prices for X. Therefore, the equation for the corresponding demand curve is $P_xX = $150.

In Figure 5.8a we present another indifference map and four budget lines for $\bar{I} = \$300$ with $P_x = \$30$, $\$10$, $\$3$, and $\$2$; and we derive the price-consumption curve. In this case the price-consumption line is

FIGURE 5.10

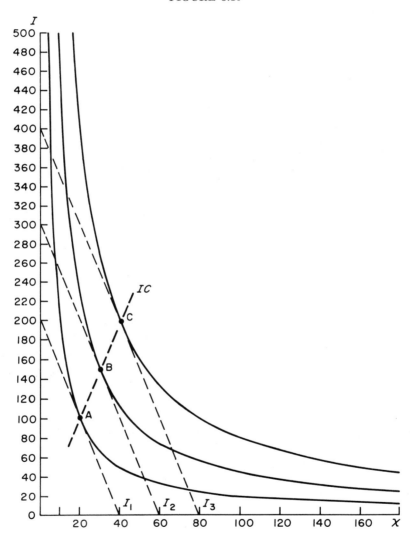

downward sloping, which means that as P_x decreases (that is, the budget lines swing out farther to the right) and the equilibrium quantities of X increase, the total expenditure on X increases.[11] In other words, the demand for X is elastic. Figure 5.8b shows the corresponding demand curve.[12]

We derive an upward-sloping price-consumption line in Figure 5.9a. As P_x decreases and X increases, total expenditure on X decreases; that is, the equilibrium values of I increase.[13] The demand curve for this good, with $E < 1$ (inelastic), is shown in Figure 5.9b.[14]

Income-Consumption Curve

In drawing a demand schedule, we assume income to be constant at a given level. The level of income is an important factor in determining the quantities that will be purchased at alternative prices. We now investigate this relationship.

In Figure 5.10 we have redrawn the indifference map of Figure 5.7a. The three budget lines shown are based on the same P_x of $5 per unit; thus, since the slopes of the lines are equal, the lines are parallel. Budget line I_1 represents consumption possibilities when $\bar{I}$ is $200; I_2 when $\bar{I}$ is $300; and I_3 when $\bar{I}$ is $400. Points A, B, and C represent equilibriums; they are tangency points between a budget line and an indifference curve.[15] An income-consumption curve is derived by connecting the

[11]If we had assumed a large number of prices for X and had generated many more budget lines and equilibrium points, the price-consumption line could have been drawn as a smooth curve.

[12]The equation for this demand curve is $X = (300 - 10P_x)/2P_x$.

[13]We have shown indifference maps yielding demand curves that are completely elastic, inelastic, or unitary elastic over their entire range. It is, of course, possible to have an indifference map that yields a demand curve (e.g., a linear demand curve) that moves

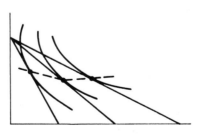

through the range of elasticity from elastic to inelastic. A sketch of such an indifference map is given here.

[14]The equation for this demand curve is $X = (300 + 10P_x)/2P_x$.

[15]Note that point B here corresponds to point B in Figure 5.7a.

points of tangency.[16] Each point on this line shows the equilibrium quantity of X the individual will consume at alternative income levels, with the price of X held constant. Therefore, the points on an income-consumption curve correspond to points on different demand curves — a different demand curve for each level of income. An upward-sloping income-consumption curve indicates that the good is a superior one; a downward sloping one indicates an inferior good.[17]

We can derive the *income elasticity* of good X from the income-consumption curve. Income elasticity is the responsiveness of quantity demanded of a good to a change in income. The coefficient of income elasticity of good X for a discrete change in income can be computed as

$$E_{X\bar{I}} = \frac{\Delta X/(X_1 + X_2)}{\Delta \bar{I}/(\bar{I}_1 + \bar{I}_2)} = \frac{\Delta X}{\Delta \bar{I}} \cdot \frac{\bar{I}_1 + \bar{I}_2}{X_1 + X_2} \tag{5.12}$$

For a very small change in income, we can write

$$E_{X\bar{I}} = \frac{dX/X}{d\bar{I}/\bar{I}} = \frac{dX}{d\bar{I}} \cdot \frac{\bar{I}}{X} \tag{5.13}$$

Thus, income elasticity depends upon two components: the reciprocal of the slope of the income-consumption curve and a proportionality factor (that is, a ratio of the income to the quantity being considered).

Income elasticity between points A and B in Figure 5.10 is

$$E_{X\bar{I}} = \frac{\Delta X}{\Delta \bar{I}} \cdot \frac{\bar{I}_1 + \bar{I}_2}{X_1 + X_2} = \frac{10}{100} \cdot \frac{300 + 400}{30 + 40} = 1 \tag{5.14}$$

Between points B and C

$$E_{X\bar{I}} = \frac{\Delta X}{\Delta \bar{I}} \cdot \frac{\bar{I}_1 + \bar{I}_2}{X_1 + X_2} = \frac{10}{100} \cdot \frac{300 + 400}{30 + 40} = 1* \tag{5.15}$$

When $E_{X\bar{I}} = 1$, a given percentage change in income results in an equal percentage change in quantity demanded.[18] If $E_{X\bar{I}} > 1$, the resulting percentage change in quantity is greater than the initiating percentage change in income; and if $E_{X\bar{I}} < 1$, the percentage change in quantity is

[16]The indifference map drawn in Figure 5.10, as well as those in Figures 5.11 and 12 results in straight-line income-consumption curves. Thus, two budget lines are sufficient to generate the curve.

[17]See page 73. It is possible for the income-consumption curve to change direction; that is, the good is a superior one at some income levels and an inferior one at others.

*Income elasticity all along the curve is unitary. Since it is a linear income-consumption curve, the reciprocal of its slope is a constant, $1/10$; and it will be noted that the proportionality factor is also a constant — $(\bar{I}_1 + \bar{I}_2)/(X_1 + X_2)$ or $\bar{I}/X$ is always 10.

[18]$E = -1$ means a given percentage change in income results in an equal percentage change in quantity demanded in the opposite direction.

FIGURE 5.11

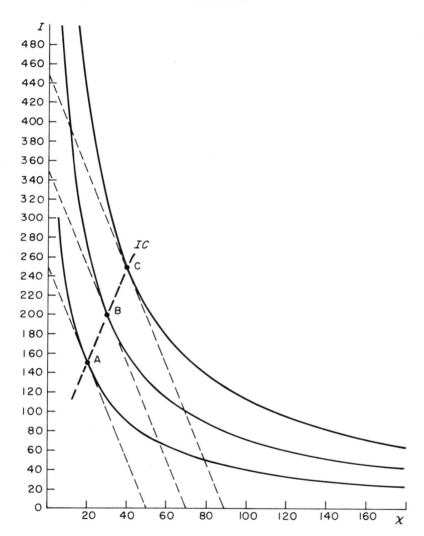

less than the percentage change in income. For normal (that is, superior goods) the coefficient of income elasticity is positive and for inferior goods it will be negative.

Income elasticity between points A and B in Figure 5.11 is $1\frac{1}{5}$; between points B and C it is $1\frac{1}{7}$. In Figure 5.12 $E_{X\bar{I}} = \frac{4}{5}$ between A and B and $E_{X\bar{I}} = \frac{6}{7}$ between B and C. Thus, in Figure 5.11 we have a case of a good

FIGURE 5.12

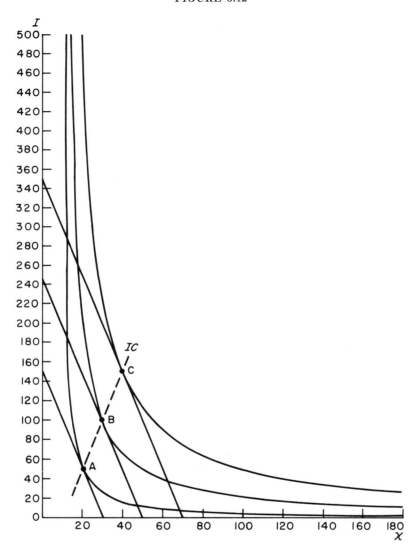

that is income elastic over the range considered and in Figure 5.12 we have
the case of an income-inelastic good.[19]

[19]It is possible to have an indifference map that would yield an income-consumption
curve that reflects income-elasticity for certain incomes and $E_{X\bar{I}} < 1$ for other incomes;
and, as we mentioned before, the income-consumption curve can also have $E_{X\bar{I}} > 0$
for some levels of income and $E_{X\bar{I}} < 0$ for others.

FIGURE 5.13

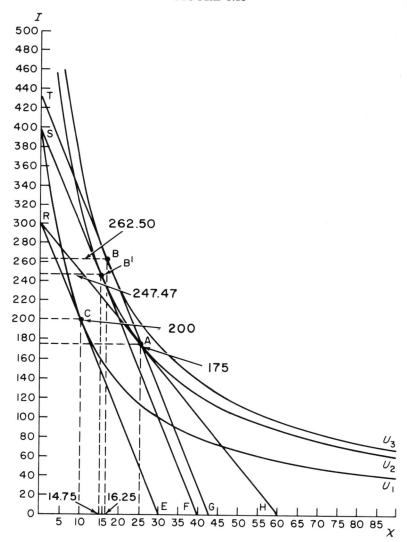

Income and Substitution Effects

In our discussion of utility we saw that it was useful to break down the total effect of a price change into income and substitution effects. This can be done much more readily with the use of indifference curves. We shall demonstrate the procedure with reference to Figure 5.13, in which we have reproduced the indifference map of Figure 5.8a (with the horizontal scale enlarged). It is assumed that the individual initially has an income of $300 ($OR$) and that $P_x = \$5$. He is in equilibrium at point A on indifference curve U_2. The price is then assumed to rise to $10; whereupon the individual's new equilibrium moves to point C on indifference curve U_1.

Analogously to the procedure used in our utility analysis, we now give the individual an increase in his income equal to the decrease in his purchasing power due to the price increase. His purchasing power goes down by the increase in price times the number of units the individual used to buy of the commodity ($\$5 - \$10)25 = -\$125$. In other words, we give him enough additional income so that he can, if he so desires, buy the same quantities of X and all other commodities as before. This is shown graphically by drawing a budget line, parallel to the new one, that goes through point A and intersects the vertical axis at $425. (Remember that parallel budget lines are based on the same P_x.) Although the consumer can now purchase the same combination as before, we note that he does not choose to do so; because X has become relatively more expensive compared with other goods, he would rather consume less of X and more of other goods. This brings him to equilibrium at point B on a higher indifference curve.

The movement from A to B represents the substitution effect of the price change, since it was the result of the change in relative prices alone. The actual change in price, however, also reduced the individual's purchasing power by RT so that he arrived at point C on indifference curve U_1. The movement from B to C, therefore, is the result of the decrease in real income that occurs as a consequence of the price rise; this movement, then, is the income effect.

In numerical terms, we can summarize the income and substitution effects as follows:

Initial equilibrium (A)	25.00 units of X	
Equilibrium after compensated price increase (B)	16.25	
Substitution effect		-8.75 units of X
Final equilibrium (C)	10.00	
Income effect		-6.25
Total effect		-15.00

This approach to analyzing the income and substitution effects was developed by E. Slutsky. An alternative approach developed by J. R. Hicks is also demonstrated in Figure 5.13. Once again we assume the consumer is initially in equilibrium at point A and that P_x changes from $5 to $10 — or the budget line changes from RE to RH. With the Slutsky approach we changed the individual's *nominal* real income so that he could buy his original combination of goods at the new price. But we did not, in fact, bring him to the same level of real income as at point A, since he did not buy the same combination as he bought before the price change and, therefore, ended on a higher indifference curve, U_3. Hicks has suggested that the correct increase in income in order to compensate for the loss in real income due to the price increase is one that will bring the consumer to the same indifference curve (this *really* just restores his level of real income) that he was on before, U_2. In the Hicksian analysis, therefore, we give to the individual an increment in income, RS, that brings him to equilibrium at B' on indifference curve U_2. Thus, the substitution effect is measured by the movement from A to B' and the income effect as the movement from B' to C. We now summarize the Hicksian approach in numerical terms:

Initial equilibrium (A)	25.00 units of X	
Equilibrium after compensated price increase (B')	14.75	
Substitution effect		-10.25 units of X
Final equilibrium (C)	10.00	
Income effect		-4.75
Total effect		-15.00

FIGURE 5.14

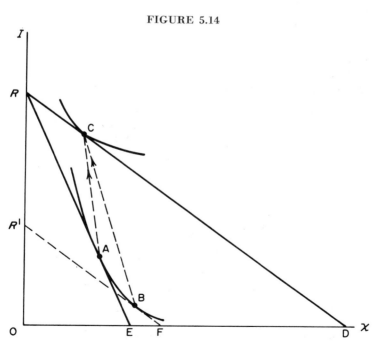

The Hicksian approach is the theoretically more correct one since it just restores to the individual his initial level of real income, while the Slutsky approach "overcompensates" the consumer for his loss of purchasing power by bringing him to a higher indifference curve. The Slutsky method has the virtue of depending only on observable market data, whereas the Hicks approach necessitates a knowledge of the indifference curves. The Slutsky measure is a good approximation of the Hicks measure for small price changes. In our example, the difference between the two measures depends upon the distance between points B and B' and this distance can be seen to decrease as the change in price approaches zero.

With the use of income and substitution effects we can investigate the conditions under which we will have negatively sloping demand curves. First, the convexity of the indifference curve ensures that the substitution effect will always be in the opposite direction to the price change.[20] Second, the income effect depends upon whether the good is normal or inferior. In our discussions of utility and the income-consumption curve, we saw that the income effect for a superior good will also be in the opposite direction of the price change. Therefore, the net effect (substitution + income) of a price change will always be in the opposite direction of a price change.

We also saw that the income effect for an inferior good is in the same direction as the price change. Therefore, if the income effect is greater than the substitution effect, the net effect will be in the same direction as the price change. In Figure 5.14 we have a case of such a Giffen good. When the consumer is in initial equilibrium at A and then the price de-

[20]We can see this intuitively using the Hicksian approach. The budget line is originally RS and then P_x declines so that the new budget line is RT. Equilibrium changes from A to C. PQ is parallel to $RT;$ that is, PQ is based on the new lower P_x. With

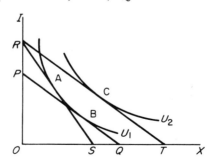

convex indifference curves, MRS_{XI} declines, moving from left to right. Therefore, since the slope of PQ is less than the slope of RS, PQ must be tangent to U_1 to the right of A (e.g., B), where the amount of X is greater than at A.

creases from RD to RE, the consumer moves to the new equilibrium, C. Note that at point C the consumer buys less of X even though its price has gone down. This effect, which results in a positively sloped demand curve, is caused by the combination of two circumstances: (1) the good is inferior and (2) the income effect is stronger than the substitution effect; that is, $A \to B < B \to C$. Although a Giffen good is a theoretical possibility, an empirical case of such a good has, as yet, not been found.

An Application of Indifference Curves

An interesting application of indifference curves is the demonstration, with an Edgeworth box, of the gains to be derived from free trade. In Figure 5.15 we assume two individuals, A and B, each with an endowment of two goods, X and Y. We show the indifference curves of these individuals on the same graph. A's origin is at the lower left and B's origin is at the upper right. Therefore, A's indifference curves $(A_1 - A_8)$ are

FIGURE 5.15

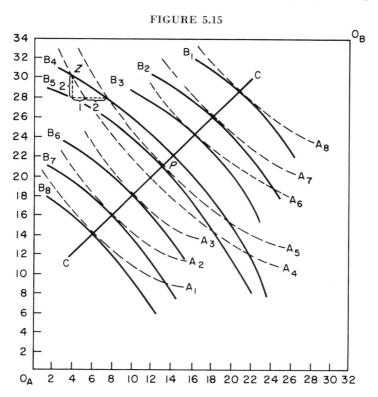

convex to A's origin, and B's indifference curves $(B_1 - B_8)$ are convex to B's origin. Point Z represents their original endowments. The width of the box represents the sum of the endowments of X held by A and B; the length represents the sum of the endowments of Y. Therefore, A's initial endowment is 4 units of X and 30 units of Y while B's endowment is 28 units of X and 4 units of Y; or the total endowment of X is 32 units and of Y, 34.

Now assume that A and B are free to trade with one another. Prior to trading, A was on A_4 and B was on B_4. Will it now be profitable for them to trade? At point Z, A could be compensated for giving up 2 units of Y by receiving 1 unit of X in exchange. B, on the other hand, would be willing to give up 3 units of X in exchange for 2 units of Y. In other words,

$$\frac{\Delta Y_A}{\Delta X_A} = \frac{2}{1} > \frac{\Delta Y_B}{\Delta X_B} = \frac{2}{3} \tag{5.16}$$

It is clearly to the benefit of both to trade at any ratio in between $\frac{2}{1}$ and $\frac{2}{3}$. For instance, if A got 2 units of X for 2 of Y, he would move to a higher indifference curve since he would have stayed on the same indifference curve if he had received one unit of X. Similarly, if B received 2 units of Y for giving up only 2 units of X, he also must move to a higher indifference curve, since giving up 3 units of X to gain 2 units of Y would have kept him at the same level of satisfaction.

As long as the individuals remain within the elliptical area encompassed by B_4 and A_4 and continue to trade, each is moving to a higher indifference curve and each benefits. Once they have reached a point such as P, where the indifference curves are tangent $(\Delta Y_A/\Delta X_A = \Delta Y_B/\Delta X_B)$, no further movement beneficial to both is possible, a gain by one representing a loss to the other. The locus of points such as C is called a contract curve and is shown on the diagram as CC.

The condition of diminishing absolute MRS_{xy} is not the same as that of diminishing marginal utility; it is less restrictive.

By definition the level of satisfaction along an indifference curve is constant; this means that the total differential is zero. Using some of the symbols used in Appendix 4A, we have

$$\mu_a dA + \mu_b dB = 0 \qquad (A5.1)$$

or

$$-\frac{dB}{dA} = \frac{\mu_a}{\mu_b} \qquad (A5.2)$$

This simply says that the absolute slope of the indifference curve is equal to the ratio of the marginal utilities of the commodities.

We want to know what happens to MRS_{xy} as we move along the indifference curve and so we differentiate μ_a/μ_b again.

Decreasing MRS_{xy} means that

$$\frac{d}{dA}\left(-\frac{dB}{dA}\right) = \left\{\frac{1}{\mu_b^3}[\mu_{aa}\mu_b^2 - 2\mu_{ab}\mu_a\mu_b + \mu_{bb}\mu_a^2]\right\} < 0 \qquad (A5.3)$$

From Appendix 4A we have:

$$\mu_a = \mu_b\left(\frac{P_a}{P_b}\right) \qquad (A4A.7)$$

We substitute this in expression A5.3 above and obtain

$$\left\{\frac{1}{\mu_b^3}\left[\mu_{aa}\mu_b^2 - 2\mu_{ab}\left(\mu_b\frac{P_a}{P_b}\right)\mu_b + \mu_{bb}\left(\mu_b\frac{P_a}{P_b}\right)^2\right]\right\}$$

This simplifies to

$$\left\{\frac{1}{\mu_b}\left[\mu_{aa} - 2\mu_{ab}\left(\frac{P_a}{P_b}\right) + \mu_{bb}\left(\frac{P_a}{P_b}\right)^2\right]\right\} < 0$$

We now multiply and divide the expression by P_b^2, which leaves the inequality unchanged:

$$\left\{\frac{1}{\mu_b P_b^2}[\mu_{aa}P_b^2 - 2\mu_{ab}P_aP_b + \mu_{bb}P_a^2]\right\} < 0 \qquad (A5.4)$$

The first term on the left must be positive if the commodity is an economic, utility-yielding commodity selling at a positive price. The condition, therefore, that the expression on the left be negative amounts to saying that the second and bracketed expression must be negative. But we have shown above in Appendix 4A that this is exactly the second-order condition for maximum utility. Furthermore, we have shown that it does not necessarily imply diminishing marginal utility.

MARKET
STRUCTURES

6

Types of Market Structures

The demand schedule facing an individual producer shows the quantities he can sell at various alternative prices. The nature of this demand schedule depends upon the structure of the industry of which the producer is a member. We may classify market structures according to the number of sellers in the industry and the degree of homegeneity of the good. Pure monopoly and perfect competition are the extremes of market organization and we shall describe these situations first; the in-between cases follow.

Monopoly exists when there is a single seller of a homogeneous good: the seller *is* the industry. The demand schedule facing a monopolist is the aggregate demand for the good; and the elasticity of this demand is the elasticity of the total demand.

A perfectly competitive industry is one in which a large number of firms sell a homogeneous product. To investigate the nature of the demand schedule facing one of these firms, consider a numerical example.

Aggregate demand for the product of a competitive industry is given by the equation $Qd = 11,000,000 - 100,000P$. There are 10,000 firms within this industry, all with the supply schedule $q_s = P$; thus, the industry supply schedule is $Q_s = 10,000P$. The equilibrium price is $100 per unit and the equilibrium quantity is 1,000,000 units, with each firm supplying $1/10,000$ of aggregate output or 100 units. We now wish to determine the effect on equilibrium price and quantity if one firm should stop producing. The industry supply schedule becomes $Q_s = 9999P$ and the new equilibrium price and quantity are approximately (to 4 decimal places) $100.0009 and 999.910 units. The initial equilibrium situation is shown in Figure 6.1a. The area in the vicinity of the equilibrium point is magnified in Figure 6.1b in order to show the effects of the shift on supply and the new equilibrium.

FIGURE 6.1

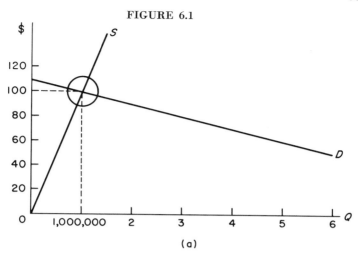

(a)

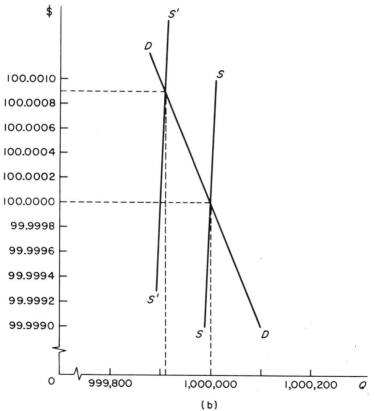

(b)

We can now derive the demand curve facing the individual perfect competitor, which is shown in Figure 6.2a. When the firm produces no output, the price it faces is $100.001; and when the firm produces 100

FIGURE 6.2

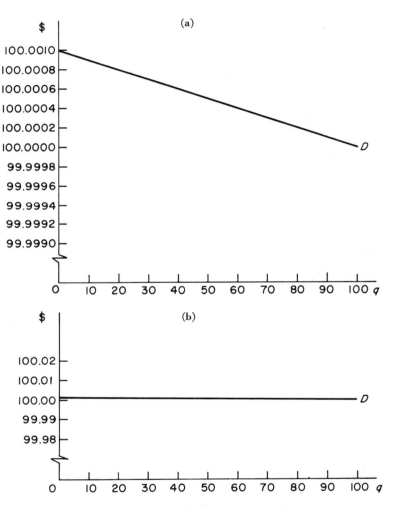

units, it can sell at $100 per unit. The elasticity of this demand curve at $100 is computed as follows:

$$\frac{\Delta q}{\Delta P} \cdot \frac{P}{q} = \frac{100}{-0.001} \cdot \frac{100}{100} = -100,000 \qquad (6.1)$$

The elasticity of the aggregate demand curve at $100 is

$$\frac{\Delta Q}{\Delta P} \cdot \frac{P}{Q} = \frac{90}{-0.001} \cdot \frac{100}{1,000,000} = -9 \qquad (6.2)$$

Notice that the slopes (and, therefore, the reciprocals of the slopes) of the total demand curve and that of the individual firm are not very different; it does not appear this way graphically because of the difference in scales that are used. However, the fact that the elasticity coefficients are quite different is based on the difference in the magnitude of output of the entire industry as compared with that of a single firm. The usual practice is to draw the demand curve facing the individual firm as being horizontal and to say that the coefficient of elasticity is infinite. What is implied by this is that the individual competitive firm has no influence on the market price and can sell as much as it can produce at the price given to it. We can see from the above discussion that the correct statement should be that the individual competitive firm has only an imperceptible influence on the market price, that the demand curve for its output is "highly" elastic, and that when drawn upon the industry price scale it cannot be distinguished from a horizontal line. For example, in Figure 6.2b, with the price-axis fairly elongated — in pennies — the demand curve appears almost horizontal. If the price-axis scale of Figure 6.1a had been used, it would be virtually impossible to distinguish the demand curve from a horizontal line.

It is important to make this distinction in order to understand the mechanism by which the equilibrium market price is arrived at in a perfectly competitive industry. When there is a disequilibrium situation in a market — say, an excess of supply over demand — the equilibrium price would be arrived at by a process of competitive price shading. In our current example we can see that if the 10,000th firm were not able to sell its output at the market price of $100.001, it would need to shade the price by only $.001 in order to dispose of its output and to bring the market into equilibrium.[1]

Monopolistic competition is a market situation in which there are a large enough number of firms selling differentiated goods so that there is no interdependence among them; that is, the action taken by one firm will not have any appreciable effects upon the other firms. In a sense each firm is a monopolist since it is the only seller of the good, narrowly defined. The nature of the demand schedule facing an individual monop-

---

[1]The student should be warned that we shall keep the conventions of drawing horizontal demand curves facing individual competitive firms and stating that the elasticity of these demand curves is infinite — but these are only convenient approximations.

olistic competitor depends, first, on the number of sellers of the broad category of goods and, second, on the degree of differentiation (that is, uniqueness) of the seller's particular good. Because the individual monopolistic competitor has some degree of "monopoly" power based on the fact that consumers consider his product to be in some sense different,[2] he is able to increase the price of his product without running the risk of losing his entire market, as would a perfect competitor.

The notion of an equilibrium price loses its uniqueness in monopolistic competition. Since the goods are not perfect substitutes for one another, there may be more than one price at a time.

An example of monopolistic competition may help to clarify the concept. Imagine a large number of barber shops in a community, and consumers indifferent among the haircuts and other services offered in the respective shops. We would consider this a competitive industry. Suppose, alternatively, that the owner of shop *A* is a raconteur, that barber *B* is capable of a critique of last night's opera, that barber *C* is a fount of baseball scores; and so on for the rest of the firms. Although each provides haircuts, consumers — with varying tastes for chitchat — will prefer one barber to the others. Each may charge a price somewhat, but not too, different from the others and still retain his customers. Clearly, however, at a substantial price difference, haircuts with baseball talk (perhaps one could take along some plugs of cotton) would compete with haircuts with opera talk.

The identifying characteristic of *oligopoly* is interdependence among the firms in the industry. By this is meant that the number of firms is small enough so that the action of any one firm will affect the others. The product of such an industry can be either homogeneous or differentiated; but in making his decisions, the oligopolist must always be concerned with the reactions of the other firms in the industry.

The shape of the demand curve facing a single oligopolist depends on the assumptions made concerning the exact nature of the interdependence among the firms in the industry. One of the most frequently made of these assumptions is that the oligopolist thinks his rivals will match any price reduction but will not follow a price increase. (We shall discuss other possible assumptions in Chapter 11.) Under this assumption the demand curve facing the oligopolist will be highly elastic at prices above the prevailing market price and relatively inelastic at prices below this one. This type of demand curve is shown in Figure 6.3; it is "kinked" at the prevailing market price ($7). The demand curve faced by the oligopolist

---

[2]This difference can be real or imagined on the part of consumers, and can be created through advertising.

FIGURE 6.3

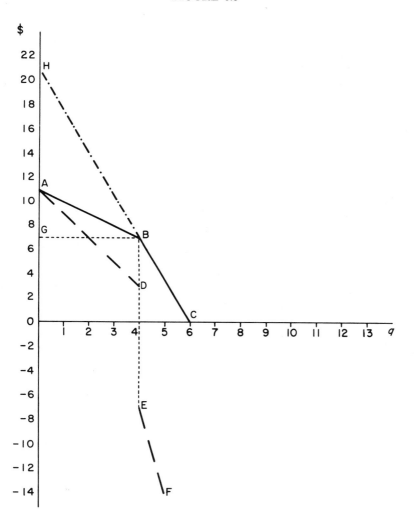

at a price above $7 is relatively elastic because the other firms in the in-
dustry will not follow a price rise so that consumers have available several
fairly good substitutes at lower prices. Below the prevailing price the
demand curve is shown to be relatively inelastic. Because the other firms
follow a price cut, the only increase in sales the price-cutting firm experiences is its proportionate share of the increase in quantity demanded
along the industry demand curve.

The Relationships among Average Revenue, Marginal Revenue, and Elasticity

We can now utilize the relationship among average revenue, marginal revenue, and elasticity derived in Chapter 3 to show the relationships among them for various market structures. The relationship derived was

$$MR = AR\left(1 + \frac{1}{E_d}\right) \quad \text{where } E_d < 0 \qquad (3.9a)$$

or

$$MR = AR + \frac{AR}{E_d}, \text{ where } E_d < 0 \qquad (3.9b)$$

For the perfectly competitive firm, elasticity approaches infinity; therefore, the term $1/E_d$ approaches zero and may be disregarded. It follows that $MR = AR$, and that the demand curve and the marginal revenue curve facing the perfect competitor are coincident (or approximately so).

Since the monopolist faces the aggregate demand for a good for which it is assumed there are no good substitutes, the demand for the product will not generally be infinitely elastic. Therefore, the term $1/E_d$ will be greater than zero (disregarding sign) and MR will be equal to AR minus $(1/E_d)(AR)$ so that MR is less than AR. The more inelastic is the demand schedule at any particular price, the greater will be the gap between AR and MR.[3]

Since the monopolistic competitor faces a downward-sloping demand curve, the relationship between AR and MR will be the same as that of the monopolist except that generally elasticity will be greater for the monop-

---

[3]The marginal revenue curve corresponding to a linear demand curve has twice the slope of the demand curve and the same y-axis intercept. This may be proved as follows:

$$AR = P = a + bq$$

$$TR = AR \times q = Pq = aq + bq^2$$

$$MR = \frac{dTR}{dq} = a + 2bq$$

It follows from this that the MR-curve corresponding to a linear demand curve may be derived by drawing a line from the vertical-axis intercept of the demand curve, which has a slope twice that of the demand curve. At their common point of intersection with the vertical axis, AR and MR are equal. As we move downward along the linear demand curve and elasticity diminishes, the gap between AR and MR increases.

olistic competitor and, therefore, the gap between AR and MR will be less.

In Figure 6.3 we have derived the discontinuous MR-curve, $ADEF$, which corresponds to the kinked demand curve, ABC. This MR-curve may be derived as follows, using the technique discussed in the footnote. Draw a line from point A through the mid-point of line GB. The line AD gives the MR-curve corresponding to the segment of the demand curve AB; we now extend the segment BC until it hits the vertical axis at H. We then derive the MR-curve corresponding to HC by the same method as above; but only the segment for outputs greater than 4 units is relevant; that is, EF. Note that our result is that MR just to the left of 4 units is \$3 and just to the right it is $-\$7$. We may check this result by using the relationship

$$MR = P\left(1 + \frac{1}{E_d}\right)$$

For the segment BC

$$E_d = -\frac{2}{7} \cdot \frac{7}{4} = -\frac{1}{2}$$

$$MR = 7\left(1 - \frac{1}{\frac{1}{2}}\right) = -7$$

For the segment AB

$$E_d = -1 \cdot \frac{7}{4} = -\frac{7}{4} = -1\frac{3}{4}$$

$$MR = 7\left(1 - \frac{1}{\frac{7}{4}}\right) = 3$$

THE THEORY
OF PRODUCTION

The Production Function

In Chapters 2–5 we investigated the determinants of the demand schedule. Thus far we have stated that the shape and position of the supply curve are determined by costs of production. In 'order to understand fully the relationship between costs of production and supply, it is necessary to understand first the technological conditions facing the firm. The economist summarizes these conditions with the *production function*, which gives the functional relationship between rates of input of factors of production and rates of output per time period. Presumably, this type of information is made available to the firm by engineers and other technical personnel.

In general terms, we may represent a production function as follows:

$$q = q(A,B,C,\cdots,N) \tag{7.1}$$

where $A \ldots N$ represent quantities of productive inputs per time period and q represents output per time period.

For ease of exposition, we shall deal with the case of two homogeneous factors of production that combine to produce a single homogeneous product.[1] Here again, as in the analysis of consumer behavior, we restrict ourselves to one dependent and two independent variables permitting

[1]Most firms produce more than one product. If the firm produces independent goods, it is possible to treat each good in the way we suggest above. If the firm produces a main product with by-products in fixed proportions (for example, the production of hides as a consequence of meat slaughtering), then the unit of output is good X plus by-products, adding no additional problems. Even when the firm can produce alternative output mixes with a given level of inputs, our results do not change substantially. Therefore, our assumption of a single homogeneous good is not overly restrictive.

the use of two-dimensional diagrams. In functional notation, then, we assume that

$$q = q(X, Y) \qquad (7.2)$$

The three-dimensional representation of this function is shown in Figure 7.1; and as we did in Chapter 5, we can reduce this to two-dimensional

FIGURE 7.1

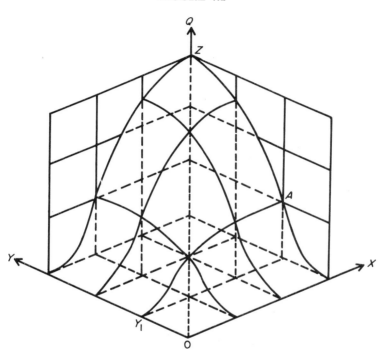

representation with the use of contour lines, which in the case of the production function are called equal-product curves or *isoquants*. In other words, each contour line in Figure 7.2 is a line of equal output for various combinations of inputs X and Y.

In contradistinction to the indifference map, however, each contour line represents a specific level of output that is assumed to be known since it is based on technological data. Therefore, as we move to higher isoquants, we know that output is increasing as well as by how much.

The data contained in the production function can also be presented in tabular form as in Table 7.1. Thus it will be noted that the output level of 500 units can be produced alternatively with $2X$ and $12.5Y$,

$10X$ and $2.5Y$ and $20X$ and $1.25Y$.* That we assume a given output can be produced with varying factor inputs implies that the technological process permits factor substitution between X and Y; and further, since we draw continuous isoquants, we are also assuming that the factors of production are continuously variable.

FIGURE 7.2

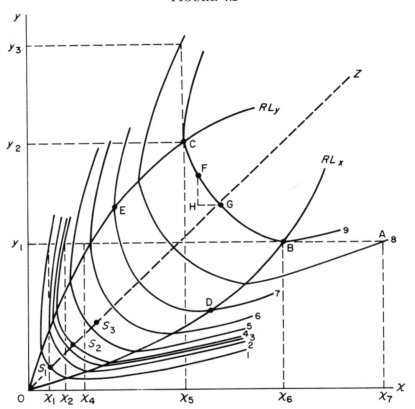

The characteristics of an isoquant will be discussed with reference to isoquant 9 (q_9) in Figure 7.2. (Note that successive isoquants are assumed to represent equal increments of output.) We have assumed that the factors are substitutes for one another in the production of the good.

*Production functions can be presented in tabular form in various ways. We have chosen to show the combinations of X and Y that can be used to produce different given levels of output. (This gives us the contour lines — isoquants — we shall be using subsequently.) An alternative method is to show, for various combinations of X and Y, the different output levels that will be produced.

TABLE 7.1

**Input of Factor Y Needed with a Given Input of Factor X to
Produce a Given Level of Output**

Isoquant Values										
1000	50.000	25.000	16.667	12.500	10.000	8.333	7.143	6.250	5.556	5.000
900	40.500	20.250	13.500	10.125	8.100	6.750	5.786	5.062	4.500	4.050
800	32.000	16.000	10.667	8.000	6.400	5.333	4.571	4.000	3.556	3.200
700	24.500	12.250	8.167	6.125	4.900	4.083	3.500	3.062	2.722	2.450
600	18.000	9.000	6.000	4.500	3.600	3.000	2.571	2.250	2.000	1.800
500	12.500	6.250	4.167	3.125	2.500	2.083	1.786	1.562	1.389	1.250
400	8.000	4.000	2.667	2.000	1.600	1.333	1.143	1.000	0.889	0.800
300	4.500	2.250	1.500	1.125	0.900	0.750	0.643	0.562	0.500	0.450
200	2.000	1.000	0.667	0.500	0.400	0.333	0.286	0.250	0.222	0.200
100	0.500	0.250	0.167	0.125	0.100	0.083	0.071	0.062	0.056	0.050
Q / X	2	4	6	8	10	12	14	16	18	20

However, unless the factors are perfect substitutes (in which case the problem is trivial, since they become in effect the same factor), it is reasonable to expect that a specific level of output requires some minimum amount of each factor. On isoquant 9, at point B, we have the minimum quantity of Y (Y_1) necessary to produce q_9. Similarly, at point C, we have the minimum quantity of X (X_5) needed to produce q_9. If the firm were to acquire a quantity of X greater than OX_6 without acquiring any more of Y, it would find that the level of output would decrease or at best remain the same. If the input of X were to increase from OX_6 to OX_7, with Y remaining constant, then output would decrease from q_9 to q_8. We may say that beyond point B, X is a redundant factor. In order to remain on q_9 beyond point B, the input of both X and Y must be increased. This results in the isoquant's being upward-sloping past B. Analogously, if Y were increased from OY_2 at point C to OY_3 with the quantity of X remaining constant, the level of output would go from q_9 to q_8. Thus, beyond point C, Y is a redundant factor and the isoquant is positively sloped, indicating that to remain on q_9 more of both factors must be used.[2]

[2]In drawing the isoquant upward-sloping beyond B and C, we are assuming that the redundant factors become a nuisance; that is, they actually interfere with the production process. *At* point B, the isoquant is horizontal and *at* point C it is vertical. Later we shall see that it is at these two points that the marginal productivities of the factors become zero.

If the excess factors do not create a nuisance, then it is more appropriate to draw the isoquant horizontal past B and vertical past C, as the redundant factors add nothing to output.

Between points C and B both factors are above their respective minimum requirements for q_9, so that substitution is possible between X and Y: output can be maintained at a given level by increasing one factor and decreasing the other. This is reflected in the downward slope of the isoquant between C and B.

Another characteristic of isoquants is that they are *nonintersecting*. Intersection would mean that a given combination of X and Y could produce two different outputs with given technology.

The curves RL_x and RL_y, called the *ridge lines*, connect points, such as E and C and D and B, where the isoquants become respectively vertical and horizontal. In the area between these ridge lines, the isoquants are negatively sloping and convex to the origin. This means that the MRS_{xy} (the slope of the isoquant, $\Delta Y/\Delta X$) decreases as we move from left to right along an isoquant. (Once again when we speak of declining MRS_{xy}, we mean in absolute terms.) The implication of this is that as the firm substitutes X for Y and approaches the minimum quantity of Y necessary to produce a level of output, X becomes a poorer and poorer substitute for Y; therefore it takes more and more X per unit of Y given up to maintain the given level of output.

The Short Run

In the theory of production we define two analytical time periods: the short run and the long run. The *short run* is a period in which at least one factor of production cannot be varied, while in the long run all factors of production are presumed to be variable. The calendar time period corresponding to the analytical short-run and long-run periods will vary from industry to industry and among firms within an industry. Thus, the short run for a tailor shop is likely to be a short calendar period whereas the short run for a steel plant is likely to be fairly lengthy.

In Figure 7.1 assume the firm to be operating in the short run; that is, it has OY_1 of factor Y and can vary its output only through varying the input of factor X. In terms of the diagram, this involves moving along the production surface at the level of Y, OY_1; or, in other words, tracing the curve Y_1A on the production surface in Figure 7.1. In the two-dimensional terms of Figure 7.2, this amounts to moving along line Y_1A at the level of Y, OY_1, parallel to the X-axis.

Notice that the line Y_1A passes through isoquants that are initially closer and closer together: the distance along Y_1A from the vertical axis to q_1 is greater than the corresponding distance between q_1 and q_2, which is greater than the distance between q_2 and q_3. Beyond q_4 the distance between successive isoquants increases. In other words, if the firm uses OX_1 along with the fixed Y input of OY_1, output is q_1. Then if the firm increases its input of factor X to OX_2 (which means an increase in X of OX_1, since $X_1X_2 = OX_1$), the new output level is q_4. Thus, adding the same quantity of the variable input as before has resulted in a greater increase of output; the first increment increased output by 1 unit and the second by 3 units.[3] If the input of the X factor is increased to OX_4 (which again represents the same increment: $OX_4 = X_1X_2 = X_2X_4$), we find that output goes to a level somewhat greater than five units; the increment of output is, therefore, less than 3. Clearly, therefore, $\Delta q/\Delta X$ (the marginal physical product of X) is increasing over the range $0 - X_2$ and decreasing thereafter. The first stage is called the stage of increasing returns and the second stage, diminishing returns. It should be noted, however, that beyond the point where line Y_1A cuts the ridge line RL_x, it cuts through isoquants that are backward-bending and, as we saw above, this means that the factor X is being used to redundancy and output declines; $\Delta q/\Delta X$ becomes negative and this is called the stage of negative returns. At the ridge line where $\Delta q/\Delta X$ is zero, the firm may be said to be momentarily at zero returns.

In Figure 7.3 is shown the exact relationship between output and the input of factor X, with Y held constant at OY_1. This relationship is called the total physical product of X (TP_x). In terms of the three-dimensional representation in Figure 7.1 we have sliced the production surface by dropping a plane perpendicular to the X-Y plane at the level of Y, OY_1; and then we have shown how the "altitude" of the slice varies as the input of factor X changes.

Note the following relationships between Figures 7.2 and 3. As the horizontal line Y_1A in Figure 7.2 cuts through successive isoquants that are closer and closer together — the stage of increasing returns — TP_x increases at an increasing rate; that is, the curve in Figure 7.3 is convex to the origin from 0 to OX_2. TP_x in the range of OX_2 to OX_6 is concave to the origin (or, in other words, is rising at a decreasing rate); in Figure 7.2 this corresponds to line Y_1A cutting through successive isoquants that are spaced farther and farther apart. Finally, beyond OX_6 where X becomes redundant in Figure 7.2, TP_x declines, showing negative returns. Of course, TP_x is at a maximum at OX_6.

The stage of increasing returns exists because too little of the variable factor is being used with the fixed factor; the variable factor is spread "too thin." Therefore, using additional units of the variable factor results

---

[3]The quantity measure might be units of a hundred or a thousand, not necessarily one. Thus, q_1 might represent 100 units and q_2 200 units, and so on.

FIGURES 7.3 and 7.4

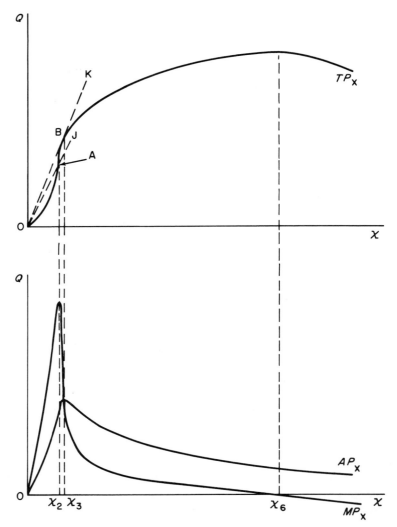

in output's increasing at an increasing rate. After the optimum proportion of the variable factor to the fixed factor has been passed, diminishing returns set in. Finally, when the quantity of the variable factor has increased to such an extent that additional units impede the efficiency of the operation of previous units, output declines.

Increasing and negative returns are probable but may not occur; the fixed factor may be efficient with little of the variable factor, and the variable factor may never become a nuisance. Economists have found, however, that diminishing returns are characteristic of all productive processes in the short run and have consequently formulated the law of diminishing returns, which states: When a variable factor is added to the fixed factor or factors in a productive process, output will increase, but after a while at a decreasing rate. It is to be noticed that the "law" does not specify when diminishing returns are to set in, but if the "law" is to be anything but a curiosity it must happen within relevant ranges of factor input. It should also be noted that the law is valid only under the assumption that at least one factor is held fixed and that technology (the production function) remains the same.

In Figure 7.4 we show the average physical product of factor X (AP_x) and the marginal physical product (MP_x) that correspond to the TP_x schedule in Figure 7.3 — that is, with Y held constant at OY_1.*

$$AP_x = \frac{TP_x}{X} \quad \text{or} \quad \frac{q}{X} \quad \text{(with } Y \text{ constant at a given level)} \qquad (7.3)$$

$$MP_x = \frac{\Delta TP_x}{\Delta X} \quad \text{or} \quad \frac{\Delta q}{\Delta X} \quad \text{(with } Y \text{ constant at a given level)} \quad (7.4)$$

in the discrete case; in the continuous case, we have

$$MP_x = \frac{\partial q}{\partial X}† \qquad (7.4a)$$

The usual relationships exist among TP_x, AP_x, and MP_x. First AP_x at a given level of X can be derived by drawing a line such as OJ from the origin to the appropriate point on the TP_x schedule; thus, AP_x for OX_2 units of X, is equal to the ratio AX_2/OX_2. Therefore, from O to OX_2, when TP_x increases at an increasing rate, MP_x rises; from OX_2 to OX_6, when TP_x increases at a decreasing rate, MP_x declines; and beyond X_6, MP_x becomes negative as TP_x declines. TP_x, can, of course, be derived from either the AP_x or the MP_x schedule in the usual manner. The relationship between AP_x and MP_x can be stated as

$$MP_x = AP_x + \frac{\partial AP_x}{\partial X} X \qquad (7.5)$$

The Slope of the Isoquant as the Ratio of Marginal Products. The slope of an isoquant, MRS_{xy}, is measured as $\Delta Y/\Delta X$. The slope can also be expressed in terms of the marginal products of the factors. On isoquant

*It should be noted that there is a different TP_x schedule for every different level of Y held constant and, therefore, different AP_x and MP_x schedules.
†The notation "∂" signifies a partial derivative; that is, the change in q as X changes by an infinitesimal amount, with Y held constant at some given level.

9 in Figure 7.2, F and G represent two of the many different factor combinations that can produce q_9. The factor combination at point H can produce a smaller level of output than q_9. The movement from F to H represents a decrease in input Y while X is held constant. The resulting loss in output can be expressed as $-\Delta Y \cdot MP_y$. The movement from H to G represents an increase in input X with Y being held constant. The resulting increase in output can be expressed as $+\Delta X \cdot MP_x$. Since output at F and G are the same, the loss in output due to the decrease in Y must equal the gain in output resulting from the use of more X. Therefore,

$$-\Delta Y \cdot MP_y = \Delta X \cdot MP_x \tag{7.6}$$

or

$$\frac{\Delta Y}{\Delta X} = -\frac{MP_x}{MP_y} \quad \text{and} \quad -\frac{MP_x}{MP_y} = MRS_{xy} \tag{7.7}$$

This definition of MRS_{xy} will be useful in our later discussion.[4]

The Long Run

Whereas in the short run, one of the factors of production is assumed fixed at some level (OY_1 in Figure 7.1), in the long run all factors are assumed to be variable. In Figure 7.1, if we assume that factors X and Y are used in a one-to-one ratio, this amounts to slicing the production surface along the line OZ.* In terms of the isoquant map in Figure 7.2, it means moving along line OZ, which is equidistant from the X and Y axes — since we have assumed equal amounts of the factors being used. It should be noticed that as we move along OZ from the origin, successive isoquants are at first spaced closer and closer together and then farther and farther apart. If we increase the inputs from combination S_1 to combination S_2 (i.e., a doubling of inputs, since $OS_1 = S_1S_2$), output increases from 1 to 4 "units." In other words, doubling the inputs causes output to more than double; in this instance, output quadruples. As we increase inputs by 50 percent from S_2 to S_3 ($S_1S_2 = S_2S_3$), output increases to a level somewhat greater than 5 "units" and less than 6.

[4]In continuous notation we can write $dY/dX = (-\partial q/\partial X)/(\partial q/\partial Y) = -MP_x/MP_y$. For a more rigorous treatment see Appendix 5, where the slope of an indifference curve was derived. The same technique can be used for isoquants: Output is a constant along an isoquant; utility is a constant along an indifference curve.

*We discuss below the determinants of the factor proportion used by the firm in the long run.

This means the 50 percent increase in inputs results in a less than 50 percent increase in output.

The behavior of output for proportional increases of inputs up to combination S_2 is said to show increasing returns to scale, and after S_2 decreasing returns to scale. Constant returns to scale, which are not shown on this diagram, would show output increasing at the same rate as the inputs.

Increasing returns to scale reflect the opportunities of using specialization of the factors of production (of which division of labor is the most frequently mentioned, but by no means the only variant). Decreasing returns to scale arise because of the inefficiencies involved in switching from an entrepreneur to a "management team." For example, doubling the scale of operation would require a doubling of entrepreneurs, but it is highly unlikely that this will double the "entrepreneurial capacity"; that is, with one entrepreneur, there is no communications problem; with two entrepreneurs, two lines of communications are necessary; with three, six lines; and so on.

Assume that we increase all inputs in the same proportion, k, and that output also increases in the proportion k — in other words, constant returns to scale. In terms of the generalized production function equation

$$q = f(X, Y, \cdots, N) \tag{7.8}$$

this amounts to

$$kq = f(kX, kY, \cdots, kN) \tag{7.9}$$

This type of production function is called *linear and homogeneous*. The word "linear" as used here means that for given percentage increases in all inputs, we obtain an *equal* percentage increase in output. The word "homogeneous" means that these constant returns to scale apply for the entire production function.

It is mathematically possible, but economically improbable, to have a production function that exhibits homogeneity and increasing (or decreasing) returns to scale. In the first case, the production function can be written as follows:

$$k^i q = f(kX, kY, \cdots, kN) \tag{7.10}$$

where $i > 1$. For example, if $i = 2$ and $k = 2$, then a doubling of all inputs will quadruple output. And in the case of decreasing returns to scale, assume $k = 4$ and $i = \frac{1}{2}$. Then a quadrupling of inputs results in a doubling of output — k^i would be $4^{1/2} = 2$.*

---

*Now it should be clear why a homogeneous production function showing constant returns to scale is called a linear homogeneous production function; that is, $i = 1$.

It is likely that a firm experiences first increasing and then decreasing returns to scale (with perhaps constant returns in between) rather than operating with a homogeneous production function. An economically realistic production function, therefore, does not lend itself to simple mathematical expression. Since it would have to fulfill the following conditions — in the long run, a stage of increasing returns to scale followed by decreasing returns to scale; and in the short run, increasing returns followed by diminishing returns and perhaps negative returns — the mathematical formulation would be exceedingly complex and, therefore, for our purposes not very useful.

The Symmetry of the Stages

With a linear homogeneous production function, it is instructive to view the short run once again. We have seen that in the initial stages of production, the firm experiences increasing returns as a result of too little of the variable factor being used with the fixed factor; and after a certain quantity of the variable factor is used, diminishing returns set in as a consequence of more than the optimum amount of the variable factor being used with the fixed factor. Finally, we introduced the possibility of negative returns that occur when the variable factor "overwhelms" the fixed factor. We can state with equal validity that increasing returns take place because too much of the fixed factor is being used along with the variable; that diminishing returns occur because less than the optimum amount of the fixed factor is being used with the variable factor; that negative returns occur because the fixed factor is highly insufficient for the quantity of the variable factor. In other words, the proportions of the factors determine the behavior of output.

The linear homogeneous production function is particularly interesting in this regard since it is *only* the factor proportions that determine output per "dose" of the inputs. The linear homogeneous production function thus permits us to isolate the effects of proportions of the factors from that of absolute amounts of factor inputs (scale). For example, if 10 units can be produced with 2 units of factor X and 1 of Y, then $2 \times 10 = 20$ units can be produced with $2 \times 2 = 4$ units of X and $2 \times 1 = 2$ of Y; and $\frac{1}{2} \times 2 = 1$ unit of X together with $\frac{1}{2} \times 1 = \frac{1}{2}$ unit of Y can produce 5 units of output. In general then, if we increase (decrease) both inputs by the proportion k, output will increase (decrease) by k. If we know output for any X and Y input combination, then so long as the ratio of X to Y remains constant, we can determine output for any other combination of X and Y inputs. This is demonstrated in Table 7.2.

In section A of the table, we show the behavior of output as the input X is varied from 1 to 14 units with the input of Y held constant at 1 unit. Column 3 shows the proportion of factor inputs — X/Y. In section B of

FIGURE 7.5

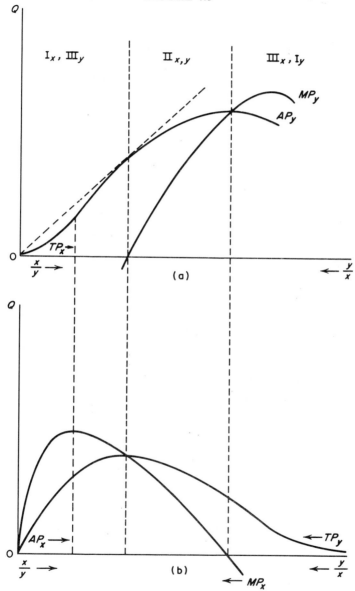

TABLE 7.2

(A)							(B)				
(1)	(2)	(3)	(4)	(5)	(6)		(7)	(8)	(9)	(10)	(11)	(12)
X	Y	X/Y	TP_x	MP_x	AP_x		Y	X	Y/X	TP_y	MP_y	AP_y
0	1		0									
1	1	1/1	5	5	5	STAGE I	1	1	1/1	5	−1	5	STAGE III
2	1	2/1	11	6	5½		1/2	1	1/2	5½	−3	11	
3	1	3/1	18	7	6		1/3	1	1/3	6	−6	18	
4	1	4/1	26	8	6½		1/4	1	1/4	6½	2	26	
5	1	5/1	32	6	6⅗		1/5	1	1/5	6⅗	7	32	
6	1	6/1	37	5	6⅙		1/6	1	1/6	6⅙	13	37	
7	1	7/1	41	4	5 6/7	STAGE II	1/7	1	1/7	5 6/7	27	41	STAGE II
8	1	8/1	43	2	5⅜		1/8	1	1/8	5⅜	35	43	
9	1	9/1	44	1	4 8/9		1/9	1	1/9	4 8/9	44	44	
10	1	10/1	44	0	4⅖		1/10	1	1/10	4⅖	54	44	
11	1	11/1	43	−1	3 10/11		1/11	1	1/11	3 10/11	65	43	
12	1	12/1	41	−2	3 5/12	STAGE III	1/12	1	1/12	3 5/12	67	41	STAGE I
13	1	13/1	37	−4	2 11/13		1/13	1	1/13	2 11/13	115	37	
14	1	14/1	31	−6	2 3/14		1/14	1	1/14	2 3/14	31	31	

the table, reading from the bottom to the top, we show the behavior of output as Y is varied from 0 to 1 unit with X held constant at 1 unit. Note that the factor proportions listed in column 9 are in terms of the ratio Y/X, not X/Y as in column 3. In other words, even though the factor proportions are the same in both columns, the ones in column 9 appear as the reciprocals of those in column 3.

In column 4 we assume a series of output figures that show increasing and then diminishing returns with respect to increases in the ratio X/Y. This TP_x schedule is plotted in Figure 7.5a. Columns 5 and 6 are derived in the usual fashion and are plotted in Figure 7.5b.

Notice that when we move from left to right in this figure the ratio X/Y increases, and in moving from right to left, Y/X increases or X/Y decreases. Consequently, column 9 should be read from bottom to top, which is equivalent to reading Figure 7.5 from right to left.

We shall explain the derivation of the figures in column 10 with reference to $Y/X = 1/14$. TP_x was defined as output when X is varied on 1 unit of Y; or, in other words, output for various ratios of X/Y per unit of Y. Similarly, TP_y is defined as output when Y is varied on 1 unit of X — or output for various ratios of Y/X per unit of X. Since we assumed $TP_x = 31$ when 14 units of X are used with 1 unit of Y (a factor ratio of $X/Y = 14/1$), if we desire to maintain this ratio with the X factor now being held at 1 unit, we multiply both inputs and output by $1/14$.* There-

---

*The changes in the proportion of the fixed (Y) factor to the variable (X) factor take place through changes in X, the Y factor being indeed *fixed*. Because of the nature of

fore, for a Y input of $\frac{1}{14}$ ($\frac{1}{14} \times 1 = \frac{1}{14}$) and an X input of 1 ($\frac{1}{14} \times 14 = 1$), TP_y is $2\frac{3}{14}$ ($\frac{1}{14} \times 31 = 2\frac{3}{14}$). The rest of column 10 is derived in analogous fashion. Columns 11 and 12 are derived from column 10 in the usual manner.[5]

The student should notice the following symmetry in Figure 7.5, where the numbers from Table 7.2 are plotted. Over the range where AP_x increases, MP_y is negative; conversely, over the range in which AP_y is rising (measured from right to left), MP_x is negative.[6] We stated

---

a homogeneous production function, however, we may involve ourselves in a hypothetical experiment in which the proportion of Y to X is kept the same as before but it is Y that is being varied and this permits us to compute total, marginal, and average product of Y. This will perhaps be clearer in the following example. We have as-

X	Y	TP_x	MP_y
[0	1]	0	
[1	1]	5	
[2	1]	11	
2	2	$2 \times 5 = 10$	-1.0
[3	1]	18	
3	1.5	$\frac{3}{2} \times 11 = 16.5$	-3.0
[4	1]	26	
4	$\frac{4}{3}$	$\frac{4}{3} \times 18 = 24$	-6.0
[5	1]	32	
5	$\frac{5}{4}$	$\frac{5}{4} \times 26 = 32.5$	$+2.0$
[6	1]	37	
6	$\frac{6}{5}$	$\frac{6}{5} \times 32 = 38.4$	$+7.0$

sumed that the input of X is varied on a unit of Y and that we know the associated output figures (these are shown in brackets).

Thus with 1 unit of X used on 1 unit of Y, 5 units of output are produced. We also know that when input of X is increased to 2 units (keeping Y constant at 1 unit) output goes to 11 units. Now by the definition of a linear homogeneous production function we know that had both X and Y been doubled (from $1X$ and $1Y$ to $2X$ and $2Y$), output would have doubled from 5 to 10. Therefore adding one unit of Y causes output to go from 11 to 10 and clearly $MP_y = -1$. We now repeat this process: we know that output for $3X$, $1Y$ is 18. If both X and Y had been increased by 1.5, output would have gone to 16.5. We compute MP_y as follows:

$$\frac{\Delta q}{\Delta Y} = \frac{-1.5}{0.5} = -3.0$$

The other MP_y's are computed in similar fashion.

[5] Notice that TP_y is the same as AP_x and AP_y is the same as TP_x. Since we defined TP_y as output per unit of X for a given input of Y and AP_x as the output per unit of X at a given quantity of Y, these two are equivalent. The same relationship holds between TP_x and AP_y.

[6] This relationship can be shown as follows: If q/X is rising, a doubling of X must more than double q. But we know that if we double both X and Y, q will just double (the linear homogeneous production function gives constant returns to scale). The effect of increasing the amount of Y must be to decrease output; MP_y is, therefore, negative.

before that the firm will, if possible, never operate in a stage where a factor is subject to negative returns. Hence the firm will attempt to operate in the stage where neither factor has a negative marginal product (that is, between the ridge lines), which is Stage II for both X and Y in Figure 7.5. It should be noted that in Stage $II_{x,y}$ both factors are subject to both declining marginal and average product.

Long-Run Least-Cost Conditions

Recall that the isoquant map in Figure 7.2 showed the different combinations of X and Y that the firm could use to produce various levels of output when all factors of production are variable. From a technological point of view, all points along an isoquant represent equal efficiency — that is, the same output can be produced with the different factor combinations. Because a firm must pay positive prices for the factors it employs, the total cost of producing a particular level of output will vary along an isoquant, depending on the factor combination and the factor prices. Thus, while all factor combinations along an isoquant represent equal *technological* efficiency, the combination with which the particular output level can be produced at lowest total cost represents the *economically* most efficient combination. And since firms try to maximize their profits which are equal to the difference between total revenue and total cost, a firm will try to select that combination of factors which minimizes the total cost for any given level of output. Or, what amounts to the same thing, for a given level of expenditure, the firm will try to maximize output.

Assume that a firm with the production function of Figure 7.2 must pay $1 per unit of X and $2 per unit of Y and that both these factor prices remain the same regardless of the quantities the firm purchases.[7] With these factor prices, we want to determine which factor comination the firm will use to produce each of the output levels included in Figure 7.2. In other words, we wish to find the least cost of producing these outputs.

Nine different *isocost lines* are drawn in Figure 7.6. Each isocost (or equal-cost line) shows the different combinations of factors X and Y the firm *can* produce when $P_x = \$1$ and $P_y = \$2$ for a given level of total expenditure. Thus, along isocost line $TC = \$695$, the firm can purchase the sample quantities of X and Y shown in Table 7.3.

[7] It is also possible that a firm pay either higher or lower per unit prices for its factors as it increases the quantities of the factors which it purchases or hires. The case of rising factor prices will be considered in Chapter 12.

FIGURE 7.6

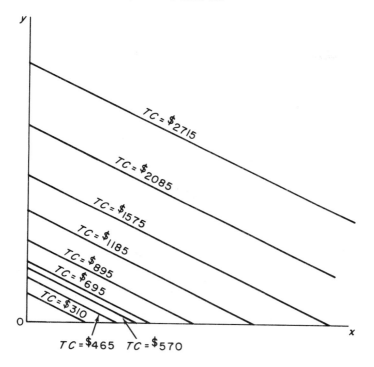

TABLE 7.3

X	Y	$P_x X$	$P_y Y$	Total Cost
695	0	$695	$ 0	$695
645	25	645	50	695
595	50	595	100	695
545	75	545	150	695
495	100	495	200	695
445	125	445	250	695
395	150	395	300	695
345	175	345	350	695
295	200	295	400	695
245	225	245	450	695
195	250	195	500	695
145	275	145	550	695
95	300	95	600	695
45	325	45	650	695
0	347½	0	695	695

Since the factor prices are assumed to be constants, the isocost lines are all parallel with slopes equal to $-P_x/P_y$.*

FIGURE 7.7

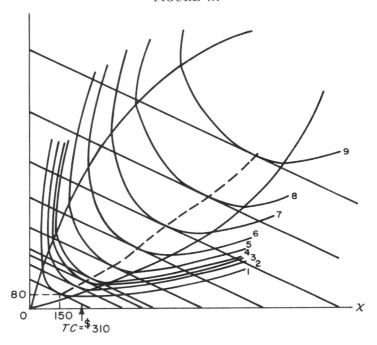

In Figure 7.7 we have redrawn the isoquant map of Figure 7.2 and have superimposed on it the isocost lines of Figure 7.6. From the infinite number of possible isocost lines, we have selected those that are tangent to the isoquants. The coordinates of the point of tangency between isoquant 1 and isocost line 1 (150 units of X and 80 units of Y) are those quantities of X and Y that ensure 100 units of output being produced at minimum cost, which is $310. We show in Figure 7.7 the least-cost combination of X and Y for the different output levels and we summarize this information in Table 7.4. The curve drawn connecting these tangency points is called the scale line or expansion path of the firm.[8]

*See page 84, where the slope of the budget line was derived. An isocost line has the same properties as a budget line, as it is based on given prices and a given level of expenditure.

[8]For their esthetic appeal, most textbooks show the expansion path and ridge lines as being smooth curves. However, the complexities of the set of choices that the production function summarizes mean that no such regularity in the shape of these curves is necessary.

It will be recalled that the slope of an isocost line is equal to $-P_x/P_y$ and the slope of an isoquant is equal to $-MP_x/MP_y$. Since at each point of tangency, the slope of the isocost line is equal to the slope of the isoquant,

---

In pages 123–124 and in Appendix 5, we showed that the slope of an isoquant was equal to the ratio of marginal products:

$$\frac{dY}{dX} = -\frac{MP_x}{MP_y}$$

We also showed there that, with a linear homogeneous production function, the marginal products are functions simply of the factor proportions. If P_x and P_y are constants, the expansion path for this special type of production function will be a straight line. We can see this with reference to the diagram.

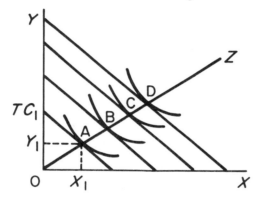

All combinations of X and Y along OZ are in the same proportion. Therefore,

$$\frac{MP_x}{MP_y} \text{ at } A = \frac{MP_x}{MP_y} \text{ at } B = \text{ and so on}$$

If A is the tangency between isoquant 1 and isocost line 1 (i.e., X_1 and Y_1 yield the lowest cost to produce q_1), then at A,

$$\frac{MP_x}{MP_y} = \frac{P_x}{P_y}$$

With the assumption of constant P_x/P_y, the slopes of the isocost lines are equal. Therefore, all least-cost combinations (tangency points between isoquants and isocost lines) must lie along line OZ where the slopes of the isoquants, $-MP_x/MP_y$, are all equal to the slope of isoquant q_1 at A.

The ridge lines also will be straight with a linear homogeneous production function. RL_x is the locus of points where $MP_x/MP_y = 0$, RL_y where $MP_x/MP_y = \infty$; and MP_x/MP_y is a function of the factor proportion used.

TABLE 7.4

(1)	(2)	(3)	(4)	(5)	(6)
q	X	Y	P_xX	P_yY	TC
100	150	80	$150	$160	$310
200	235	115	235	230	465
300	270	150	270	300	570
400	305	195	305	390	695
500	435	230	435	460	895
600	535	325	535	650	1185
700	685	445	685	890	1575
800	905	590	905	1180	2085
900	1125	795	1125	1590	2715

Column 4 = Column 2 $\times$ \$1
Column 5 = Column 3 $\times$ \$2
Column 6 = Column 4 + Column 5 = Total Cost

we can state that

$$\frac{MP_x}{MP_y} = \frac{P_x}{P_y} \tag{7.11}$$

or

$$\frac{MP_x}{P_x} = \frac{MP_y}{P_y}* \tag{7.11a}$$

This tangency condition holds all along the expansion path.

A numerical example should make clear why this tangency condition represents the minimum cost of producing a given level of output or the maximum output for a given level of expenditure. With $P_x = \$1$ and $P_y = \$2$, assume this firm is using a combination of factor quantities such that $MP_x = 10$ and $MP_y = 15$. Then the following inequality would hold:

$$\frac{MP_x}{P_x} > \frac{MP_y}{P_y}; \quad \frac{10 \text{ units}}{\$1} > \frac{15 \text{ units}}{\$2}$$

or 10 units per \$ $> 7\frac{1}{2}$ units per \$.

*Appendix 4A can be used to demonstrate rigorously that this is a necessary condition if output is to be maximized subject to a given level of total cost. If A and B represent two factors of production, P_a and P_b the given constant prices of those factors, I the given level of total cost, and U output, the proof is identical with Appendix 4A. (Of course, marginal products would be relevant, rather than the marginal utilities of Chapter 4.) Furthermore, the second-order condition, ensuring that output is at a maximum rather than a minimum is identical with that in Appendix 4A.

FIGURE 7.8

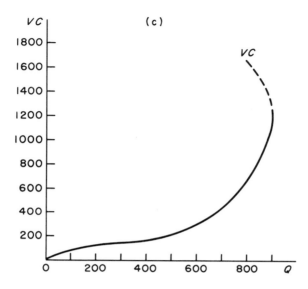

If the firm were to spend $1 less on factor Y, it would lose $7\frac{1}{2}$ units of production; but if the firm kept its expenditure constant by spending the dollar on factor X, it would gain approximately 10 units of output. This means there would be a net increase in output of $2\frac{1}{2}$ units with expenditure the same. Further transfers of expenditure from Y to X would continue to result in additional output as long as $MP_x/P_x > MP_yP_y$. As discussed previously, however, the use of more X and less Y will cause MP_x to decline and MP_y to increase; and since P_x and P_y are constants with continuously divisible factors, MP_x/P_x and MP_y/P_y will become equal to each other.

The total cost figures in column 6 of Table 7.4 are the minimum costs for producing the various levels of output. And for each level of output, the factor combination of columns 2 and 3 is the economically most efficient one.

Short-Run Equilibrium of the Firm

Given the fact that it cannot vary all its factors of production, the firm, in the short run, will attempt to produce any level of output at the least possible cost. First, we shall consider the short-run situation presented on pages 120 – 124: factor X is the only variable factor and Y the

FIGURE 7.8

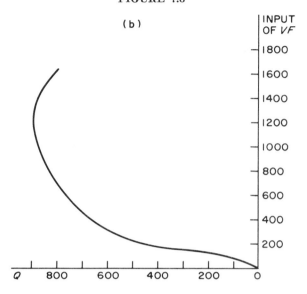

(b)

INPUT
OF *VF*

1800
1600
1400
1200
1000
800
600
400
200

Q   800   600   400   200   O

only fixed one, which we shall assume is at the level OY_1 (750 units). In Figure 7.2, moving along Y_1A, we can see that for any output a specific input of the one variable factor is necessary if redundancy is to be avoided. In this case the fact that the firm has no technological choice in producing any level of output makes the economically and the technologically most efficient methods of production the same. These conclusions are, however, merely the result of the simplifying assumption that there is only one variable factor of production.

The short-run total product schedule of Figure 7.3 (which was derived from the isoquant map of Figure 7.2 by holding Y constant at $OY_1 = 750$ units) can be converted into a short-run total cost curve. This procedure is demonstrated with reference to Figures 7.8 a–c. In Figure 7.8a we merely replot Figure 7.3. In Figure 7.8b we replot the same input-output relationship but with the axes reversed. (Alternatively, this may be described as rotating Figure 7.8a 90 degrees around the 0-point as an axis.) In Figure 7.8b the vertical axis gives us the input of the variable factor; and when we have multiplied these factor quantities by the price of the factor ($1 in this example), we obtain the variable cost for each level of output shown on the horizontal axis. Figure 7.8b with the $-vertical axis, then, is the variable cost curve of the firm. It is a convention, however, to read positive quantities from left to right. Turning Figure 7.8b over we

FIGURE 7.8

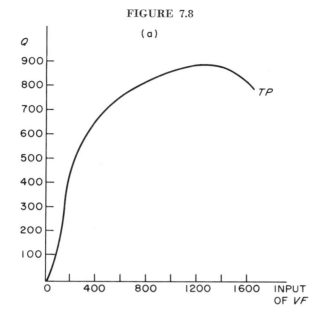

(a)

get Figure 7.8c, which is the same as Figure 7.8b except that the quantity-axis now reads from left to right. Since we have assumed Y constant at 750 units and P_y a constant of \$2 per unit, the "fixed cost" is \$1500. If we were to add this fixed cost to the variable cost at each level of output, we would obtain a new curve, with the same shape as the variable cost curve, but above it by the constant amount of \$1500. This is the short-run total cost curve of the firm. The derivation of these cost curves is summarized in Table 7.5.

Once we make the more realistic assumption that the firm has two or more variable factors, it is again faced with more than one technological alternative and must choose among them on economic grounds. A relationship among three inputs and output is represented by a four-dimensional production surface.[9]

The reader has seen that when we cut a three-dimensional surface at some fixed level of one of the variables, the resulting surface is two-dimensional. Analogously, cutting a four-dimensional surface at a fixed level of one of the variable factors produces a three-dimensional surface. Figure 7.2 might be a representation of a relationship among

[9]The concept of four dimensions is outside the experience of human beings, who live in a three-dimensional world; it is, however, both mathematically and analytically a useful abstraction to talk about n-dimensional relationships.

TABLE 7.5

X	Y	q	VC(= $1 · X)	FC(= $2 · 750)	TC = VC + FC
90	750	100	$ 90	$1500	$1590
125	750	200	125	1500	1625
150	750	300	150	1500	1650
170	750	400	170	1500	1670
210	750	500	210	1500	1710
300	750	600	300	1500	1800
450	750	700	450	1500	1950
690	750	800	690	1500	2190
1270	750	900	1270	1500	2770

three inputs and output when one of the inputs is being held constant at some level. The resulting problem is similar to the one considered above in which the firm was operating in the long run with two factors of production. We demonstrated then that the firm would combine its factors in the long run (and in the long run all factors are variable) so that the following equality would hold for any level of output:

$$\frac{MP_a}{P_a} = \frac{MP_b}{P_b} = \cdots = \frac{MP_n}{P_n} \qquad (7.12)$$

COSTS OF PRODUCTION

8

Short-Run Costs

In this section we shall consider the costs of the firm in the short run, when at least one factor of production is fixed.[1] We now derive the average and marginal cost curves.

Variable costs (VC) are those costs that vary with the output of the firm and that will be zero when output is zero.

Fixed costs (FC) are those costs that remain constant as output varies and are incurred even if output is zero.[2]

Total cost (STC) is the sum of variable plus fixed costs:[3]

$$STC = VC + FC \qquad (8.1)$$

Marginal cost (SMC) is the rate of change of total cost with respect to changes in output. In the continuous case:

$$SMC = \frac{dSTC}{dq}, \qquad (8.2a)$$

[1]It has been pointed out that the "fixed factor" is many times fixed in cost but, within the fixed cost, the entrepreneur has built a flexible plant adaptable to a wide range of outputs. For instance, he may build ten small machines that can be brought into use as needed to produce a wide range of outputs, rather than a single large machine of equal cost that, although more efficient in producing large outputs, is not as flexible. For a full discussion of this point, see George J. Stigler, "Production and Distribution in the Short Run," *Journal of Political Economy*, XLVII (1939), 105–127. Reprinted in A.E.A., *Readings in Income Distribution* (Richard D. Irwin, Homewood, Ill., 1951).
[2]Another category of short-run costs is quasi-fixed costs. These are costs that are zero when output is zero but assume a certain value when output is increased above zero and then remain at that level for all outputs above the initial one.
[3]Included in all the cost concepts are not only the explicit or expenditure cost but the cost of forgone opportunities — or implicit cost. For example, the wages lost by the entrepreneur when he works for his own firm rather than in his most remunerative alternative occupation are included as implicit costs.

and in the discrete case:

$$SMC = \frac{\Delta STC}{\Delta q} \qquad (8.2b)$$

Since the difference between total cost and variable cost is a constant — a fixed cost — marginal cost can also be computed as

$$SMC = \frac{dVC}{dq} \quad \text{or} \quad SMC = \frac{\Delta VC}{\Delta q} \qquad (8.2c)$$

Average variable cost (AVC) is the variable cost per unit of output:

$$AVC = \frac{VC}{q} \qquad (8.3)$$

Average fixed cost (AFC) is the fixed cost per unit of output:

$$AFC = \frac{FC}{q} \qquad (8.4)$$

Average total cost (ATC) is the total cost per unit of output:

$$SAC = \frac{STC}{q} = \frac{VC}{q} + \frac{FC}{q} = AVC + AFC \qquad (8.5)$$

We now derive the relationships defined above for the cost data that was obtained from the production function on page 119, where $P_x = \$1$ and $P_y = \$2$. With reference to Table 8.1, the student should note the following relationships: When AP_x rises, $MP_x > AP_x$, and when AP_x declines, $MP_x < AP_x$ (columns 7 and 9). When AP_x rises, AVC falls, and when AP_x declines, AVC increases (columns 7 and 8). Since X is the only variable factor and its price is a constant, when the average productivity of X rises — that is, increasing returns to X — the cost per unit of output (AVC) must decline. There is an analogous relationship between MP_x and SMC (columns 9 and 10). When the marginal productivity of X rises, the extra cost per unit of output (SMC) must fall.[4]

Therefore, if there is an initial stage of increasing returns, followed by a stage of decreasing returns, the AVC-curve will be U-shaped; it declines, reaches a minimum, and then rises. Analogously, the SMC-curve will be U-shaped. The usual relationship holds between the AVC- and SMC-curves and is shown graphically in Figure 8.1: when AVC declines, SMC

---

[4] These relationships can be shown as follows:

$$\frac{q}{x} = AP_x$$

If q/x rises, x/q falls and $(x/q)P_x$, with P_x constant, falls. If $\Delta q/\Delta x$ rises, $\Delta x/\Delta q$ falls, and $(\Delta x/\Delta q)P_x$ falls, with P_x constant.

FIGURE 8.1

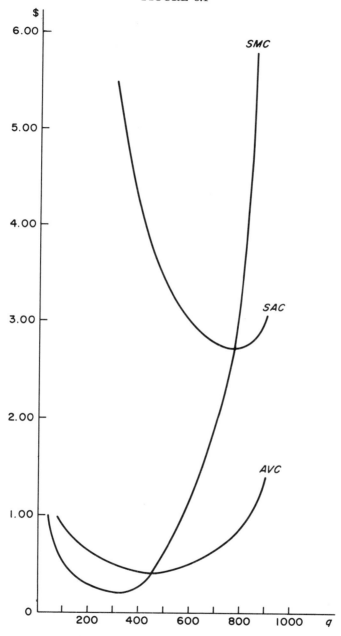

FIGURE 8.2

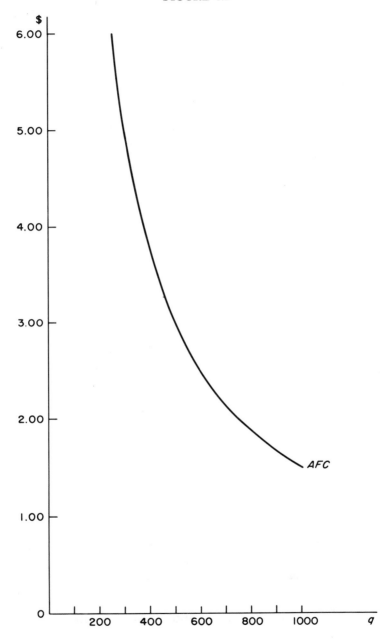

lies below AVC; when AVC rises, SMC lies above AVC; and when AVC is at its minimum level, it is equal to SMC.

We show the AFC schedule (column 11 in Table 8.1) in Figure 8.2. Fixed costs being constant, AFC continuously declines as output is increased. When output reaches high levels, AFC approaches zero but, of course, must remain positive.[5] In graphical terms, then, AFC is a rectangular hyperbole.

The shape of the SAC schedule in Figure 8.1 (column 12) depends on the shapes of the AVC- and AFC-schedules since $SAC = AVC + AFC$. Over

TABLE 8.1

(1) X	(2) Y	(3) q	(4) VC	(5) FC	(6) STC	(7) AP_x	(8) AVC	(9) MP_x	(10) SMC	(11) AFC	(12) SAC
0	750	0	$ 0	$1500	$1500					$ → ∞	$ → ∞
								1.11	$0.90		
90	750	100	90	1500	1590	1.11	$0.90			15.00	15.90
								2.86	0.35		
125	750	200	125	1500	1625	1.60	0.625			7.50	8.125
								4.00	0.25		
150	750	300	150	1500	1650	2.00	0.50			5.00	5.50
								5.00	0.20		
170	750	400	170	1500	1670	2.35	0.425			3.75	4.175
								2.50	0.40		
210	750	500	210	1500	1710	2.38	0.42			3.00	3.42
								1.11	0.90		
300	750	600	300	1500	1800	2.00	0.50			2.50	3.00
								0.67	1.50		
450	750	700	450	1500	1950	1.56	0.6428			2.14	2.785
								0.42	2.40		
690	750	800	690	1500	2190	1.16	0.8625			1.88	2.737
								0.17	5.80		
1270	750	900	1270	1500	2770	0.71	1.411			1.67	3.077

(1), (2), and (3) were obtained from Figure 7.8a.
(4) = (1) × $1 (See Figure 7.8c.)
(5) = (2) × $2
(6) = (4) + (5)
(7) = (3) ÷ (1)
(8) = (4) ÷ (1)
(9) = Δ(3) ÷ Δ(1) = discrete MP_x
(10) = Δ(4) ÷ Δ(3) = Δ(6) ÷ Δ(3) = discrete MC
(11) = (5) ÷ (3)
(12) = (8) + (11) = (6) ÷ (3)

[5] We have seen that $AFC = FC/q$; clearly also $AFC \times q = (FC/q)q = FC = $ constant. In graphical terms, this means that the rectangles cut off by the ordinates and abscissas of the points of the AFC-curve must all have areas equal to FC.

the range of output where AVC is declining (up to 500 units in Table 8.1), SAC will also fall, since AFC always declines. However, when AVC starts to increase, SAC can continue to decline, if the decrease in AFC more than offsets the increase in AVC. Thus, in our example, SAC declines up to 800 units of output. SMC has the same relationship to SAC as it does to AVC, since $SMC = \Delta STC/\Delta q = \Delta VC/\Delta q$; that is, when SAC declines, $SMC < SAC$; when SAC increases, $SMC > SAC$; and $SMC = SAC$ when SAC is at its minimum level. This relationship is shown in Figure 8.1.

For some firms evidence indicates the variable costs of production increase at a constant rate over a range of outputs. This situation is presented in Table 8.2 for the range of outputs between 4 and 8 units. Thus, AVC reaches a minimum of \$7 at 4 units; but instead of rising as output expands, remains at \$7 through 8 units and rises thereafter. Note that

FIGURE 8.3

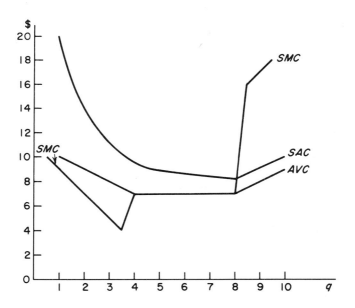

since SMC is equal to AVC at the minimum level of AVC, SMC and AVC are coincident over a range of outputs. With a flat-bottomed AVC curve, SAC will still be ∪-shaped; SAC will decline while AVC is a constant and will rise when the increases in AVC start to outweigh the decreases in AFC. The cost schedules of Table 8.2 are drawn in Figure 8.3.

Long-Run Costs

Since in the long run all factors of production can be varied, the relevant cost concepts are *total cost* (*LTC*, which is the same as total variable cost) and the corresponding average and marginal costs.

TABLE 8.2

q	VC	FC	STC	SMC	AVC	AFC	SAC
0	$ 0	$10	$10			$ → ∞	$ → ∞
				$10			
1	10	10	20		$10	10.00	20.00
				8			
2	18	10	28		9	5.00	14.00
				6			
3	24	10	34		8	3.33	11.33
				4			
4	28	10	38		7	2.50	9.50
				7			
5	35	10	45		7	2.00	9.00
				7			
6	42	10	52		7	1.67	8.67
				7			
7	49	10	59		7	1.43	8.43
				7			
8	56	10	66		7	1.25	8.25
				16			
9	72	10	82		8	1.11	9.11
				18			
10	90	10	100		9	1.00	10.00

Marginal cost (*LMC*) is the rate of change of total cost with respect to changes in output:

$$LMC = \frac{dLTC}{dq} \quad \text{(continuous)} \qquad (8.6a)$$

$$LMC = \frac{\Delta LTC}{\Delta q} \quad \text{(discrete)} \qquad (8.6b)$$

Average cost (*LAC*) is the total cost per unit of output:

$$LAC = \frac{LTC}{q} \qquad (8.7)$$

The relationships that exist among *LTC*, *LAC*, and *LMC* are the same as the short-run ones. This is demonstrated with respect to Table 8.3 and Figure 8.4. When *LTC* increases at a decreasing rate, *LMC* falls; and

FIGURE 8.4

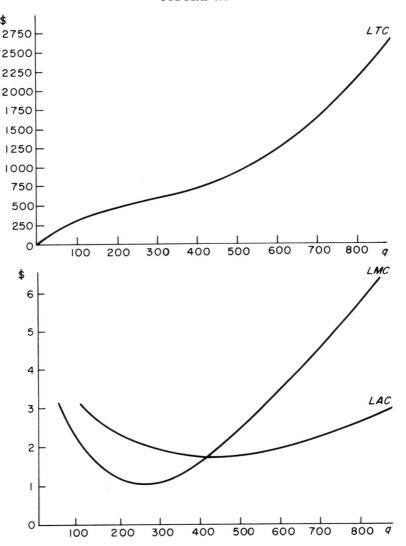

LMC rises when *LTC* increases at an increasing rate. Observe how the declining stage of *LMC* is over the range of outputs where the isoquants were closer and closer together in Figure 7.7. Similarly, for those outputs where the isoquants were drawn farther and farther apart in Figure 7.7, *LMC* increases. When *LAC* decreases, *LMC* < *LAC*; when *LAC* increases, *LMC* > *LAC*; and when *LAC* is at its minimum level, *LMC* = *LAC*.

If there is a wide range of output over which there are constant returns to scale, the *LAC*-curve will be flat-bottomed and the *LMC*-curve will coincide with *LAC* over this portion.

The Relationship between Long-Run and Short-Run Costs

We have seen above that, depending upon the period that it has available to adjust its size of plant, either the firm will be able to achieve a completely optimum combination of factors, when all factors are variable (the long run), or it will achieve a less-than-optimum combination because of the constraint of some fixed factor or factors (the short run).

TABLE 8.3

q	*LTC*	*LMC*	*LAC*
0	$ 0		
		$3.10	
100	310		$3.10
		1.55	
200	465		2.32
		1.05	
300	570		1.90
		1.25	
400	695		1.74
		2.00	
500	895		1.79
		2.90	
600	1185		1.90
		3.90	
700	1575		2.25
		5.10	
800	2085		2.61
		6.30	
900	2715		3.02

SOURCE: Table 7.6.

At any moment in time, the firm will be operating in the short run. However, if we conceive of a firm that has not yet entered an industry or an operating firm planning for the future over a time period long enough so that all factors affecting operations can be varied, then the relevant production and cost data for the decision making of the firm are the long-run ones.

In Figure 8.5, we assume the firm to be producing q_1 in the short run with OY_1 of the fixed factor and OX_1 of the variable factor. If it became

FIGURES 8.5, 8.6, and 8.7

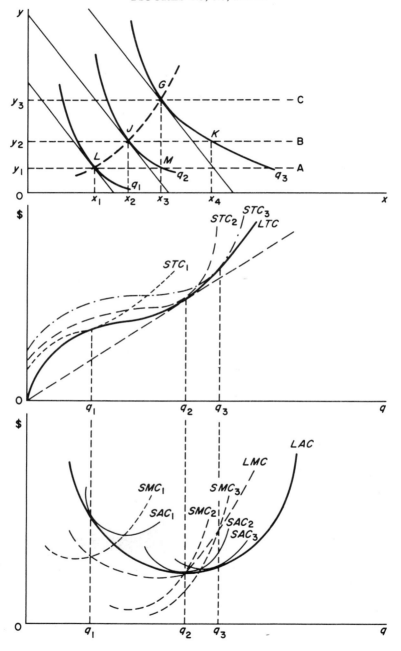

necessary for the firm to increase output to q_2 in the short run, it would produce q_2 using its fixed factor, OY_1, and OX_3 of the variable factor. It would move from point L on isoquant q_1 to point M on isoquant q_2. On the other hand, if the firm were planning to increase output to q_2 in the long run, it would choose to do so by utilizing OY_2 of the now variable Y-factor and OX_2 of the X-factor. This amounts to a movement from L on isoquant q_1 to J on isoquant q_2, along the expansion path. Analogously, if the firm were to increase output from q_2 to q_3, in the short run it would move from J to K, and in the long run from J to G on the expansion path.

It should be noted that if the firm happens to have OY_1 of the fixed factor in the short run and desired to produce q_1, it will, of necessity, use X_1 of the variable factor. And this is the factor combination that will be used in the long run. In the same way, if the firm happened to have OY_2 of the fixed factor in the short run, it would be forced to utilize OX_2 to produce q_2. Finally, if fortuitously the firm had OY_3 of the fixed factor in the short run, it would end using OX_3 of the variable factor to produce q_3; and this is just the combination the firm would choose in the long run. In other words, points L, J, and G lie on the long-run expansion path and, therefore, on the long-run output curve of the firm; and these points also lie on the respective short-run product curves cut out by Y_1A, Y_2B, and Y_3C.

In Figure 8.6 we show, first, the long-run total cost curve derived from the expansion path in Figure 8.5. We also show the short-run total cost curves tangent to the LAC-curve at q_1, q_2, and q_3. STC_1 corresponds to the short run in which the fixed factor is at the level OY_1, STC_2 to the short run with OY_2, and STC_3 to the short run with OY_3 the fixed factor. Clearly, for each point on the LTC-curve there will correspond a point of tangency with an STC-curve. Another way of stating this is that the LTC-curve consists of the minimum cost points for particular outputs on an infinite number of STC-curves.

The same relationship can be explained in terms of the average and marginal schedules in Figure 8.7. Like the relationship between LTC and STC, the SAC-curve consists of the minimum per-unit-cost points for particular outputs on an infinite number of SAC-curves. The LAC-curve is called an envelope curve to the SAC-curves since no point on an SAC-curve can ever lie below the LAC-curve. In other words, each point on the LAC-curve represents the absolute minimum per-unit cost of producing a given output when all factors are variable. We have assumed that the Y-factor can be varied continuously and so get a smooth envelope curve. If Y can be varied only discretely, the envelope curve would give a scalloped effect.

We have assumed that the X-Y combination at point J in Figure 8.5

represents not only the least-cost combination of inputs for producing q_2, but also the minimum per-unit-cost of producing any output in the long run. Therefore, in Figure 8.6, a line drawn from the origin is tangent to the LTC-curve at q_2; as a consequence, LAC in Figure 8.7 is at a minimum and equal to LMC at q_2. Furthermore, since $STC_2 = LTC$ to produce q_2, $SAC_2 = LAC$ and $SMC_2 = LMC$. Therefore $SAC_2 = SMC_2$; or, in other words, at q_2, SAC_2 is at its minimum and $SAC = SMC = LMC = LAC$.

It will be noticed that for all outputs less than that at which LAC is a minimum, the tangency with an SAC-curve occurs to the left of the minimum SAC on the relevant SAC-curve. And for outputs greater than q_2, the tangencies take place at outputs greater than the respective minimum SAC. This means that when a firm is operating subject to increasing returns to scale (from 0 to q_2), it can achieve minimum SAC by building plants larger than those that would produce given outputs at their minimum cost points and underutilizing these plants (that is, at outputs less than those that result in minimum SAC). Similarly, for outputs greater than q_2, where the firm experiences decreasing returns to scale, the firm will achieve lowest SAC for a particular level of output by building plants smaller than those that would produce a given output at minimum SAC and overutilizing them. To summarize, a firm is not interested in achieving the minimum cost output for a given plant but is interested in producing a given output at minimum cost.

A concrete example will perhaps make it easier to see why the firm may choose to operate plants at other than minimum cost outputs. Suppose that a housewife has ten pounds of wash per day that can be done by hand, be washed in a machine, or be sent to a steam laundry. The following are the relevant long-run cost data:

Cost per pound if done by hand	Cost per pound if done by washing machine	Cost per pound if done by laundry
10¢	10 lbs. (1 hr.): 6¢ 50 lbs. (5 hrs.): 5¢	10 lbs.: 7¢ 50 lbs.: 4.2¢

Based upon the fact that her cost per pound is minimized this way, she chooses to buy a washing machine and run it one hour a day. A friend points out that if she were to run the machine the maximum time per day permitted by the landlord (5 hours) and wash 50 pounds, her per-pound cost would be reduced to 5¢. She replies that she is interested in washing 10 and not 50 pounds of laundry per day, and for 10 pounds the washing machine gives lowest unit cost; and that if she wanted to wash 50 pounds per day, the steam laundry would be more economical, since its unit cost for this quantity is lower than that of the washing machine.

THE RELATIONSHIP BETWEEN *LMC* AND *SMC* AND *LAC* AND *SAC*

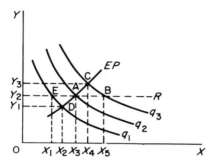

Assume a firm is producing q_2 using OX_3 of X and OY_2 of Y. We want to demonstrate that, if the firm were to expand output to q_3 (assuming that $q_3 - q_2$ represents a small increase), $SMC > LMC$.

At point A,

$$\frac{MP_{x_3}}{MP_{y_2}} = \frac{P_x}{P_y} \qquad (A8.1)$$

which we can rewrite as

$$\frac{MP_{x_3}}{P_x} = \frac{MP_{y_2}}{P_y} \qquad (A8.2)$$

Since these ratios are equal, their reciprocals are equal:

$$\frac{P_x}{MP_{x_3}} = \frac{P_y}{MP_{y_2}} \qquad (A8.3)$$

Note that

$$\frac{P_x}{MP_x} = \frac{P_x}{\Delta Q/\Delta X} = \frac{\Delta TC}{\Delta Q} = MC$$

Since $P_x/MP_x = P_y/MP_y$ along the expansion path, the addition to cost will be the same no matter which factor is used to produce a small increment of output. Therefore, at A,

$$\frac{P_x}{MP_{x_3}} = \frac{P_y}{MP_{y_2}} = LMC \qquad (A8.4)$$

Similarly, in the short run, if the firm employs only one variable factor of production,

$$\frac{P_x}{MP_x} = SMC$$

Therefore, at A, along line Y_2R,

$$\frac{P_x}{MP_{x_3}} = SMC \qquad (A8.5)$$

and at A, therefore,

$$LMC = SMC \qquad (A8.6)$$

If the firm expanded output to q_3 and was free to vary both X and Y, it would produce at C on the expansion path. At C

$$\frac{P_x}{MP_{x_4}} = \frac{P_y}{MP_{y_3}} = LMC \qquad (A8.7)$$

If the firm operates in the short run with OY_2 of Y, it would produce q_3 at B where

$$\frac{P_x}{MP_{x_5}} = SMC \qquad (A8.8)$$

Note that, if we exclude the possibility of the firm's operating in an area where a factor is redundant,

$$MP_{x_4} > MP_{x_5} \qquad (A8.9)$$

since at B there is more X and less Y than at C.

If

$$MP_{x_4} > MP_{x_5}, \quad \frac{P_x}{MP_{x_4}} < \frac{P_x}{MP_{x_5}}$$

and, therefore, from equations A8.7 and A8.8 we see that

$$LMC < SMC \qquad (A8.10)$$

We can use the same procedure to demonstrate that if the firm were to decrease output from q_2 to q_1, $SMC < LMC$. If the firm could vary X and Y, it would produce at D on the expansion path. At D,

$$\frac{P_x}{MP_{x_2}} = \frac{P_y}{MP_{y_1}} = LMC \qquad (A8.11)$$

If the firm had a fixed amount of Y, OY_1, it would produce q_1 at E.

At E,

$$\frac{P_x}{MP_{x_1}} = SMC \qquad (A8.12)$$

Since at E there is less X and more Y than at D,

$$MP_{x_1} > MP_{x_2} \qquad (A8.13)$$

Thus,

$$\frac{P_x}{MP_{x_1}} < \frac{P_x}{MP_{x_2}}$$

and following from equations A8.11 and A8.12:

$$SMC < LMC \qquad (A8.14)$$

Note that this means when the firm cuts back output, costs are reduced less in the short run than in the long run.

We showed on page 150 that when a firm produces at minimum LAC,

$$LAC = LMC = SMC = SAC$$

We now explain why for outputs less than the one where LAC is a minimum, the tangency with an SAC-curve occurs to the left of the minimum SAC.

When LAC declines, $LMC < LAC$. If LAC is tangent to SAC, $LAC = SAC$, $LMC = SMC$, and SAC must also be declining. When SAC falls, $SMC < SAC$. Therefore, it will be at some greater level of output at which SAC stops declining and reaches a minimum, or where $SMC = SAC$.

Analogously, when LAC and SAC are tangent for outputs greater than the one at which LAC is a minimum, the tangency occurs to the right of minimum SAC. If LAC rises, SAC must also be rising at the point of tangency. If SAC is increasing, $SMC > SAC$ and $SMC = SAC$ at a smaller level of output than the one at the point of tangency.

9

PRICING AND OUTPUT DECISIONS UNDER PERFECT COMPETITION

Profit Maximization

In his model of the firm, the economist assumes that a firm will attempt to maximize its profits (or minimize its losses); that is, maximize the difference between total revenue and total cost. The economist does not mean to say that this is the only motive influencing the behavior of the firm. There are other factors based on sociological, political, and psychological considerations. However, for contemporary, free-market economies, the economist does claim that the assumption of profit maximization is the crucial one; furthermore, in this system, the other considerations are many times measured in monetary terms. For example, if a firm were operating with the purpose of maximizing the prestige of the entrepreneur, it would probably attempt, in our type of economy, to maximize its profit since wealth and prestige are highly correlated. If the behavior of the firm is expressed as follows:

Economic behavior $= f$ (profits and sociological, political, and
other factors)

the economist assumes that predictions as to the behavior of the firm, based on the assumption of profit maximization, will yield better predictions than those based on any other variable or variables, given the difficulty of measuring these other variables and of incorporating them into a model of firm behavior. The profit maximization assumption will stand or fall depending on its ability to predict more accurately than any alternative assumption.

In this chapter we deal with profit maximization under conditions of perfect competition; and in the following chapters, we deal with the other market structures discussed in Chapter 6.

TABLE 9.1

(1) q	(2) VC	(3) STC	(4) AVC	(5) SAC	(6) SMC	(7) TR (P=$5.80)	(8) II (P=$5.80)	(9) MII (P=$5.80)	(10) TR (P=$0.90)	(11) II (P=$0.90)	(12) MII (P=$0.90)	(13) TR (P=$0.30)	(14) II (P=$0.30)	(15) MII (P=$0.30)
0	$ 0	$1500		$→∞		$ 0	$-1500		$ 0	$-1500		$ 0	$-1500	
100	90	1590	$0.90	15.90	$0.90	580	-1010	$4.90	90	-1500	$ 0	30	-1560	$-0.60
200	125	1625	0.625	8.125	0.35	1160	-465	5.45	180	-1445	0.55	60	-1565	-0.05
300	150	1650	0.50	5.50	0.25	1740	90	5.55	270	-1380	0.65	90	-1560	+0.05
400	170	1670	0.425	4.175	0.20	2320	650	5.60	360	-1310	0.70	120	-1550	+0.10
500	210	1710	0.42	3.42	0.40	2900	1190	5.40	450	-1260	0.50	150	-1560	+0.10
600	300	1800	0.50	3.00	0.90	3480	1680	4.90	540	-1260	0	180	-1620	-0.60
700	450	1950	0.6428	2.785	1.50	4060	2110	4.30	630	-1320	-0.60	210	-1740	-1.20
800	690	2190	0.8625	2.737	2.40	4640	2450	3.40	720	-1470	-1.50	240	-1950	-2.10
900	1270	2770	1.411	3.077	5.80	5220	2450	0	810	-1960	-4.90	270	-2500	-5.50
1000	2270	3770	2.27	3.77	10.00	5800	2030	-4.20	900	-2870	-9.10	300	-3470	-9.70
1100	3770	5270	3.427	4.791	15.00	6380	1110	-9.20	990	-4280	-14.10	330	-4940	-14.70
1200	6070	7570	5.058	6.308	23.00	6960	-610	-17.20	1080	-6490	-22.10	360	-7210	-22.70

SOURCE: Columns 1–6 are from Table 8.1.

Profit Maximization in the Short Run

We shall demonstrate profit maximization with reference to the costs derived in the first section of Chapter 8. In Table 9.1 we reproduce the cost data of Table 8.1 and, in addition, we include data for several more levels of output.

In Chapter 6 we saw that a perfectly competitive firm accepts the going market price as a given; in other words, the demand schedule faced by the perfectly competitive firm has elasticity approaching infinity. As we argued before, this type of demand curve will appear visually as a horizontal line at the market price. Further, since $TR = p \times q$, the TR-schedule of the perfectly competitive firm will be q times the constant p. This will appear graphically as a straight line from the origin with slope (MR) equal to price.

In Figure 9.1a we show the STC-schedule from Table 9.1 and the TR-schedule corresponding to an assumed market price of \$5.80 per unit. Since profit (π) is measured as

$$\pi = TR - STC \qquad (9.1)$$

in graphical terms, it is measured as the vertical distance between the TR- and STC-curves. This vertical distance will be a maximum when the slope of the TR-curve is equal to the slope of the STC-curve; in other words, where $MR = MC$. These vertical distances (profits) are shown in Figure 9.1b, where it will be seen that they reach a maximum at approximately 850 units.[1]

---

[1]When profit is being maximized, the slope of the profit curve is momentarily zero (at about 850 units in Figure 9.1b). Since $\pi = TR - TC$, we can write the slope of the profit curve in continuous terms as

$$\frac{d\pi}{dq} = \frac{dTR}{dq} - \frac{dTC}{dq}$$

When profit is being maximized,

$$\frac{d\pi}{dq} = 0 \text{ or } \frac{dTR}{dq} - \frac{dTC}{dq} = 0$$

Therefore,

$$\frac{dTR}{dq} = \frac{dTC}{dq}$$

However, both the minimum and the maximum of a curve have zero slope. To ensure a maximum, the second derivative of the profit curve must be negative; that is,

$$\frac{d^2\pi}{dq^2} = \frac{d^2TR}{dq^2} - \frac{d^2TC}{dq^2} < 0$$

We can arrive at these same results in Table 9.1. In column 7 TR is computed at the assumed price of $5.80 and in column 8 profit is the difference between TR and STC (column 7 − column 3). The highest profit is attained at 850 units.

Another way of viewing profit maximization is in terms of the marginal and average schedules. In Figure 9.2a we plot the AVC, SAC, and SMC schedules from Table 9.1. In addition we show the demand (and MR) schedule facing the firm with the assumed price of $5.80. Since profits are maximized when $MR = MC$ (or $P = MC$ with perfect competition since $P = MR$), the firm will produce at the output level of approximately 850 units. In column 9 of Table 9.1 and in Figure 9.2b we show marginal profit ($M\pi$), which is equal to $MR - MC$. As long as $M\pi > 0$, the firm can increase its total profit by increasing output; and when $M\pi < 0$, the firm can increase total profit by decreasing output; and when $M\pi = 0$, the firm is maximizing its profit. If output is discontinuous, the firm will stop producing at the level of output where marginal profit is as close to zero as possible without becoming negative.

Total profit can be measured in Figure 9.2a by taking the difference between price (AR) and SAC at the profit-maximizing level of output and then multiplying this profit per unit by the level of output. In algebraic terms, this can be written as follows:

$$\frac{TR}{q} - \frac{STC}{q} = \frac{\pi}{q} \qquad (9.2)$$

$$\frac{\pi}{q}(q) = \pi \qquad (9.3)$$

---

or

$$\frac{dMR}{dq} - \frac{dMC}{dq} < 0$$

Therefore, for *maximum* profit,

$$\frac{dMR}{dq} < \frac{dMC}{dq}$$

Thus, at the profit-maximizing level of output,

(1) $MR = MC$ and

(2) the slope of the MR-curve is less than the slope of the MC-curve.

Another way of stating this condition is:

for outputs greater than the equilibrium one: $MC > MR$
for outputs less than the equilibrium one: $MR > MC$

Thus in Figure 9.2a we can measure profits as follows:

$\pi = AB \times 850$ units
  $= (\$5.80 - \$2.80)\ 850$ units
  $= \$3.00 \times 850$ units
  $= \$2550$

Although it is not as frequently used, an alternate method of graphically measuring total profit is to take the area under the marginal profit curve.[2]

Next, we assume the price facing the firm is $0.90 per unit and determine the profit-maximizing output. In Figure 9.1a we draw in the new *TR*-schedule. At no output does *TR* lie above *STC*. This means, of course, that the firm cannot make a positive profit at any level of output. The problem then becomes one of minimizing loss, rather than one of maximizing profit.[3] We follow the same procedure as before and choose that output at which the slope of the *TR*-curve (*MR*) is equal to the slope of the *STC*-curve (*SMC*). This occurs at 55Q units of output.

In Figure 9.2a we show the new horizontal demand (and *MR*) curve at $0.90. It will be noticed that in applying our rule for profit-maximization (or loss-minimization), we are faced with a conundrum: there are two outputs at which $MR = SMC$, 50 units and 550 units. But if the firm desires to produce 50 units, it is not minimizing its loss; if it were to increase output beyond 50, $MR > SMC$ (in other words, $M\pi > 0$), and the firm could reduce its loss. If the firm decreased output below 50 units, $SMC > MR$, and the firm's losses would be smaller. Thus, at 50 units, the firm would be better off either expanding output or cutting back to zero. In fact, at 50 units, it is maximizing its losses (or minimizing its profit). On the other hand, at an output of 550 units, if the firm were to expand output, $SMC > MR$ and marginal profit would be negative; or if it were to decrease output, $MR > SMC$, marginal profit would be positive and this would mean a positive loss of profit.[4]

[2]This amounts to integrating the following expression:

$$\frac{d\pi}{dq} = \frac{dTR}{dq} - \frac{dTC}{dq}, \int_0^{q_e} \left[\frac{dTR}{dq} - \frac{dTC}{dq} \right] dq$$

where q_e is profit-maximizing output. This gives $TR - TC = \pi$.

[3]If $STC > TR$ at every level of output, then losses are minimized when $STC - TR$ is a minimum. Algebraically, this is the same as stating that $TR - STC$ should be a maximum and we showed before that this occurs when $MR = SMC$.

[4]In note 1 above we showed that for the output at which $MR = SMC$ to be a maximum profit (or minimum loss) output, the slope of the *MR*-curve must be less than the slope of the *SMC*-curve. At 50 units of output, this condition is not fulfilled: the slope of the *MR*-curve is zero, while the slope of the *SMC* curve is less than zero. However, at 550 units, the slope of $SMC > 0$ and the slope of *MR* is still zero and, therefore, the condition is fulfilled.

FIGURE 9.1

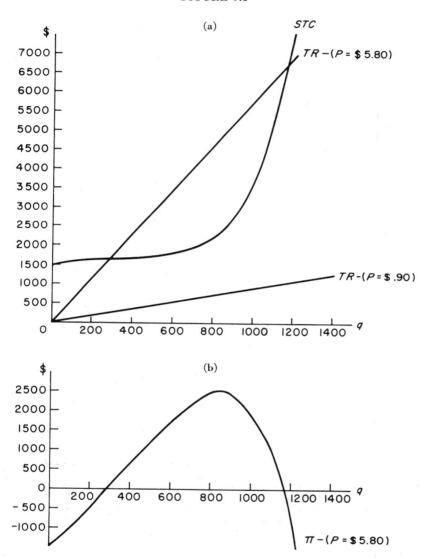

Column 11 in Table 9.1 lists profits at the different output levels when the price faced by the firm is $0.90. The minimum loss occurs between 500 and 600 units of output, and Figure 9.2a shows the minimum loss (of approximately $1255) to occur at 550 units.

We have now investigated a case in which the firm is not making profits; the best it can do is to minimize losses. The natural question

FIGURE 9.2(a)

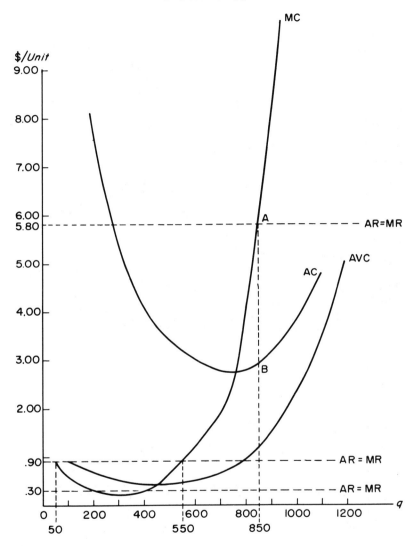

then is this: How large must losses be in the short run before the firm will leave the industry?

Our definition of fixed costs makes them, in effect, the unavoidable costs: those costs that would exist even if output were to fall to zero. Variable costs, on the other hand, are the avoidable costs: those that vary with output and would be zero if output were zero. In the short run, since

FIGURE 9.2(b)

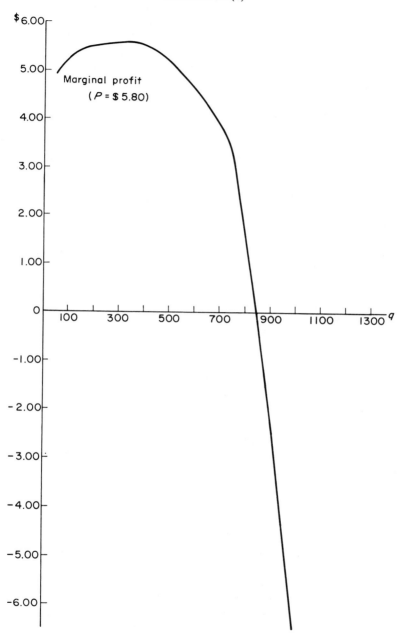

Marginal profit
(P = $ 5.80)

only variable costs can be avoided by shutting down, it is these costs that must be covered if the firm is to stay in the industry. A numerical example will make this clear.

In the case above with the price being $0.90, the best the firm can do is to make a loss of $1255. Now suppose the firm decides to leave the industry; its fixed or unavoidable cost (loss) would be $1500. Clearly, the firm will find it preferable to remain in operation because in this fashion it reduces its losses by approximately $245 ($1500 − $1255). These conclusions are valid only so long as the $1500 cost remains unavoidable — that is, in the short run.

As our last example, we assume a price of $0.30 per unit and once again we see that positive profits are impossible. Column 14 in Table 9.1 indicates that losses are minimized when the firm produces nothing, so that it would be better off to cease operation.

We have seen that, in the short run, the firm would be willing to stay in the industry at a loss when the price was $0.90 but would not be willing to stay when the price was $0.30. In the first instance, the loss at the optimum output was less than the fixed, unavoidable cost and, in the second, it was greater than the fixed cost at every output. We may then ask, What is the minimum price at which the firm would stay in the industry? It must be that price at which the firm would at least cover its avoidable, variable costs. If it just covers variable costs, its losses will equal fixed, unavoidable costs, which would be incurred even if output were zero. Therefore, the minimum price at which the firm will remain in the industry is that at which variable costs are being covered by total revenue; to put it another way, where $P = $ minimum AVC. In terms of Figure 9.2a, this minimum price is $0.40. For prices above this level, it will produce the quantity given by the intersection of the price ordinate with the SMC-curve above minimum AVC. At a price equal to minimum AVC, the firm will incur the same loss whether it shuts down or produces where $SMC = P$. Here the firm is indifferent between staying in or leaving the industry as far as short-run variables are concerned; the decision will be based on expectations for the long run.

Note that what we have said concerning the output decision of the firm for prices above minimum AVC amounts to the assertion that the SMC-curve, above minimum AVC, gives us the output that the firm will produce for various prices. In other words, this portion of the SMC-curve is the supply curve of the perfectly competitive firm in the short run.

If we know the SMC for each of the many firms within the perfectly competitive industry and if we assume these SMC-curves are stable for changes in industry output, we can derive the industry short-run supply curve by summing horizontally. If all firms are identical, then the industry's short-run supply curve would have the same shape as the individual firm's short-run supply curve with the quantity axis multiplied by the number of firms.

If this industry is only one of many that employ the same factors of production, then an increase in industry output, resulting in an increased demand for these factors of production, will have only slight effect on the prices of the factors.[5] In other words, our assumption of stable SMC-curves with changes in industry output will be valid.

If, however, the industry purchases enough of a factor to have a substantial effect upon price, the industry's short-run supply curve cannot be obtained by a simple summation of the firms' supply curves. The reason for this is illustrated in Figure 9.3 (where we assume an industry com-

FIGURE 9.3

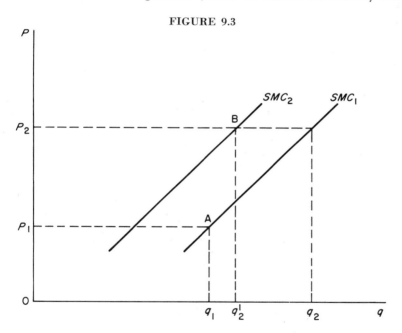

posed of 1000 identical firms). Assume the price to be P_1 with the firm producing the profit-maximizing output of q_1. Then assume an increase in industry demand that results in an increase in price to P_2. If factor prices remained constant, the firm would increase its output along SMC_1 to q_2. But under the assumption that changes in the industry's demand for factors of production increase the prices of these factors, the SMC-curve is

[5]In effect, the supply curves of these factors of production are approximately horizontal to the firm. See Chapter 12.

assumed to shift to SMC_2.[6] Now the new profit-maximizing output for the firm will be q_2'. Note that the firm's output at P_1 and P_2 is read from two different SMC-curves; we cannot simply add the firms' SMC-curves in order to obtain the supply of the industry. It is possible, however, to find the output of the industry at various prices by adding together the quantities produced at P_1, P_2, $\cdots$, P_n, which would be at points such as A, B, $\cdots$, N, on a succession of SMC-curves.[7]

Profit Maximization in the Long Run

In the long run as in the short run, the firm finds its profit-maximization output by equating marginal cost to marginal revenue. In the long run, however, all costs are variable; therefore, the firm must cover total cost in order to remain in the industry. We illustrate long-run profit maximization in Table 9.2 and Figure 9.4.

If the firm faces a price of \$2 per unit, $MR = LMC$ at 450 units in Table 9.2 and Figure 9.4.

Maximum profit in Table 9.2 is seen to be in excess of \$105 at 450 units.

[6]These shifts in the cost curves should not be confused with the movements along cost curves due to the output decisions of the firm; these were discussed above in Chapters 5 and 6. The shifts take place because of changes in variables not under the control of the firm.

[7]

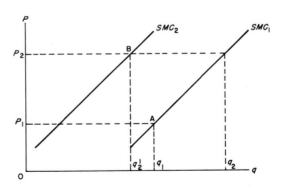

In Figure 9.3, point B on SMC_2 must always lie to the right of point A; in other words, q_2' must be greater than q_1. If $q_2' \leq q_1$ it would mean that after the increase in price the representative firm (and, therefore, the industry) is producing the same as, or less than, it did before. But this would mean it was hiring the same or a smaller amount of the factors of production as before and, therefore, SMC_2 could not be above SMC_1. Thus a situation such as the one in the accompanying diagram is an impossible one.

TABLE 9.2

q	LTC	LAC	LMC	TR $(P=\$2)$	π $(P=\$2)$
0	$ 0			$ 0	$ 0
			$3.10		
100	310	$3.10		200	−110
			1.55		
200	465	2.32		400	−65
			1.05		
300	570	1.90		600	30
			1.25		
400	695	1.74		800	105
			2.00		
500	895	1.79		1000	105
			2.90		
600	1185	1.98		1200	15
			3.90		
700	1575	2.25		1400	−175
			5.10		
800	2085	2.61		1600	−485
			6.65		
900	2715	3.02		1800	−915

FIGURE 9.4

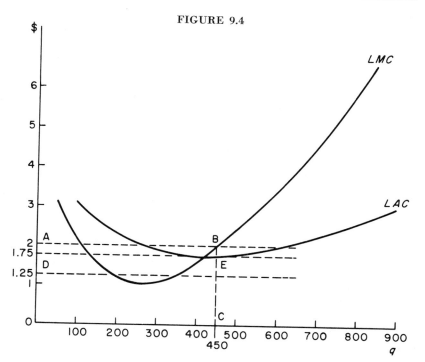

According to Figure 9.4, $\pi = \$112.50$. This can be calculated in the following way:

$$TR = OABC = \$2.00 \times 450 \text{ units} = \$900.00$$

$$LTC = ODEC = \$1.75 \times 450 \text{ units} = \underline{\$787.50}$$

$$\pi = DABE = \$0.25 \times 450 \text{ units} = \$112.50$$

Next we consider the price of \$1.25/unit in Figure 9.4 and see that the price is below *LAC* at all levels of output. All costs being variable in the long run, the firm will leave the industry; for all prices below minimum *LAC*, the firm will leave the industry. Thus, the long-run supply curve of the perfectly competitive firm is that portion of *LMC* that lies above *LAC*.

The Long-Run Supply Schedule of the Perfectly Competitive Industry

When we derived the industry's short-run supply curve, we simply horizontally summed the firms' short-run supply curves on the assumption that changes in industry output do not change factor prices. With the assumption that factor prices (and, therefore, the firms' cost curves) change as industry output changes, the industry's supply curve was derived by summing horizontally the short-run profit-maximizing outputs for alternative prices — after the changes in the firms' cost curves.

Since in the long-run all factors of production can be varied, there can be entry into and exit from an industry. In deriving the industry's long-run supply curve, it will not do to add the firms' profit-maximizing outputs at different prices when the number of firms within the industry is a variable.

Before we demonstrate the derivation of the long-run supply curve, consider the meaning of economic profit. Recall that costs of production include not only the expenditure (or explicit) costs of the firm but the nonexpenditure (or implicit) costs. Thus, when $\pi = TR - LTC = 0$, it does not mean that the entrepreneurs of the firm are not "making any money;" $\pi = 0$ means that the earnings of the entrepreneurs are equal to what their factors (labor and capital) could earn in alternative occupations. Thus, their remuneration is just sufficient to keep them in the industry. In fact, as we shall see below, the meaning of long-run equilibrium for the perfectly competitive firm is that $\pi = 0$.

We shall derive the long-run supply schedule for a hypothetical industry. We assume, for the present, that all firms in this industry, as well as potential firms, have identical cost schedules and that changes in industry output do not affect these cost schedules.

FIGURE 9.5

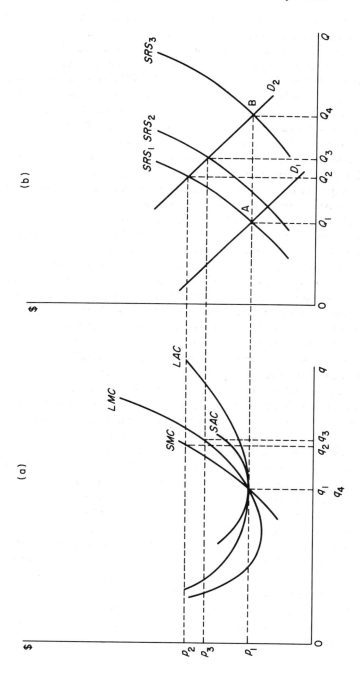

Figure 9.5a depicts a representative firm in long-run equilibrium ($\pi = 0$), producing Oq_1 at a price of OP_1, as well as the relevant *SAC*- and *SMC*-curves for the initial equilibrium point. In Figure 9.5b we show the corresponding short-run industry supply curve, SRS_1, with the equilibrium output of OQ_1 and the price of OP_1. Now let demand increase to D_2 and the resulting change in price to OP_2. Industry output expands in the short run to OQ_2. The individual firm moves along its *SMC* curve, adjusting output as best it can with existing capacity, to Oq_2. When the firm is producing Oq_2 at OP_2, its profit is $(P_2 - SAC) \cdot Oq_2$.

If we assume that demand does not change in the long run, there will be two long-run reactions to this increase in price: (1) existing firms will adjust capacity so as to produce a given output most efficiently; that is, they will base their output decisions on long-run costs; and (2) potential firms will enter the industry in response to the positive profits. For the sake of simplicity, we shall assume that the individual firms' adjustments precede the entry of new firms into the industry.

As the firms increase output along *LMC* (and produce on new *SMC*-curves to the right of the initial *SMC*-curve), industry supply increases to SRS_2 and the new short-run equilibrium output is OQ_3. This, however, reduces price to OP_3, and the firm's output is Oq_3. At this new price, profits are still being made by the firm, however, so that potential firms now enter the industry and continue to enter as long as positive profits exist. Long-run equilibrium will not occur until price has fallen to OP_1, or until the new industry short-run supply schedule is SRS_3.

It will be noted that the individual firm's new long-run equilibrium is at the output at which *LAC* is a minimum — Oq_1. Further, the output of the industry in the long run has grown through an increase in the number of firms, not by an increase in output of existing firms; though in the adjustment period, the existing firms' outputs did increase.

If we connect points such as A and B, which represent long-run equilibriums, we obtain the long-run supply curve for the industry. In this case, it is a horizontal line at the level of minimum *LAC*, showing that industry output can be increased by any amount in the long run at this constant price. This is called a constant-cost industry.

We now change the assumption that alterations in industry output have no effect on costs of production to the new assumption that, as industry output expands, the costs of the individual firms increase. (Again, for simplicity's sake, let costs increase only as a result of substantial increases in industry output; in other words, when new firms enter.) We shall once again show the derivation of the industry's long-run supply curve under these new conditions.

FIGURE 9.6

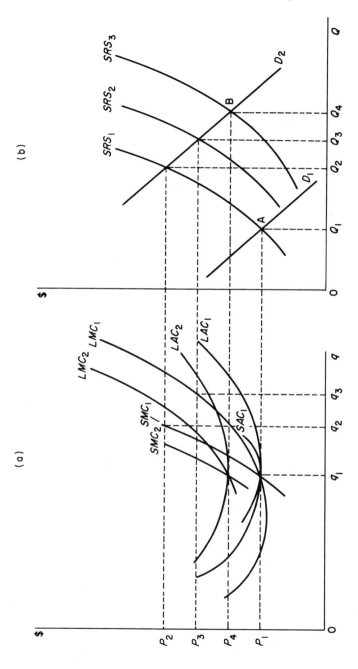

In Figure 9.6a, Oq_1 and OP_1 represent the firm's long-run equilibrium and in Figure 9.6b, OQ_1 is the corresponding industry equilibrium output when the demand curve is D_1. If demand increases to D_2, the industry will increase output to OQ_2, and the firm will maximize its short-run profit by producing Oq_2 at the price of OP_2. In the long run, the firm will adjust capacity so as to produce profit-maximizing output most efficiently. This increase in output is reflected in the increase of the industry short-run supply curve to SRS_2. Thus, industry output is OQ_3, price is OP_3, and the individual firm produces Oq_3. Profits are still greater than zero. Therefore, new firms enter the industry and keep doing so until $\pi = 0$.

By our assumption of increasing costs as industry output expands, the cost curves of the individual firms shift upward;[8] this involves short-run adjustments of output of the type discussed above. We show, however, only the final long-run equilibrium, which is at OP_4 and OQ_4 for the industry, and Oq_4 for the firm.

Note that long-run changes are now of three types: (1) the increase in output of the existing firms; (2) the entry of new firms into the industry and the resulting increase in output; and (3) the shift upward of the cost curves of the firms that results in the new long-run equilibrium price being greater than the original.

Note also that the new long-run equilibrium quantity for the firm is the same as the old equilibrium quantity. The reason for this is that, in deriving the new cost curves, we implicitly assumed the same percentage increase in all factor prices. Therefore, minimum LAC is at the same level of output as it was before.[9] If all factor prices do not change proportionately, there is no necessity for the cost curves to shift parallel to themselves, and output of the individual firm can either increase or decrease.

To get the long-run industry supply curve, we once again connect points such as A and B and find that we have a positively sloping long-run supply curve for the industry; such an industry is called an increasing-cost industry.

[8]To avoid cluttering the diagrams, we shift only the long-run cost curves, but short-run costs increase as well.

[9]This can be seen by considering the least-cost condition for selecting the optimum factor proportions:

$$\frac{MP_a}{P_a} = \frac{MP_b}{P_b} = \cdots = \frac{MP_n}{P_n}$$

At the initial equilibrium, this condition must have been fulfilled. If we multiply all factor prices by a constant, k, the equality still holds:

$$\frac{MP_a}{kP_a} = \frac{MP_b}{kP_b} = \cdots = \frac{MP_n}{kP_n}$$

FIGURE 9.7

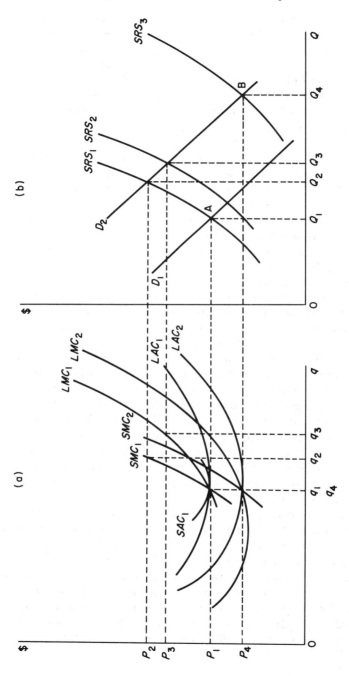

Turning to the case of external economies (decreasing-cost industry), we assume the industry initially to be in long-run equilibrium, producing OQ_1 at OP_1 (Figure 9.7b), and the firm's initial long-run equilibrium to be at Oq_1 (Figure 9.7a). As a result of an increase in demand to D_2, the price in the short run rises to OP_2 and the firm increases output to Oq_2 along SMC_1. The long-run adjustment of the firm is to produce along LMC_1; this shifts the industry's short-run supply curve to SRS_2, the price falls to OP_3, and the firm produces Oq_3.

In response to the still existing profits, new firms enter the industry; and with the assumption of decreasing costs, the cost schedules of the firms fall. New firms continue to enter until long-run profit is zero and the new long-run equilibrium price is OP_4. Once again we have assumed that the new equilibrium output of the firm is the same as before. When we connect points such as A and B, we find the long-run industry supply curve to be downward-sloping and we have a decreasing-cost industry.

It should be obvious that, if an industry is initially in equilibrium, a decrease in demand will result in losses; and in the long run, adjustments through exit of firms from the industry will result.

There is no necessity that external economies or diseconomies be reversible. We shall illustrate this with regard to two examples. The first concerns an industry that grows up in an area because of the availability of needed raw materials. When the density of firms has reached a certain point, a railroad spur is built to connect this area to the main line, thereby reducing the per-unit transportation costs of the firms. If the number of firms (and industry output) decreases as a result of a reduction in industry demand, it is probable that the spur will remain and, therefore, the reduction in per-unit costs will continue. (The long run for a railroad is substantially longer than for most other industries because of the durability of equipment. But, of course, if the spur is unprofitable for the railroad over a period long enough for the equipment to be depreciated, then it will abandon the spur and, at that time, per-unit transportation costs would revert to their original level.)

Our second example concerns surface mining in a locality. As a result of an increase in the demand for the mineral, new firms enter the industry. As long as the density of firms is such that when surface deposits are exhausted, a firm can move to virgin land, inexpensive strip-mining techniques will continue to be used. However, if no virgin land is available, then more expensive and intensive methods of mining will become necessary. Now suppose that after these intensive methods have been utilized for a time, the demand for output declines and firms leave the industry. The remaining firms will still need to use the intensive techniques because surface deposits have been exhausted. Clearly, the external diseconomies in this case are not reversible.

Until this point we have assumed all firms to be identical and, therefore, it has been correct to say that when price reached the level of minimum *LAC* for one firm, all firms had zero profit. Even if all firms are not identical, it is still true that the *LAC* for all firms, when costs are properly defined, will be at the same level. Under conditions of perfect competition, differences between firms due to superior knowledge and lower factor prices are ruled out. However, it is possible for a firm to have a unique factor of production. But with perfect knowledge, the superior productivity of this factor will be known to the industry, and other firms will bid for the services of the factor. As long as the differential between this factor's remuneration and the payments to comparable factors of lesser productivity is less than the new revenue that the superior factor adds to the total revenue of the firm that utilizes it, firms will continue to bid for its services, and so drive up its rate of remuneration until it is just equal to the differential value of its service. Therefore, the firm that does use this factor will have a cost curve at the same level as the firms have that do not use the factor. The cost curve of the former will, however, include a rental element to a superior factor.[10] A simple numerical example will explicate this point. Assume an industry in which all firms but one have average costs of $10 at an output level of 100 units. The other firm, because of a superior factor, has an average cost of $9 for the same output level. Therefore, the superior factor gives rise to a differential of $1 $\times$ 100 units of output = $100. Competitive bidding will, therefore, force up the factor's remuneration until it is $100 higher than that for ordinary comparable factors. This will raise the average cost of the firm utilizing this factor by $100/100 units or $1, so that the new average cost at 100 units will be $9 + $1 = $10, which is the same as average cost for the other firms.

[10]See Chapter 12.

We now investigate the possibility of a negatively sloping supply curve. This can intersect a negatively sloping demand curve in one of two ways shown below.

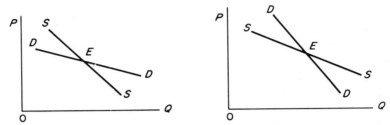

Which of these represents a stable equilibrium? Marshall considered Figure 9.A(b) stable and Figure 9.A(a) unstable. To the left of the intersection, demand price is greater than supply price and output will expand, he argued; to the right of the intersection, supply price is greater than demand price and consequently supply will contract. Walras considered the situation shown in Figure 9.A(a) to be stable and 9.A(b) unstable. To the left of the intersection, quantity supplied is greater than quantity demanded at any price and price must fall; to the right of the intersection, quantity supplied is less than quantity demanded and price must rise.

Actually both figures represent stable equilibriums, but for different time periods. Walras was thinking of the short run in which the burden of adjustment is upon price; thus in Figure 9.A(a) an excess of supply to the left of E will drive the price down and an excess of demand over supply to the right of E will drive the price up. Marshall, on the other hand, was concerned with the long run. An excess of demand price over supply price to the left of E in Figure 9.A(b) could cause an expansion of output, and a reduction of price and an excess of supply price over demand price in the long run will result in a contraction of output and an increase in price.

The comparison of these seemingly contradictory positions is important because it demonstrates how important it is to specify the process involved in achieving an equilibrium. Simply comparing two static equilibriums is not enough, as is clear above.

PRICING AND OUTPUT DECISIONS UNDER MONOPOLY

10

Pure Monopoly

Monopoly exists when the following conditions are fulfilled:

1. There is a single seller of a good.
2. There are no close substitutes for the good.
3. Effective barriers to entry into the industry exist.[1]

We saw in Chapter 6 that the demand schedule facing the monopolist is coincident with the industry demand.

The principles of profit-maximization for monopoly are the same as for perfect competition. Thus, in general, profit will be maximized where $MR = MC$ and the slope of MC is greater than the slope of MR at the point of intersection.[2]

Profit maximization in the short run is shown in Figure 10.1. Notice that $P > MR$. The student is reminded of the following relationship:

$$MR = AR + \frac{AR}{E} = AR\left(1 + \frac{1}{E}\right) \quad \text{(where } E < 0\text{)} \qquad (10.1)$$

Under conditions of perfect competition, $E \rightarrow -\infty$, and, therefore, $1/E \rightarrow 0$ and $MR = AR$ (at the limit). However, E is finite under

---

[1]Effective barriers to entry can exist for the following reasons:

  (1) The market is limited and will not support more than one firm.
  (2) The existing firm follows a price policy calculated to reduce the attractiveness of entry.
  (3) The firm may have control over strategic raw materials or an important process through ownership of patent rights.
  (4) The firm might operate through government licensing or the imposition of trade barriers such as tariffs and quotas.

[2]The second condition can be stated as $MR > MC$ for outputs less than the profit-maximizing one, and $MR < MC$ for greater outputs.

FIGURE 10.1

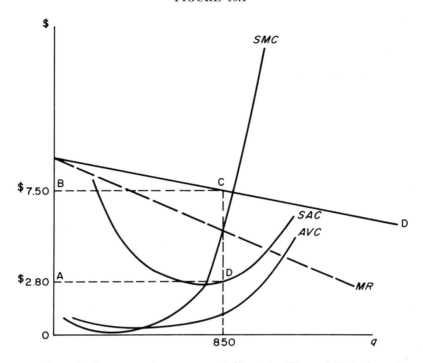

monopoly, which means that $-\infty < 1/E < 0$. Thus, MR is less than AR by this amount: $AR (1/ \mid E \mid)$.

We may look at this relationship another way. MR is defined as the change in total revenue due to producing and selling an extra unit of output. Since a perfect competitor sells at a given market price, the additional revenue he receives for selling an extra unit is equal to the market price. But, since a monopolist faces a downward-sloping demand curve, the price must be reduced in order to sell an additional unit. If the monopolist sells a homogeneous good in a market that cannot be segmented, then a reduction in price on the $(n + 1)$ unit must result in a similar price reduction on the previous n units. This can be summarized by the following relationship, which we derived in Chapter 1:

$$MR = AR + \frac{dAR}{dq} q \qquad (10.2)$$

or in discrete terms

$$MR = AR_2 + \frac{\Delta AR}{\Delta q} q_1 \qquad (10.2a)$$

For the competitive firm, dAR/dq (the slope of the demand schedule) $= 0$; therefore, $MR = AR$. For the monopolist, $dAR/dq < 0$ and, therefore, $MR < AR$.

Figure 10.1 and Table 10.1 illustrate the determination of profit-maximizing output and price for the monopolist in the short run. The output produced will be 850 units, which is the level at which SMC intersects MR from below. The price for that output is then found by going vertically up to the demand curve. Thus, $7.50 is the equilibrium price and the short-run profit is $ABCD = \$3995$.

TABLE 10.1

(1) q	(2) STC	(3) AVC	(4) SAC	(5) SMC	(6) P	(7) TR	(8) MR	(9) π
0	$1500		$\to\infty$		$9.20	$ 0		−$1500
				$0.90			$9.00	
100	1590	$0.90	15.90		9.00	900		−690
				0.35			8.60	
200	1625	0.625	8.125		8.80	1760		135
				0.25			8.20	
300	1650	0.50	5.50		8.60	2580		930
				0.20			7.80	
400	1670	0.425	4.175		8.40	3360		1690
				0.40			7.40	
500	1710	0.42	3.42		8.20	4100		2390
				0.90			7.00	
600	1800	0.50	3.00		8.00	4800		3000
				1.50			6.60	
700	1950	0.64	2.785		7.80	5460		3510
				2.40			6.20	
800	2190	0.86	2.74		7.60	6080		3890
				5.80			5.80	
900	2770	1.41	3.08		7.40	6660		3890
				10.00			5.40	
1000	3770	2.27	3.77		7.20	7200		3430
				15.00			5.00	
1100	5270	3.43	4.79		7.00	7700		2330
				23.00			4.60	
1200	7570	5.06	6.31		6.80	8160		590

SOURCE: Columns 1–5 are derived from Table 8.1.

It is of interest to note that although the perfect competitor has only one decision alternative — that is, he must make an output decision on the basis of a given price — the monopolist has two decision alternatives. He can set the price and allow profit-maximizing output to be determined; or he can set output and then charge the price that will maximize profits. In either case there is only one price-output combination that is optimum for profit-maximization.[3]

Long-run profit maximization is achieved when $LMC = MR$. The extent of monopoly power in the long run will probably be less than in the short run. One reason for this is the likelihood that demand will be more elastic in the long run than in the short run since people have more opportunity to adjust to prices and to seek out appropriate substitutes. Another reason is that the threat of potential entry exists in the long run. A monopolist, concerned with maximizing profit in the long run, may in the short run forgo the temporary advantages to be gained from maximizing short-run profit. This may happen because of the fear of attracting punitive legislation (such as antitrust), new firms into the industry, and foreign rivals into the domestic market.

An Aside on Average Cost Pricing

Based upon the fact that businessmen generally set price by adding a markup to an estimate of average cost, some individuals have attacked the relevance of marginal-cost pricing in explaining price behavior. There are two main lines of counterattack. First, as we pointed out in the beginning of Chapter 9, the validity of a model does not depend on its descriptive accuracy but on its ability to predict behavior more accurately than alternative models. Second, on the basis of empirical evidence concerning the shape of typical cost curves, markup pricing can give approximately the same results as marginal-cost pricing.

The empirical evidence indicates that long-run average cost curves are flat-bottomed over a wide range of output. As we showed in Chapter 8, this means that LMC and LAC are coincident over the flat-bottomed portion. With marginal-cost pricing, the following long-run equilibrium condition exists:

$$LMC = MR \qquad (10.3)$$

[3]Since the monopolist equates MC and MR, the MC-curve of the monopolist may be said to give a relationship between MR and output, rather than between price and output as is true of the perfect competitor.
There are an infinite number of prices corresponding to each MR; the particular price corresponding to any MR depends on the elasticity as shown in

$$P = \left(\frac{E}{E + 1}\right) MR$$

Therefore, no supply schedule of the ordinary kind exists for the monopolist.

For a firm that is not a perfect competitor

$$MR = P(1 + 1/E)$$

where

$$E \leq -1* \tag{10.4}$$

Therefore, in equilibrium:

$$LMC = P\left(\frac{E+1}{E}\right) \tag{10.5}$$

or

$$P = LMC\left(\frac{E}{E+1}\right) \tag{10.6}$$

Over the range where LAC is flat-bottomed, $LAC = LMC$, so that in equilibrium

$$P = LAC\left(\frac{E}{E+1}\right) \tag{10.7}$$

Now suppose $E = -3$. Then

$$P = LAC\left(\frac{-3}{-3+1}\right) = 1.5 \, LAC \tag{10.8}$$

In other words, the markup would be 50 percent. Furthermore, notice that the greater the inelasticity (the smaller the coefficient in absolute terms), the greater will be the markup.

If, in the short run, the firm were to mark up on average variable cost, and AVC was flat-bottomed (and the empirical evidence indicates it often is), then the results obtained would be the same as those obtained with marginal-cost pricing. If, however, as is much more likely, businessmen mark up on the basis of SAC, a discrepancy arises between average-cost pricing and marginal-cost pricing, the size of which is based on the magnitude of AFC.

Price Discrimination

Price discrimination exists when a seller charges different prices for units of

---

*Note that an imperfect competitor will never operate on an inelastic portion of a demand curve; this would mean that $MR < 0$, and consequently by increasing price and decreasing output, he can both increase TR and decrease TC and thus increase π.

a homogeneous commodity. The following conditions must be fulfilled if price discrimination is to be practiced:

1. The seller has some degree of monopoly power.
2. The seller is able to segment his market. Segmentation exists when consumers who buy at a low price are not able to resell the commodity at a higher price. Segmentation can arise because of the physical character- istics of the good (for example, physicians' services, electricity), or such barriers as transport costs and tariffs.

Take-It-or-Leave-It Price Discrimination. Ordinarily, the monopolist sets a profit-maximizing price and permits buyers to purchase as much as they wish at that price. Under perfect price discrimination the monopolist deals with each buyer separately and instead of permitting him to buy all that he wants to at a stated price, the monopolist specifies both the quanti- ty the buyer can receive of the good and the total amount of money he must pay to get it. The monopolist in effect makes the buyer pay the maximum amount that he will, for the amount that the monopolist de- cides to supply to him, under threat of denying the good to him altogether — he gives him a take-it-or-leave-it choice. This kind of discrimination is called perfect because it permits the seller to squeeze the greatest revenue from the buyer for any given output.

In effect, then, the demand curve of the consumer becomes the marginal revenue curve facing the monopolist.[4] This is shown in column 3 of Table 10.2, where we show the original demand schedule considered by the monopolist to be his MR-schedule (with the MR figures placed at the mid-points of their respective intervals) and, corresponding to this MR- schedule, we show an "all-or-nothing" demand schedule P'. The total revenue collected by the monopolist for four units with perfect discrimina- tion can be found as the sum of the MR figures up to and including MR for the fourth unit — [(5 + 4 + 3 + 2) = $14] or as $P' \times 4$ units ($3.50 $\times$ 4 = $14).

The monopolist attempting to do so would find it extremely difficult to discriminate perfectly along a consumer's demand schedule, since he would be charging different prices for each unit for infinitesimal incre- ments of output sold to the consumer. In practice, perfect discrimination

---

[4]This is only true when the practice of perfect price discrimination by the monopolist does not reduce the consumer's purchasing power enough to cause him to reduce his purchase of all goods, including the one subject to take-it-or-leave-it price discrimina- tion. This will generally be true if expenditure on the good in question is a small proportion of his total expenditures. If the good should have an important place in the consumer's budget, the perfect discrimination curve will be somewhat below the ordinary demand curve. For further discussion of this point see Appendix 10.

is usually "lumpy." For example, electricity rates are often quoted on the basis of different prices for successive "lumps" of the service, rather than declining continuously as the consumer uses more electricity.

TABLE 10.2

(1) P	(2) Q	(3) MR'	(4) TR	(5) TR'	(6) P'
6	0		0	0	
		5			
5	1		5	5	5
		4			
4	2		8	9	$4\frac{1}{2}$
		3			
3	3		9	12	4
		2			
2	4		8	14	$3\frac{1}{2}$
		1			
1	5		5	15	3
		0			
0	6		0	15	$2\frac{1}{2}$

Columns 1 and 2 are the ordinary demand schedules.
Column 4 is the ordinary TR-schedule: $(1) \times (2)$.
Columns 2 and 3 are the perfect discriminator's MR when the consumer is forced to pay the maximum price he is willing to pay for each unit.
Column 5 shows the total revenue corresponding to MR'.
Column 6 is derived as $TR'/q = (5)/(2)$.

Imperfect Discrimination. In order to demonstrate price discrimination of this kind, we assume a monopolist sells in two separate markets, each with its own demand schedule. We also assume that the marginal cost of supplying a unit of output to either market is the same. In Figures 10.2a–c we demonstrate the determination of the equilibrium price and quantity for each market. Figures 10.2a and b show the demand and marginal revenue schedules for the respective markets. Figure 10.2c shows the aggregate demand (D_T) and its corresponding MR schedule (MR_T). The aggregate demand, marginal-revenue, and marginal-cost curves in Figure 10.2c are the same as the ones we assumed for the nondiscriminating monopolist discussed in the first section above.

The monopolist determines his optimum output of 850 units in the usual fashion by equating MR_T to MC_T (Figure 10.2c). Once the monopolist has decided to produce a given output at given cost, he can maximize his total revenue (and, therefore, his profit) by allocating the output between the two markets in such a way that the marginal revenues are

FIGURE 10.2

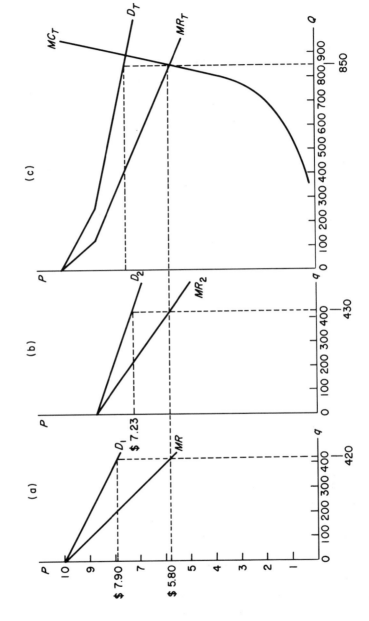

equal — that is, $MR_1 = MR_2 = MR_T = MC_T = \$5.80.$* For example, if sales had been allocated in such a way that $MR_1 = \$7$ and $MR_2 = \$2$, then transferring a unit from the second market to the first would result in an increase in total revenue of approximately $5.

Therefore, the monopolist will sell 420 units in market 1 and charge $7.90 per unit, and in market 2 he will sell 430 units at a price of $7.23. It should be noted that $q_1 + q_2$ is equal to q_T in Figure 10.2;[5] that is, $420 + 430 = 850$.

*If we assume the cost of supplying the commodity to the two markets 1 and 2 to be the same, then the firm will maximize total revenue (and total profits) for any given output by dividing its sales between the two markets so that

$$\text{(a)} \qquad MR_1 = P_1\left(1 + \frac{1}{E_1}\right) = MR_2 = P_2\left(1 + \frac{1}{E_2}\right)$$

The firm will be producing the maximum profit output where $MR_1 = MR_2 = MC$ in which MC is the marginal cost (the same for both markets) of producing a unit of output. In equilibrium, then,

$$\text{(a')} \qquad \frac{P_1}{P_2} = \left[\frac{(E_2 + 1)/E_2}{(E_1 + 1)/E_1}\right]$$

$$= \left[(E_2 + 1)/E_2\right]\left[E_1/(E_1 + 1)\right]$$

A more general formulation that makes no assumptions about costs in the two markets states that in each market the firm will equate MR to MC. In equilibrium, then,

$$\text{(b)} \qquad MC_1 = MR_1 = P_1[(E_1 + 1)/E_1]$$

$$MC_2 = MR_2 = P_2[(E_2 + 1)/E_2]$$

$$\frac{P_1}{P_2} = \frac{MC_1[E_1/(E_1 + 1)]}{MC_2[E_2/(E_2 + 1)]}$$

If $MC_1 = MC_2$ as assumed in (a) above, then,

$$\frac{P_1}{P_2} = [E_1/(E_1 + 1)][(E_2 + 1)/E_2]$$

and this is the same result as that obtained in (a'). If $E_1 = E_2$, then,

$$\frac{P_1}{P_2} = \frac{MC_1}{MC_2}$$

[5]We can prove this relationship as follows: Assume linear demand curves in both markets, represented by

$$P_1 = a + bq_1 \qquad \text{and} \qquad P_2 = c + dq_2$$

or

$$q_1 = \frac{P_1}{b} - \frac{a}{b} \qquad\qquad q_2 = \frac{P_2}{d} - \frac{c}{d}$$

(Continued on page 184)

Some examples of imperfect price discrimination include different prices for theater tickets, based on the location of the seats in the theater, when the cost differential is significantly smaller than the price differential; steamship and airline companies that charge different prices for different

---

(Continued from page 183)

where b and d are the slopes and a and c are the vertical axis intercepts. The total demand schedule can be written as

$$q_T = \frac{P_1}{b} + \frac{P_2}{d} - \frac{a}{b} - \frac{c}{d}$$

The corresponding marginal revenue schedules can be derived by using the following demand equations:

$$P_1 = a + bq_1$$

$$P_2 = c + dq_2$$

$$P_T = \frac{bdq_T}{b+d} + \frac{ad}{b+d} + \frac{cb}{b+d}$$

Express total revenue for the three demand equations:

$$TR_1 = aq_1 + bq_1^2$$

$$TR_2 = cq_2 + dq_2^2$$

$$TR_T = \left(\frac{bd}{b+d}\right)q_T^2 + \left(\frac{ad}{b+d}\right)q_T + \left(\frac{cb}{b+d}\right)q_T$$

The MR equations are then

$$MR_1 = a + 2bq_1$$

$$MR_2 = c + 2dq_2$$

$$MR_T = 2q_T\left(\frac{bd}{b+d}\right) + \left(\frac{ad}{b+d}\right) + \left(\frac{cb}{b+d}\right)$$

We can now state:

$$q_1 = \frac{MR_1}{2b} - \frac{a}{2b}$$

$$q_2 = \frac{MR_2}{2d} - \frac{c}{2d}$$

$$q_T = \frac{MR_T}{2d} + \frac{MR_T}{2b} - \frac{a}{2b} - \frac{c}{2d}$$

Therefore, when $MR_1 = MR_2 = MR_T$,

$$q_1 + q_2 = q_T \text{ since } \frac{MR}{2d} + \frac{MR}{2b} - \frac{a}{2b} - \frac{c}{2d} = \frac{MR}{2b} - \frac{a}{2b} + \frac{MR}{2d} - \frac{c}{2d}$$

FIGURE 10.3

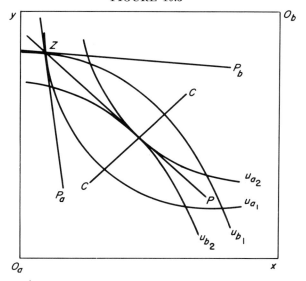

classes of service — once again, when the price differences outweigh the cost differences; and different electricity rates charged to commercial and residential users.

We can show the loss in utility that results from price discrimination with the use of the Edgeworth box diagram discussed at the end of Chapter 5. Assume initially in Figure 10.3 that price discrimination exists and that individual A is being charged the price P_a, and is therefore in equilibrium at Z on U_{a_1}; and that B is being charged a price P_b and is in equilibrium at Z on U_{b_1}. If price discrimination is removed and a uniform price, represented by ZP, is charged, each individual will adjust his purchases so that when he is at his new equilibrium, the price line (ZP) is tangent to his highest possible indifference curve. But when the indifference curves of A and B are tangent to a common price line, they are tangent to each other; and thus the common equilibrium point lies on the contract curve. We saw in Chapter 5 that a move from an equilibrium off the contract curve to one on the curve represents a gain in utility for both; we see in Figure 10.3 that A moves from U_{a_1} to U_{a_2} and B moves from U_{b_1} to U_{b_2}.

Regulated Monopolies

There are some industries in which economies of scale are so substantial (for example, many public utilities) that, in a sense, they are "natural" monopolies. The per-unit cost of providing the commodity declines substantially as the firm increases production so that the most efficient form of organization is that of monopoly. In the case in which the government permits the existence of a monopoly to achieve economies of scale, it is generally (in the United States) accompanied by government regulation to protect the public from undue exercise of monopoly power. We shall discuss several of the many alternative methods that government uses to control monopolies.

Indirect Government Control through Taxation. We assume that a *specific tax* of AC per unit is levied on the monopolist shown in Figure 10.4. Prior to the imposition of the tax, the monopolist's profit-maximizing output was Oq_1, price was OP_1, and profits were AP_1EF.

The tax raises the STC-schedule by the amount of the tax; thus, we show an upward shift in both the SAC- and SMC-curves by the amount of the tax. Profit-maximizing output is now Oq_2, price is OP_2, and profits are reduced to DP_2GH. Profits must be smaller with the tax because the monopolist was originally maximizing his profits by producing Oq_1; therefore, selling Oq_2 must result in a before-tax profit of less than the Oq_2-profit. In addition, the monopolist must pay a tax from these smaller profits.[6]

The degree to which a monopolist can shift a per-unit tax depends upon the elasticity of demand facing him. Since the demand for the product of a monopolist tends to be relatively inelastic, in all likelihood a good portion of the tax will be shifted to the consumer; and, therefore, the tax revenue collected by the government will represent mainly a burden on the consumer rather than a reduction in the gains from monopoly power.

We next analyze the effects of a *profits tax* upon the monopolist. We assume the original equilibrium in Figure 10.5 to be Oq_1 units of output, price OP_1, with profits being AP_1DE. A tax equal to a certain percentage of total profits will not result in any change in the equilibrium price and output. If t is the tax (in percentage terms) and Oq_1 is the *profit-maximizing* output prior to the tax, then $(1 - t) \times Oq_1(P_1A)$ (that is, the percentage of profits kept after the tax) is the largest after-tax profit obtainable by the firm.[7]

---

[6]Since Oq_1 was the profit-maximizing output before the tax,

$$Oq_1(P_1A) > Oq_2(P_2B)$$

With the tax, the SAC for Oq_2 units increases from OB to OD. Therefore,

$$Oq_1(P_1A) > Oq_2(P_2D)$$

[7]As currently constituted, the corporation profits tax is not a true profits tax. This is so because dividends are treated as a distribution of pure profits, whereas the payment

FIGURE 10.4

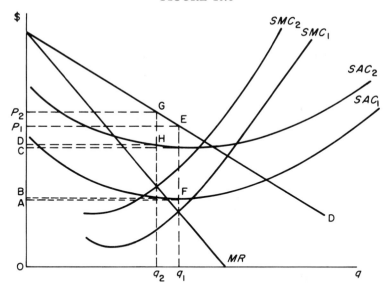

Direct Government Controls through Price Regulation. We shall discuss two major kinds of price regulation. In one the government sets a ceiling price at the level where $LMC = P$. This is the price OP_2 in Figure 10.6. In the absence of regulation, the monopolist would produce Oq_1 at a price of OP_1. With the ceiling price, the effective demand curve becomes P_2AD; the corresponding MR-curve is coincident with the demand curve over the range P_2A, is discontinuous at A, and then becomes CD. The profit-maximizing output is Oq_2, since at greater outputs, $LMC > MR$ and at smaller outputs, $LMC < MR$. The monopolist is thus forced to produce more at a lower price.

If, however, as is implied by natural monopoly, the LAC-curve is downward-sloping over the entire relevant range of outputs (see Figure 10.7), then attempting to set a price equal to LMC will result in losses to the monopolist. For example, at the price OP_2, average revenue will be less than LAC. Therefore, unless the government is willing to subsidize the firm, this type of regulation is not feasible.

In this case, the usual procedure is to permit the firm to make a "fair"

---

to the owners is really made up of two components: (1) a return on invested capital — that is, the opportunity cost of the funds tied up in the firm by the owners, and (2) pure profit — if any. This creates an incentive for the corporation to raise new funds through the bond market rather than from the sale of new stock, since bond interest is a cost that can be deducted before computation of taxable income.

FIGURE 10.5

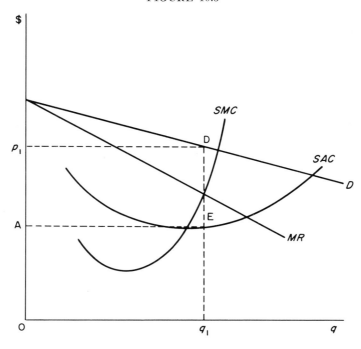

return on invested capital. If the opportunity cost of invested capital is included in the cost schedules, this procedure is the same as setting a price such that profits are zero. In Figure 10.7 this amounts to setting the price OP_1 so that the demand schedule becomes P_1AB and the mar-

FIGURE 10.6   **FIGURE 10.7**

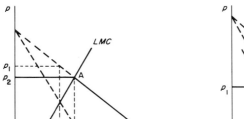

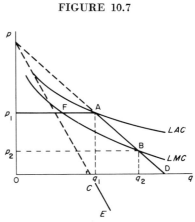

ginal-revenue schedule is coincident with demand over the range P_1A, is discontinuous at A, and thereafter is CE. At the price of OP_1, the firm will produce Oq_1 since $MR < LMC$ for greater outputs and $MR > LMC$ for smaller outputs.[8] Another way of stating this is that LMC cuts MR in its discontinuous segment.[9]

[8]It should be noted that the intersection of MR and LMC at point F does not represent an equilibrium, since for smaller outputs, $LMC > MR$ and for greater outputs, $MR > LMC$.

[9]It is sometimes possible for the government to force an output where $LMC = P$ even with continuously declining LAC, by permitting the monopolist to practice price discrimination. An example of this is the different rates charged by electrical utility companies to the different markets of commercial and residential consumers.

A consumer purchasing n commodities will fulfill the following condition in equilibrium:

$$\frac{MU_a}{P_a} = \frac{MU_b}{P_b} = \cdots = \frac{MU_n}{P_n} = Z \qquad (A10.1)$$

Z represents the common ratio of marginal utility to price in equilibrium and has been called the marginal utility of money or the marginal utility of income — the gain in total satisfaction from the marginal dollar of expenditure. Now if the consumer purchases many commodities and we choose one of these that represents only a small part of his expenditures, any ordinary change in its price will result in but a small change in purchasing power. Further, when this small change in real income is redistributed among the many commodities the individual buys, there will be very little adjustment of purchases and consequently very little change in Z, the marginal utility of money. For a commodity, therefore, that represents a small part of a consumer's budget, we may, as a simplification, assume Z to be constant; this amounts to ignoring income effects of price changes as being insignificantly small. Now if Z can be assumed constant, we may write that in equilibrium for commodity A

$$P_a = MU_a \cdot \frac{1}{Z} \qquad (A10.2)$$

where $1/Z = P_a/MU_a$ and represents the money cost of a marginal util. $MU_a \cdot 1/Z$, therefore, represents marginal utility measured in money terms. The equation states that an individual will purchase a commodity up to the point where the price of the commodity is equal to its marginal utility measured in money terms.

Further, since $1/Z$ is a constant, the demand curve becomes simply the marginal utility curve multiplied by a constant — the reciprocal of the marginal utility of

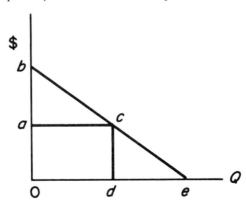

money — that converts it into a marginal utility curve along which MU is measured in dollar units.

Under the assumptions above, if the individual faces a market price of Oa he will purchase Od. His total utility from the commodity (measured in money terms) will be $Obcd$; his expenditures $Oacd$; and he therefore has excess utility of abc, which is called his consumer's surplus. Now the consumer is willing to pay for any unit of the commodity up to its marginal utility (measured in money terms) rather than go without it. This means that by charging for each unit of the commodity the maximum price the consumer will pay, the monopolist can take the consumer's surplus abc unto himself.

PRICING AND OUTPUT DECISIONS UNDER MONOPOLISTIC COMPETITION AND OLIGOPOLY

11

Monopolistic Competition: Short-Run Equilibrium

It will be recalled from Chapter 6 that monopolistic competition exists when there are many sellers of goods that are close (but not perfect) substitutes for one another. The number of sellers is too great for interdependency among the firms.

The demand schedule facing a monopolistic competitor will be somewhat downward-sloping. The degree of monopoly power will depend upon the degree of differentiation, since all the other conditions of perfect competition are being fulfilled. Of course, if a high degree of differentiation is achieved, the appropriate model is no longer monopolistic competition, but monopoly. On the other hand, if the degree of differentiation is minute, then for many problems the appropriate model is perfect competition. The monopolistic competitive model is mainly useful for explaining certain phenomena, such as advertising and selling costs, in industries considered "substantially" competitive, which are not predicted by the perfectly competitive model.

Short-run, profit-maximizing price and output are determined in the usual fashion. Thus, in Figure 11.1, $MR = SMC$ at 850 units and the price charged will be \$6.65. Since the gap between P and MR is determined by

$$MR = AR\left(1 + \frac{1}{E}\right) \tag{3.9a}$$

the difference between P and SMC at the equilibrium output will be relatively small under conditions of monopolistic competition.[1]

---

[1]For purposes of comparison, it was assumed that the monopolist in Figure 10.1 and the monopolistic competitor in Figure 11.1 have the same cost schedules and produce the same profit-maximizing output. At the profit-maximizing output of 850 units, the gap between P and SMC for the monopolist is \$1.70 (\$7.50 − \$5.80), whereas for the monopolistic competitor P exceeds SMC by \$0.85 (\$6.65 − \$5.80).

The products sold by the monopolistic competitors within an industry may differ from one another physically, but it is more likely that the differentiation is based on attendant services and amenities (for example, the conversational abilities of the barbers described in Chapter 6, packaging, convenience of location, and branding of product).

Although the perfect competitor has no incentive to advertise or to carry on other sales promotion activities, the monopolistic competitor will use these devices in an effort to differentiate further his good so that the

FIGURE 11.1

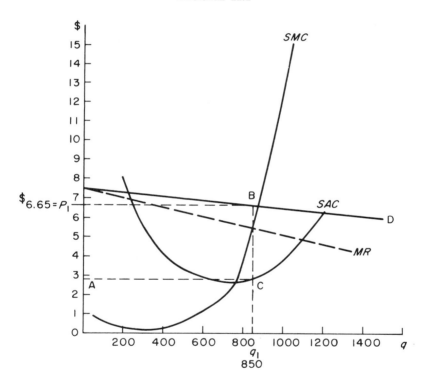

demand he faces will increase as well as become more inelastic. As a limit, he attempts to achieve the gains of monopoly. An increase in selling activities will shift the average and marginal costs of the firm upward, and they are undertaken in an attempt to shift the demand and marginal revenue schedules upward. The profitability of the selling activities will be indicated by $\Delta TR_s - \Delta TC_s$, where the subscript s represents "due to a per-unit change in selling activities."

Monopolistic Competition: Long-Run Equilibrium

The usual situation under monopolistic competition is free entry into and exit from the industry in the long run. When profits are being earned in the short run, they present an incentive to potential firms to enter the industry. If we assume that the total demand for the products remains constant and that the degree of differentiation among firms is such that consumers consider the products of the various firms to be substitutes in a broad sense, then with new firms entering, customers will be drawn from the existing firms to the new ones. Thus, as new firms enter, the demand schedule facing each member of the industry will shift downward. This downward shift in demand will continue as long as positive profits exist. Thus, in Figure 11.2 long-run equilibrium is shown as Oq_1 and OP_1. At this output, price is just equal to LAC; thus, $\pi = 0$. Note also that at Oq_1, where the demand schedule is tangent to LAC, $MR = LMC$.*

Note that if the firm were operating in a perfectly competitive industry, it would be in long-run equilibrium at an output of Oq_2, where it would be operating at minimum LAC. The monopolistic competitive firm stops short of this output. Therefore, the monopolistic competitor does not operate at the most efficient point on his LAC-curve. In other words, excess capacity exists in the long run. This model casts some light on the phenomenon of several barber shops in close proximity, with one or a few chairs rarely occupied, as well as similar situations with gas stations, drugstores, neighborhood grocery stores, and the like, all of which fulfill the conditions of monopolistic competition and exhibit excess capacity.

In Figure 11.3 we show long-run equilibrium when entry into the industry is blocked. When potential firms cannot enter the industry freely in response to positive profits, the existing firms are able to retain profits in the long run. In Figure 11.3 the long-run profits are AP_1BC.

Since the initial costs of entering a typical monopolistic competitive industry are relatively low, if barriers to entry exist they are likely to be

---

*This can be proven as follows:

$$E_d = \frac{dq}{dP} \cdot \frac{P}{q} \text{ and } E_{LAC} = \frac{dq}{dLAC} \cdot \frac{LAC}{q}$$

At Oq_1, $P = LAC$ and $\dfrac{dP}{dq} = \dfrac{dLAC}{dq}$

Therefore, $E_d = E_{LAC}$ at Oq_1

The relationship between MR and P is $MR = P(1 + 1/E_d)$ and the relationship between LMC and LAC is $LMC = LAC(1 + 1/E_{LAC})$

Therefore, since $P = LAC$ and $E_d = E_{LAC}$ at Oq_1, $MR = LMC$

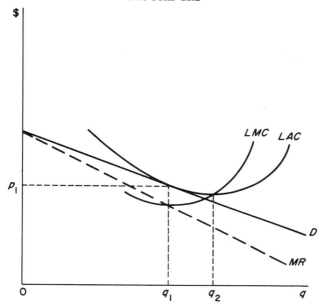

FIGURE 11.2

artificial, such as licensing or other government regulations. For example, in New York City there are a fixed number of taxi medallions that are required in order to run a cab within the city. Another example of blocked entry is the licensing of liquor stores in many states.

Most monopolistic competitive industries, however, do have free entry. This fact, together with the small initial cost of entering, tends to result in a high birth rate of new firms in these industries. The death rate will tend also to be high, partially because of the excess capacity in these industries and partially because of the fact that "hope springs eternal" when it is shrouded by ignorance: many potential small entrepreneurs have little or no experience in operating their own businesses.

It should be noted that the concept of the industry under conditions of monopolistic competition becomes rather fuzzy. Firms may be said to be in the same industry when they sell a homogeneous good; that is, the cross elasticities among the products are infinite. Thus, in perfect competition and monopoly, the concept of the industry is precise. Since in monopolistic competition, firms sell products that are different, at least in some degree, it becomes difficult to define precisely what we mean by an industry. One method of determining industry boundaries is to place goods with high positive cross elasticities into the same industry. However, what constitutes a "high" coefficient of cross elasticity is entirely arbitrary.

FIGURE 11.3

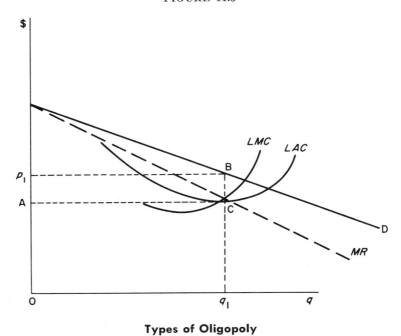

Types of Oligopoly

Oligopoly is a market structure characterized by few enough firms so that they are interdependent; that is, each firm considers how its actions will affect the policies of its rivals. The oligopolist is like the man who is playing chess: before taking any action, he must consider the possible reactions on the part of his opponent and how to counter them.

Oligopoly does not lend itself readily to theoretical analysis of the sort we have been using because there are an infinite number of reaction patterns. At one extreme is an oligopoly situation in which the firms decide to act in collusion, and, therefore, achieve a monopoly solution to pricing and output decisions. At the other extreme is the situation in which the individual oligopolist changes his price and output without regard to the reactions of his rivals because he has a misguided notion about their stupidity and/or ignorance, or he is persuaded that their reaction lag is great enough to permit him to gain a temporary advantage from these changes. Between these extremes there are, if not an infinite, at least a large number of possibilities. In our discussion we shall consider several of the more interesting ones.

It should also be noted that the product of an oligopolistic industry can be either homogeneous or differentiated. The former is likely to exist in producer goods industries such as steel, cement, and copper, and the latter in consumer goods industries such as automobiles and cigarettes. The reason for the lack of differentiation in the producer goods industries is that these are goods usually purchased according to engineering specifications. In the examples that we shall be considering, we shall assume pure (or homogeneous) oligopoly.

As in monopolistic competition, the greater the degree of differentiation, the less the interdependency among the oligopolists. When an oligopolistic industry achieves a mature status and firms realize the consequences of competitive price cutting, they tend to revert to nonprice competition (such as advertising and "quality" changes). The effort is to increase profits through a shift in their demand curves and an increased inelasticity of demand in the relevant price range.

Oligopoly with Absolute Collusion

The firms in an oligopolistic industry realize that total industry profits can be fully maximized by collusion; that is, price and output are determined for the industry by equating MR, corresponding to the aggregate demand facing the industry, to MC of the industry. The industry marginal-cost schedule is the horizontal summation of the member firms' MC-schedules. Once the industry profit-maximizing output is determined, each firm's contribution to the total output is determined in such a way that

$$MC_1 = MC_2 = \cdots = MC_n \qquad (11.1)$$

In other words, the MC for producing a unit of output must be the same for all firms if the profit-maximizing output is to be produced at minimum cost.

In Figure 11.4d, the profit-maximizing output is 1100 units, since at that level $MR_T = MC_T$ ($\$1.10 = \$1.10$). Thus, to ensure the lowest cost for 1100 units, firm 1 will produce 550 units, firm 2 will produce 330 units, and firm 3 will produce 220 units. It will be noted that $q_1 + q_2 + q_3 = Q_T$ (550 + 330 + 220 = 1100).*

There is the additional problem of allocating the now-larger industry profits among the member firms. If these profits are distributed in such a way that each firm receives the same percentage of industry profit as it did prior to collusion, then each firm's profits will increase as a result of collusion. The actual method used for allocating profits depends

*See note 5 in Chapter 10.

FIGURE 11.4

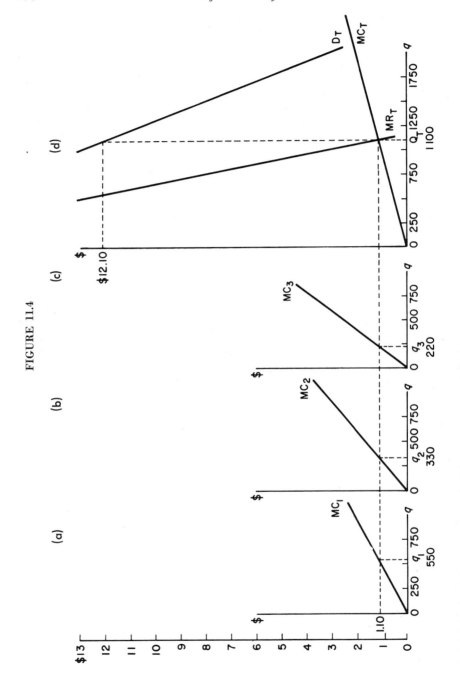

upon the relative bargaining strengths of the firms, the history of the industry, and so on. Clearly, the firm will be willing to participate in the cartel only if it is at least as well off as it was before.[3]

Oligopoly with Tacit Collusion

In the United States overt collusion is illegal. One form of tacit collusion among oligopolists is reflected by the *kinky demand curve*, which was dis-

[3]In the next section, we shall compare profits obtained under the monopoly solution with those obtained when there is less-than-complete collusion of the oligopolists.

FIGURE 11.5

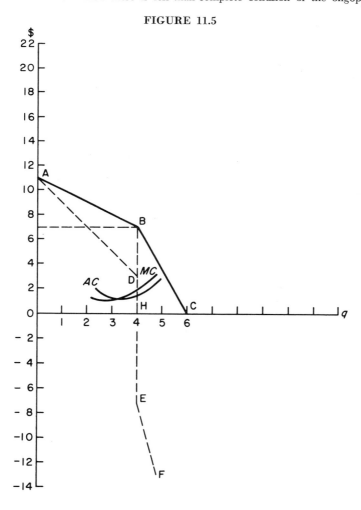

cussed in Chapter 6. This type of demand curve expresses the view of the oligopolist that his rivals will follow his price cuts but not his price increases. Although the kinky demand curve describes a particular attitude, it does not say anything about the determinants of the attitude, nor does it explain the current price at which the kink is presumed to be. Once the current price has been arrived at by some historical process of interaction between the oligopolists (perhaps disastrous experiences with competitive price cutting), the kinky demand curve helps to explain future behavior.

In Figure 11.5 we reproduce Figure 6.3 and also show the cost schedules of the firm. The equilibrium output is 4 units and price is $7, since for outputs greater than 4 units, $MC > MR$ and for smaller outputs, $MR > MC$.

It is often said that the kinky oligopoly demand curve results in rigid prices: the price remains stable over long periods of time. This is a consequence of two factors: (1) each firm believes that little is to be gained by a price rise and that a price cut will lead to a "price war" and (2) since the MC-curve cuts the discontinuous section of the MR-curve, substantial shifts in the MC- and AC-curves can take place and that, depending on the length of the discontinuity, the firm will still find its optimum output to be the same as it was at the kink price. For example, in Figure 11.5, if MC shifts within the range DH, no change in price or output will result, since MR will still be greater than MC for smaller outputs and MC will be greater than MR for larger outputs.

Empirical evidence seems to indicate that the kinky oligopoly demand curve does not accurately describe the most common form of oligopoly behavior. It is believed that oligopolists act in collusion and attempt to achieve a monopoly solution rather than behaving as posited by the kinky demand curve.[4] Recent antitrust action in the electrical equipment and steel industries tends to support this belief.

Another possible form of tacit collusion is *price leadership on the part of the low-cost oligopolist* in the industry. In Figures 11.6a–c we assume three firms in an industry and show the equilibrium price and output under the assumption that the firms have agreed to share the market equally.[5] Firm 1 would like to charge $11.91 and sell 373 units; firm 2 would like to sell 365 units at $12.15 per unit; and firm 3 would like to sell 355 units at $12.45. However, firm 1, being the lowest-cost firm,

---

[4]For a further discussion of this point, see George J. Stigler, "The Kinky Oligopoly Demand Curve and Rigid Prices," *Journal of Political Economy*, LV (October 1947), 432–449.

[5]Thus, the horizontal sum of the three demand curves represents the aggregate demand facing the industry.

FIGURE 11.6

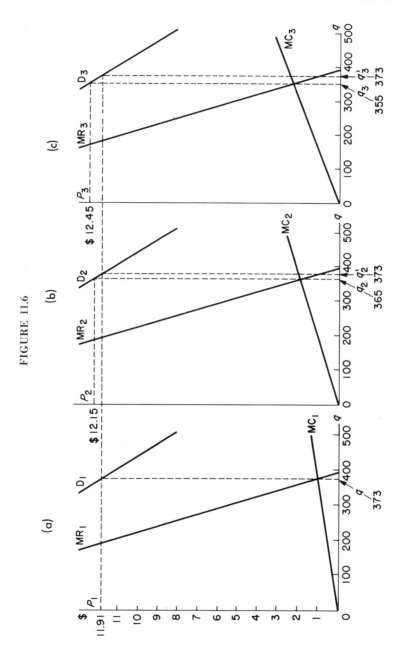

charges a price lower than that charged by the other two firms. If there is no overt agreement among the firms as to price policy, firms 2 and 3 will be forced to charge $11.91 and sell 373 units each or be faced with the danger of losing their share of the market.

It should be noted that the horizontal sum of the demand curves in Figure 11.6 is equal to the market demand that we assumed to face the cartel in Figure 11.4d; that is,

$$q_1 = 770 - 33\tfrac{1}{3}P \qquad\qquad (11.2a)$$
$$q_2 = 770 - 33\tfrac{1}{3}P \qquad\qquad (11.2b)$$
$$q_3 = 770 - 33\tfrac{1}{3}P \qquad\qquad (11.2c)$$
$$\overline{Q_T = 2310 - 100P \text{ or } P = 23.10 - 0.01Q_T} \qquad (11.2d)$$

Therefore, it is possible to compare the total profit earned by the cartel to industry profit with price leadership.

Still another type of tacit collusion is called "umbrella price leadership," which occurs when a dominant firm in the industry sets price at the level at which it can sell its profit-maximizing output and then permits the smaller firms in the industry to sell all they profitably can at that price. One of the reasons why this may be done is the desire to retain the appearance of a competitive industry in the presence of antitrust laws. We demonstrate this type of behavior in Figure 11.7, in which MC_S represents the horizontal sum of the smaller firms' MC-curves and MC_L represents the large firm's marginal cost. We shall assume that all the small firms have identical cost schedules and that there are twenty of them in the industry. Since the small firms accept the price set by the dominant firm, their MC-curves are their supply curves (in the same way that the MC-curve of the perfectly competitive firm is its supply curve since it accepts the price set by the market) and MC_S is, therefore, the total supply curve of the small firms. The demand curve facing the large firm can be derived by taking the horizontal difference at any price between the total demand and the amount supplied by the small firms. This demand is shown as D_L and the corresponding marginal-revenue curve as MR_L. Thus the large firm will produce 972 units at the point where $MC_L = MR_L$ and it will set a price of $4.46. At this price the small firms will supply a total of 892 units, or each firm will produce 44.6 units.

Oligopoly without Collusion

In this section we shall discuss unsophisticated oligopoly behavior. By "unsophisticated" we mean either that an oligopolist does not realize he and his rivals are interdependent, or that he realizes this but makes no

FIGURE 11.7

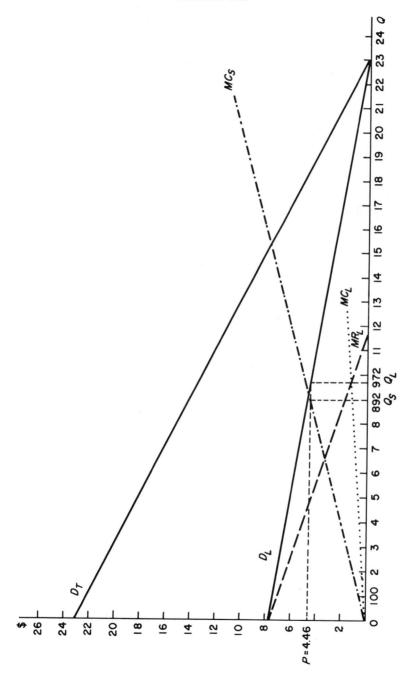

effort to establish any form of collusion with them. In the first case, we assume an oligopolist who is not aware of this interdependence or, if he is aware of it, misjudges its magnitude. We may describe this variant of oligopolistic behavior as immature, because, unless the oligopolist suffers from colossal stupidity, he will at some point learn the lessons of experience: he cannot disregard the effect that his rivals' reactions to his own actions will have upon him. For example, suppose that an oligopolist who was maximizing profit experiences a decrease in costs and, in order to achieve new maximum profits, reduces price and increases his output. His rivals discover that, as a result of this price reduction, their demand schedules shift downward; they will react to this by reducing price and output, causing reductions in their maximum profits. But this reaction shifts the demand schedule of the first oligopolist; and thus his price and output will change. But this shifts the demand curves facing his rivals, and so on and on. This type of behavior will deteriorate into a competitive price-cutting war. When the oligopolists have learned the lesson from their experiences, their behavior may be better described by the kinky demand curve or by one of the other forms of tacit collusion.

An example of unsophisticated oligopoly behavior, when the oligopolist realizes he is interdependent, was described by Augustin Cournot.[6] We shall present Cournot's treatment of the oligopoly solution for a two-firm case (duopoly), but the reasoning can be extended to several firms. Assume that the aggregate demand facing an industry is given by

$$Q_d = 10 - P \text{ (Figure 11.8a)} \qquad (11.3)$$

and that the costs of production are zero. (Cournot's two firms were owners of mineral springs producing identical mineral water.) Thus, a firm maximizing profits will produce where its TR is a maximum; in other words, where $MR = MC = 0$. Let us initially assume that there is one firm in the industry. Acting as a monopolist, it will produce 5 units at $P = \$5$, as is shown in Figure 11.8b, and its profits will be \$25.

Next, we assume that the second firm enters the industry and that its assumption concerning the behavior of the existing firm is that that firm's output will remain at 5 units regardless of its own behavior. Therefore, the second firm takes its demand equation to be

$$q_2 = (10 - P) - 5 \qquad (11.4)$$

or

$$q_2 = 5 - P \qquad (11.4a)$$

[6]Augustin Cournot, *Researches into the Mathematical Principles of Wealth*, trans. N. Bacon and Irving Fisher (New York: The Macmillan Company, 1897).

Figure 11.8c shows the determination of equilibrium price and output for the second firm; thus, $P = \$5/2$, $q_2 = 5/2$, and maximum profits are therefore $6.25 (5/2 \times \$5/2 = \$25/4)$.

Total industry output is now $7\frac{1}{2} = q_1 + q_2 = 5 + 2\frac{1}{2}$. According to the total demand curve of Figure 11.8a, market price will become $5/2$.

FIGURE 11.8

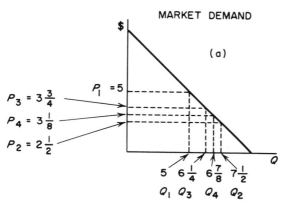

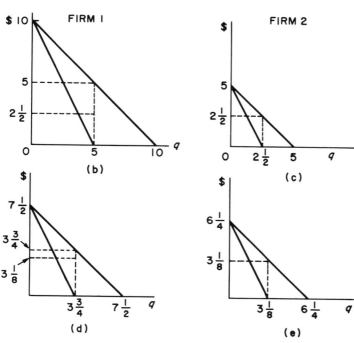

Therefore, firm 1 will now be able to sell its 5 units at $P = \$5/2$; and its profits are reduced to one half their former level — \$12.50.

If the first firm suffers from the same form of myopia as the second firm, it will assume that the $5/2$ units being sold by the second firm are fixed and the first firm then will re-estimate its demand curve, based on this assumption. This new demand curve will be

$$q_1 = (10 - P) - 2\tfrac{1}{2} = 7\tfrac{1}{2} - P \qquad (11.5)$$

In Figure 11.8d, the new profit-maximizing output is $15/4$, $P = \$15/4$, and profits have been increased temporarily from \$12.50 to \$14.06 ($15/4 \times \$15/4 = \$225/16$).

Firm 2 will now regard the $15/4$ units as constant and its demand curve becomes

$$q_2 = 10 - P - \frac{15}{4} = \frac{25}{4} - P \qquad (11.6)$$

Figure 11.8e shows the equilibrium values of $q_2 = 25/8$ and $P = \$25/8$, and profits increased to \$9.77 ($25/8 \times \$25/8 = \$625/64$) from \$6.25.

The new market price becomes \$25/8 and the first firm's profits are now \$11.72 ($30/8 \times \$25/8 = \$750/64$).

This process continues, with the fluctuations becoming progressively smaller, and the values of P, q_1, and q_2 approach limits. The limits they approach can be determined by solving the following simultaneous equations:[7]

$$q_1 = \tfrac{1}{2}(10 - q_2) \qquad (11.7)$$

$$q_2 = \tfrac{1}{2}(10 - q_1) \qquad (11.8)$$

These two equations represent conditions for the fulfillment of profit maximization if each oligopolist assumes his rival's output to be constant and if we assume linear demand curves and zero costs. Adjustments will continue to take place as long as one of these equations is being violated. Therefore, an equilibrium will be achieved when both are being simul-

---

[7]The equations are derived in the following way:
Total demand is represented by: $Q_T = 10 - P$
The demand facing firm 1 is thus: $q_1 = 10 - P - q_2$
 which can also be written as: $P = 10 - q_2 - q_1$
The total revenue of the firm 1 can be expressed as: $Pq_1 = (10 - q_2) q_1 - q_1^2$
Therefore, $MR_1 = 10 - q_2 - 2q_1$
Since the firm has zero costs, profit maximization will occur when $MR_1 = 0$
$$MR_1 = 0 = 10 - q_2 - 2q_1$$
$$2q_1 = 10 - q_2$$
$$q_1 = \tfrac{1}{2}(10 - q_2)$$
The equation for q_2 can be derived in the same way.

taneously fulfilled. In our example, in order to determine the values of q_1 and q_2 that represent equilibrium, we can solve these equations simultaneously:

$$q_1 = \frac{1}{2}(10 - q_2) = 5 - \frac{1}{2}q_2 \qquad (11.7a)$$

$$q_2 = \frac{1}{2}(10 - q_1) = 5 - \frac{1}{2}q_1 \qquad (11.8a)$$

$$q_1 = 5 - \frac{1}{2}\left[5 - \frac{1}{2}q_1\right] \qquad (11.9)$$

$$q_1 = 5 - 5/2 + \frac{1}{4}q_1$$

$$3/4q_1 = 5/2$$

$$q_1 = 10/3 \qquad (11.10)$$

We can substitute in $q_2 = 5 - \frac{1}{2} q_1$ and get $q_2 = 10/3$. To determine market price, we substitute in the aggregate demand equation:

$$q_1 + q_2 = Q_T = 10 - P \qquad (11.11)$$

$$20/3 = 10 - P$$

$$P = 10/3 \qquad (11.12)$$

A Comparison of Perfect and Imperfect Competition

The existence of antitrust legislation in many countries implies a judgment that competition is in some sense more socially desirable than other market structures. In this section we shall compare the various market structures we have discussed as to differences in price, output, and efficiency under similar conditions. The only completely accurate comparison that can be made is between perfect competition and monopoly since in the in-between cases, a host of particular assumptions can be made concerning the exact degree of monopoly power that exists and the way in which it is exercised.

PERFECT COMPETITION VS. MONOPOLY: SHORT-RUN PRICE AND OUTPUT

In Figure 11.9 ΣSMC is the short-run supply of a perfectly competitive industry (that is, it is the sum of the SMC curves of the individual member firms) and D is the aggregate demand for the output of the industry. Thus, the market price will be OP_C and the equilibrium output OQ_C.

Let us assume that a monopolist buys all the firms in the industry and operates them as individual plants, and that, as a result of this purchase, no changes take place in the costs of the individual plants. If the monopolist maximizes his profits, he will equate MR to ΣSMC and the monopoly price will be OP_M and monopoly output OQ_M. As a result of the monopolization of the industry, price is higher and quantity less than under perfect competition.

Notice also that under perfect competition $P = MC$. This means that the price to the consumer for an extra unit of output is just equal to the

FIGURE 11.9

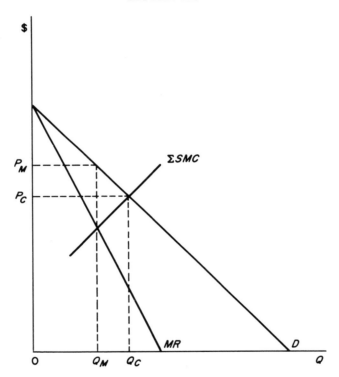

value of the factors of production that society must surrender in order to produce the extra unit of output. Under monopoly, however, $P > MR = MC$, so that the price to the consumer is in excess of the value to society of the resources used up. And although the consumer is willing to pay more for an additional unit of output than the cost to society for producing that unit of output, no further output is forthcoming from the monopolist. This means that a shift of the resources needed to produce one unit of output from a competitive industry to a monopolistic one

FIGURE 11.10

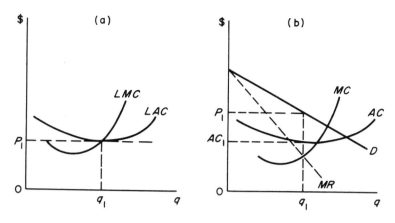

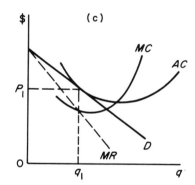

(with the same marginal costs) will increase the total money value of output produced with the same resources. If we measure economic efficiency as

$$\frac{\text{value of output}}{\text{value of input}}$$

for the economy as a whole, then if such shifts of resources can profitably take place, the ratio has not been maximized and maximum economic efficiency has not been attained.

PERFECT COMPETITION VS. MONOPOLY: LONG-RUN PRICE AND OUTPUT

We saw in Chapter 9 that when the perfectly competitive firm is in long-run equilibrium, it produces at the minimum point of its LAC-curve and has no profit. This is shown in Figure 11.10a. This means that the perfectly competitive firm produces where its per-unit cost is the lowest possible; in other words, it has taken advantage of all economies of scale and has not yet incurred any diseconomies of scale. On the other hand, as Figure 11.10b indicates, the monopolist is not subject to pressure from entering firms and thus there is no necessity for him to produce at minimum *LAC* or to make zero profit. Even if, by chance, the monopolist makes no profit, he still does not produce where *LAC* is a minimum (see Figure 11.10c). In summary, we can state that a competitive firm will utilize the optimum plant in the most efficient manner in the long run, and that the competitive entrepreneur will earn only the opportunity costs of his factors of production. The monopolist, on the other hand, need not build the optimum-size plant in the long run and may receive returns in excess of opportunity costs. It will be recalled that this excess is wasteful in the sense that it is not necessary to retain the factors of production in the industry in the long run.

SOME OTHER CONSIDERATIONS

In our comparison of perfect competition and monopoly, we assumed that the industry could be either competitive or monopolistic. However, let us consider the situation where market price in a competitive industry is such that losses are made in the short run. This will result in firms leaving the industry in the long run. And it may happen that price does not reach minimum *LAC* until relatively few firms remain in the industry. Under these conditions, perfect competition could not exist. Or consider the case in which *LAC* continues to decline until a single firm's output represents a very large proportion of total industry demand. Again, perfect competition will not be possible.

The fact that many firms do control a substantial portion of their respective industry outputs, in spite of antitrust laws, seems to indicate an attitude in the law that it is not the existence of market power that constitutes a violation of antitrust regulations but rather the "undue" exercise of this power however the court may define it. All forms of imperfect competition represent some degree of market power, monopoly being the ultimate. The inefficiencies ascribed to monopoly are therefore ascribable in part to other forms of imperfect competition, the exact degree being dependent on where they lie on the continuum between perfect competition and pure monopoly.

In Figure 11.9 we assumed that the monopolization of the industry did not result in a change in costs. It is possible, though, for the monopolization of the industry to result in either an increase or a decrease in costs. An increase in costs can occur because (1) there are inefficiencies associated with the attempt of the monopolist to run all the plants that were formerly part of the competitive industry; and (2) the monopolist may become lax and not act as a true profit maximizer in the sense that he allows costs to rise above the minimum attainable level since he is not subjected to competitive pressures.

It may be argued that monopolization can result in a decrease in costs if the monopolist uses part of his monopoly profit for research and development with the aim of reducing his costs of production. It has also been argued that the "neighborhood effects" of this research and development are substantial: the benefits of new knowledge accrue to society as a whole. On the other hand, it cannot be argued that, simply because a firm possessing market power has lower per-unit costs than comparable firms in a competitive industry, the cost difference represents a gain of technological efficiency due to monopolization. This difference can be due to the fact that the monopolist, because of his size, is capable of exerting pressure on suppliers of factors of production and to effect a transfer of income from these suppliers by extorting a noneconomically justified reduction in factor prices.

A further point that must be taken into consideration in comparing perfect with imperfect competition concerns the difference in the types of goods produced. For example, monopolistic competition affords the consumer a wide variety of choices among similar goods, whereas with perfect competition, homogeneous goods are produced. Therefore, if the satisfaction of consumers is increased as a result of the differentiation of goods, the inefficiencies ascribable to this form of imperfect competition cannot be compared in absolute terms with the efficiencies of perfect competition.

THE DETERMINATION
OF FACTOR PRICES

12

Factor Price Determination under Conditions of Perfect Competition in Both the Product and Factor Markets

In Chapter 7 we stated that, in order to produce a given level of output at the lowest cost possible, with fixed factor prices, a firm would combine the factors in such a way that

$$\frac{MP_a}{P_a} = \frac{MP_b}{P_b} = \cdots = \frac{MP_n}{P_n} \qquad (7.11a)$$

This gives us the optimum factor proportions but does not give us the absolute amounts of the factors the firm should utilize.

In making any decision, the firm compares the change in revenue, resulting from the decision, with the change in cost, resulting from the decision, in order to determine what action should be taken. If the difference between the change in revenue and the change in cost is positive, the firm will find the action profitable. This principle, of course, applies to the firm's decisions concerning the quantities of factors to utilize.

In a competitive factor market, the extra cost of an extra unit of the factor is simply equal to the market price of that factor; that is, if the firm is only one of many purchasing the services of the factor, it will have only an imperceptible influence on the price of the factor. In other words, the supply of the factor to the firm appears horizontal and has elasticity in the vicinity of infinity: the firm can purchase as many units of the service as it can utilize at the going market price.

The extra revenue that results from the use of the extra unit of the factor is equal to the extra output that the extra unit of the factor contributes — the MP of the factor — *multiplied by* the extra revenue that results from selling an extra unit of the output — the MR. In other words, the extra revenue is equal to the difference between the TR

212

obtained from selling the output produced by $n + 1$ units of the factor and the TR obtained from selling the output produced by n units of the factor.[1] Therefore, if the extra revenue resulting from the utilization of an extra factor unit exceeds the extra cost of hiring it, the firm's decision will be to hire that unit; if the reverse is true, then the unit will not be hired. In symbolic terms, we can state

$(MP_F \times MR) > P_F$ if the firm is to increase its factor hire

$(MP_F \times MR) < P_F$ if the firm is not to increase its factor hire

Therefore, if $(MP_F \times MR) = P_F$* the firm has achieved an equilibrium in the employment of the factor.

We shall demonstrate factor price determination with reference to the perfectly competitive firm of Chapter 9. In Table 12.1 we list various input levels and show output at these levels. In column 3 we show the marginal product of the factor MP_x. In column 5 we show $(MP_x \times MR)$. Since we assume the firm is a perfect competitor in the product market, $P = MR$ — in this case \$5.80. The product of the price of the good and the marginal product of the factor is called the value of the marginal product of the factor:

$$VMP_x = (MP_x \cdot P) \qquad (12.1)$$

The product of the marginal revenue of the good and the marginal product of the factor is called the marginal revenue product:

$$MR_x = (MP_x \cdot MR) \qquad (12.2)$$

It should be noted that, since for the competitive firm $P = MR$, $VMP_x = MRP$.

We show the $VMP_x (= MRP_x)$ in Figure 12.1. We show also the supply of the factor facing the firm, since in Chapter 7 we assumed \$1 was the constant factor price. The firm will continue to increase its hire of the factor until $MRP_x (= VMP_x) = P_x$. This occurs at 880 units of the factor. Since the $MRP_x (= VMP_x)$ shows the relationship between alternative prices of the factor and quantities of the factor that will be employed by the firm, it is in effect a demand curve for the factor of production.

It can be seen from Table 12.1 that, if the firm faced a factor price of, say, \$10.00, there would be two levels of factor inputs at which $MRP_x =$

[1]
$$\frac{\Delta TR}{\Delta q} \cdot \frac{\Delta q}{\Delta F} = \frac{\Delta TR}{\Delta F}$$

*This equilibrium condition should be amended to state: $MP_F \times MR = P_F$ provided that $(MP_F \times MR)$ is declining. See pages 156–157.

P_x: at approximately 90 units and 210 units. The firm would employ the greater quantity since the equilibrium conditions are not being fulfilled at 90 units. For example, if the firm employed 90 units, $MRP_x > P_x$ for increases in factor employment, and $MRP_x < P_x$ for reductions. There-

TABLE 12.1

(1)	(2)	(3) MP_x $(P_x = \$1)$	(4) $MR = P$ $= \$5.80$	(5) $VMP_x =$ $MRP_x = [(3) \cdot (4)]$	(6)	(7) $\dfrac{P_x}{MP_x} = \dfrac{\$1}{MP_x}$
X	q				MC	
0	0					
		1.11	$5.80	$6.438	$0.90	$0.90
90	100					
		2.86	5.80	16.588	0.35	0.35
125	200					
		4.00	5.80	23.20	0.25	0.25
150	300					
		5.00	5.80	29.00	0.20	0.20
170	400					
		2.50	5.80	14.50	0.40	0.40
210	500					
		1.11	5.80	6.438	0.90	0.90
300	600					
		0.67	5.80	3.886	1.50	1.50
450	700					
		0.42	5.80	2.436	2.40	2.40
690	800					
		0.17	5.80	0.986	5.80	5.80
1270	900					
		0.02	5.80	0.116	10.00	10.00
6270	1000					

fore, a movement away from 90 units in either direction would result in an increase in the profit of the firm. Thus, equilibrium is achieved when $MRP_x = P_x$ and the slope of the MRP_x-curve is less than the slope of the supply curve of the factor; it is only the downward-sloping portion of the MRP-curve that represents the demand curve for the factor.[2]

To derive the aggregate demand for this factor, we horizontally sum the MRP_x-curves (which for the competitive firm is the same as its VMP_x-curve) of all firms that are users of the factor. And the intersection of this aggregate demand schedule with the total supply schedule of the factor determines the market price of the factor, which the firms then accept as the going factor price.

[2]For a rigorous proof of this see note 1 in Chapter 9. For TR substitute TR_x; for TC, substitute TC_x; and for q, substitute X.

FIGURE 12.1

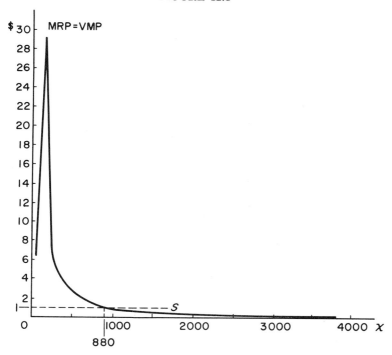

It is interesting to show the relationship between the conditions for equilibrium factor hire and the conditions for the maximization of profits in the product market.

The least-cost condition can be stated as

$$\frac{MP_a}{P_a} = \frac{MP_b}{P_b} = \cdots = \frac{MP_n}{P_n} \tag{7.11a}$$

Note that

$$\frac{P_a}{MP_a} = \frac{P_a}{\Delta q/\Delta a} = \frac{\Delta TC}{\Delta q} = MC \tag{12.3}$$

Since the ratio MP_i/P_i is equal for all factors, the addition to cost will be the same no matter which factor is used to produce a small increment of output. If the firm employs only one variable factor of production, then simply $P_a/MP_a = MC$.

Equilibrium in the factor market exists when

$$MRP_a = P_a \tag{12.4}$$

or

$$MP_a \cdot MR = P_a \tag{12.4a}$$

Dividing both sides of the equality by MP_a,

$$\frac{MP_a \cdot MR}{MP_a} = \frac{P_a}{MP_a} \tag{12.5}$$

Therefore, we can state

$$MR = MC \tag{12.6}$$

which is the equilibrium condition we derived for the product market. And for the firm that is a pure competitor in the product market, $P = MC$.

We can demonstrate this relationship by comparing Figures 12.1 and 9.1. Figure 9.1 shows the determination of equilibrium output and Figure 12.1 shows the determination of equilibrium factor employment. When 880 units are employed, $MP_x = 0.172$.[*] And from Figure 9.1 we see that when profit-maximizing output is produced, $MC = \$5.80$. Therefore, the least-cost condition is

$$\frac{P_x}{MP_x} = MC$$

$$\frac{\$1}{0.172} = \$5.80 \quad \begin{array}{l}\text{(This can be verified from column 7 of} \\ \text{Table 12.1.)}\end{array}$$

The equilibrium condition for the factor market is

$$MP_x \cdot MR = P_x$$

$$0.172 \cdot \$5.80 = \$1.00$$

Dividing both sides by MP_x,

$$\frac{0.172 \times \$5.80}{0.172} = \frac{\$1.00}{0.172}$$

$$\$5.80 = \$5.80$$

$$MR = MC$$

which is the equilibrium condition for the product market derived in Chapter 9.

We can further verify these results by comparing profits calculated in terms of the product market and in terms of the factor market. For the product market, Table 9.1 and Figure 9.1 show

$$P = \$5.80$$
$$q = 850 \text{ units}$$
$$TR = \$4930$$
$$STC = \$2380$$
$$\pi = \$2550$$

[*]In Table 12.1, we see that $MP_x = 0.17$ at 980 units of X (the mid-point of the interval 690 to 1270). The exact MP_x figure at 880 units can be obtained by finding the slope of the TP_x schedule of Figure 7.8a, provided, of course, we expanded the scales.

For the factor market,

$P_x = \$1$

$X = 880$

$VC = \$880$

We know from Chapter 9 that 750 units of the fixed factor are employed and the price of it is $2 per unit; or fixed costs are $1500:

$$STC = FC + VC = \$1500 + \$880$$

$$STC = \$2380$$

When 880 units of the variable factor are used, output is 850 units; and with $P = \$5.80$, $TR = \$4930$, and profits are clearly the same as before: $2550.

Factor Price Determination under Conditions of Perfect Competition in the Factor Market and Monopoly in the Product Market

The principles developed in the preceding section apply equally in this case. The only difference is that for the monopolist, $P > MR$; therefore, in the factor market,

$$VMP_x > MRP_x$$

Since in equilibrium, the firm will set

$$MRP_x = P_x \tag{12.7}$$

$$VMP_x > P_x \tag{12.8}$$

It should be noted that it is the MRP_x-curve that is the demand curve for the factor whether the firm is a monopolist or a competitor in the product market; but for the monopolist this curve is not coincident with, but is less than, the VMP_x-curve.

In Table 12.2 we list the relevant data for the determination of the factor market equilibrium of the monopolist of Chapter 10. We assumed there that the firm hired its variable factor at $1.00 per unit. Therefore, factor-market equilibrium in Figure 12.2 is at 880 units. Again, if we compare this equilibrium with the one shown in Figure 10.1, we will find they are equivalent.

In Chapter 11 we pointed out that the economic inefficiency of monopoly, from the point of view of the economy as a whole, may be seen by the fact that resources can be reallocated between the competitive and the monopolistic spheres of the economy without changing the value of

FIGURE 12.2

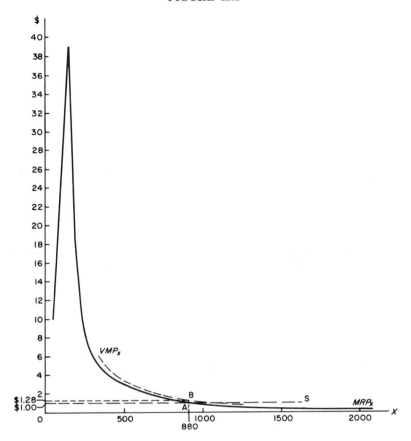

factor inputs used, and yet total money value of output is increased. We can show this in Figures 12.1 and 2. The monopolist and the perfect competitor each hires a factor at its market price of $1; therefore, for the competitor,

$$P_x = MRP_x = VMP_x$$
$$\$1 = \$1 \quad\; = \$1$$

But for the monopolist:

$$P_x = MRP_x < VMP_x$$
$$\$1 = \quad\; \$1 < \$1.28$$

Therefore, a transfer of one factor unit from the competitor to the monopolist will result first in a loss of value of output of $1 and then a gain of

$1.28; or a net gain of $0.28. It should also be noted that the factor employed by the competitive firm receives its full VMP as the price per unit of its services, whereas the factor employed by the monopolist receives less than its VMP. As a matter of fact, we can define the degree of monopolistic exploitation of a factor as

$$VMP_x - P_x$$

TABLE 12.2

(1) X	(2) q	(3) MP_x	(4) P	(5) VMP_x	(6) MR	(7) MRP_x
0	0		$9.20			
		1.11		$10.10	$9.00	$10.00
90	100		9.00			
		2.86		25.45	8.60	24.57
125	200		8.80			
		4.00		34.80	8.20	32.80
150	300		8.60			
		5.00		42.50	7.80	39.00
170	400		8.40			
		2.50		20.75	7.40	18.50
210	500		8.20			
		1.11		9.00	7.00	7.78
300	600		8.00			
		0.67		5.29	6.60	4.40
450	700		7.80			
		0.42		3.23	6.20	2.58
690	800		7.60			
		0.17		1.28	5.80	1.00
1270	900		7.40			
		0.02		0.15	5.40	0.108
6270	1000		7.20			

In Figure 12.2, the exploitation per unit is AB.

We can now restate our objection to monopoly by asserting that resources are inefficiently allocated unless VMP_x is equal in all of the factor's alternative uses. This condition is violated by the existence of monopoly.

Monopsony: Nature of the Supply Curve of Labor

Monopoly power may exist in the factor market as well as in the product market. When a single firm is the only user of a specific factor of production, it is called a monopsonist; if it is one of several firms using the factor, it is an oligopsonist. In our discussion of monopsony power, we shall assume the firm is a pure monopsonist.

Just as the monopolist faces the total demand for the product he sells, the monopsonist faces the entire supply schedule of the factor he employs. Therefore, the monopsonist must consider the effect of a change in his employment of the factor on the price of the previous units employed, just as a monopolist must consider the effect of selling the $n + 1$ unit on the price of the previous n units per time period.

In our discussion of the supply of a factor, we shall limit ourselves to labor. It is possible to have a backward-bending supply curve of labor. The point at which the worker supplies less labor in response to a higher wage may be considered to occur when the marginal utility derived from the additional income becomes less than the marginal utility derived from additional leisure. There are other supply curves of labor that are not of the usual shape. One of these is a vertical supply curve at some quantity of labor. If we assume this fixed quantity to be at the individual's capacity, it would probably describe the supply curve of a "dedicated" worker; for example, a humanitarian medical researcher with an outside source of income. Another unusual supply curve is one that is horizontal at the going wage rate and becomes vertical at capacity. This would apply for an individual who cannot obtain a "subsistence" income until his capacity is reached.

The aggregate supply of labor is the sum of the individual supply schedules. Although most individuals have backward-bending supply curves, the points at which the bends occur are randomly distributed. Therefore, the aggregate supply will continue to rise over a wide range of wages, and the relevant portion of the aggregate curve probably will be upward-sloping.

Factor Price Determination under Conditions of Perfect Competition in the Product Market and Monopsony in the Factor Market

In columns 1 and 2 of Table 12.3 and in Figure 12.3 we present the supply curve of labor faced by a perfectly competitive firm in the product market. When the firm faces an upward-sloping supply curve, the extra cost of hiring an additional unit of the factor is no longer the same as the price of the factor. The firm not only has to pay more for the extra unit; in addition it must raise the price paid to the previous units hired. In column 3 we show the total outlay for labor (TO_L) and in column 4 we derive the marginal outlay for labor:

$$MO_L = \frac{dTO_L}{dL} \tag{12.9}$$

or in discrete terms

$$MO_L = \frac{\Delta TO_L}{\Delta L} \qquad (12.9a)$$

It will be noted that MO_L is upward-sloping and greater than the supply curve of labor, P_L, since the usual relationship holds between P_L and MO_L:

$$MO_L = P_L + \frac{dP_L}{dL} L \qquad (12.10)$$

or in discrete terms,

$$MO_L = P_{L_2} + \frac{\Delta P_L}{\Delta L} L_1 \qquad (12.10a)$$

Whether the firm is a perfect competitor or a monopsonist in the factor market, the equilibrium condition for factor hire is the same: the firm will continue to employ the factor as long as the extra revenue received from the sale of the extra output produced by the extra unit of the factor — MRP_L — exceeds the extra outlay necessary to acquire the extra factor unit — MO_L. Thus, we can state the equilibrium condition as

If $MRP_L > MO_L$, the firm will increase its employment of L

If $MRP_L < MO_L$, the firm will decrease its employment of L

$$(12.11)$$

FIGURE 12.3

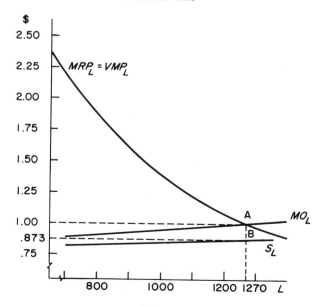

TABLE 12.3

(1) P_L	(2) L	(3) TO_L	(4) MO_L
$0.824	0	$ 0	
			$0.844
0.844	200	168.80	
			0.884
0.864	400	345.60	
			0.924
0.884	600	530.40	
			0.964
0.904	800	723.20	
			1.004
0.924	1000	924.00	
			1.044
0.944	1200	1132.80	
			1.084
0.964	1400	1349.60	

Column 1 is derived from the equation

$$P_L = 0.824 + 0.001L$$

Column 3 is derived from the equation

$$TO_L = 0.824L + 0.0001L^2 = (1) \times (2)$$

Column 4 is derived from the equation

$$MO_L = 0.824L + 0.0002L = \frac{\Delta TO_L}{\Delta L}$$

In other words, equilibrium factor employment occurs when

$$MRP_L = MO_L \text{ provided } MRP_L \text{ is declining.} \qquad (12.12)$$

When the firm is a perfect competitor in the factor market, $MO_L = P_L$, so that in equilibrium, $MRP_L = MO_L = P_L$. However, if the firm is a monopsonist, $MO_L > P_L$ and in equilibrium, then

$$VMP_L = MRP_L = MO_L > P_L \qquad (12.13)$$

We shall demonstrate the determination of factor market equilibrium in Figure 12.3. $MRP_L = MO_L = \$1.00$ at 1270 units of L, and the price per unit paid by the firm is $0.873. Thus,

$$VMP_L = MRP_L = MO_L > P$$
$$\$1.00 = \$1.00 = \$1.00 > \$0.873$$

The extent of monopsony power can be measured as the distance AB — the amount by which MRP_L exceeds P_L. This is analogous to measuring monopoly power as the distance between the price of the good and the marginal cost of producing the good at the equilibrium output.

Factor Price Determination under Conditions of Monopoly and Monopsony

The determination of factor prices under these conditions is demonstrated in Table 12.4 and Figure 12.4. The same equilibrium conditions apply;

FIGURE 12.4

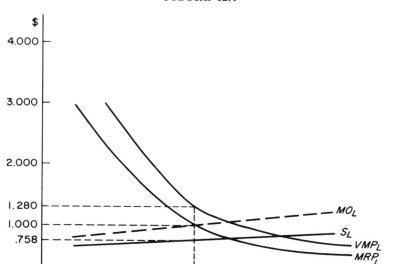

therefore, the firm will hire 880 units of labor and pay a wage of $0.758 per unit. At 880 units,

$$VMP_L > MRP_L = MO_L > P_L$$
$$\$1.28 > \$1.00 = \$1.00 > \$0.758$$

Notice that the laborer's wage is less than the value of the marginal product on two counts: first, the monopolistic exploitation of labor, measured as the gap between VMP_L and MRP_L; and, second, the monopsonistic power of the firm, measured as the gap between MRP_L and P_L.

TABLE 12.4

(1) P_L	(2) L	(3) TO_L	(4) MO_L
$0.626	400	$250.40	
			$0.791
0.681	600	408.60	
			0.901
0.736	800	588.80	
			1.011
0.791	1000	791.00	
			1.121
0.846	1200	1015.20	
			1.231
0.901	1400	1261.40	

Summary of Equilibrium Conditions

EQUILIBRIUM CONDITIONS

	Gain to firm from hiring extra unit of factor	=	Cost to firm due to hiring extra unit of factor
General case	MRP_L	=	MO_L
Perfect competition in both markets	$VMP_L = MRP_L$	=	$MO_L = P_L$
Monopolist in product; perfect competitor in factor market	$VMP_L > MRP_L$	=	$MO_L = P_L$
Perfect competitor in product; monopsonist	$VMP_L = MRP_L$	=	$MO_L > P_L$
Monopolist-monopsonist	$VMP_L > MRP_L$	=	$MO_L > P_L$

The Relevance of Monopsony

One of the best historical examples of monopsony in the United States is the "factory town," in which one concern was the chief source of employment. With the advent of the automobile and other cheap methods of transportation, this type of regional monopsony has become less likely. Even if a firm possesses monopoly power in the product market, it is unlikely that it will be able to achieve monopsony power in the factor market. For example, the largest automobile producers possess market power on the selling side; but since they are in competition for factors not only with other firms in the Detroit area but with firms in the surrounding factor market (which encompasses a much wider area than merely Detroit), if they do possess monopsony power, it is only to a small degree.

Furthermore, monopsony power has been reduced as a result of increased knowledge on the part of the workers. The increase in knowledge has been made possible by the expansion of government employment offices, recruitment by firms over a wider geographical area, and wider circulation of media that provide employment information. The improved and expanded transportation and communications facilities have also resulted in increased mobility on the part of labor. This too, of course, has the effect of lessening regional monopsony.

The Effect of Government Regulation on Monopsony

Minimum-wage laws are sometimes defended on the grounds that they help to counter the effects of monopsony power. In Figure 12.5 we show the effects of minimum-wage legislation on a monopsonist. We assume that prior to the imposition of a minimum wage, the equilibrium quantity of labor employed is L_1, and the corresponding wage rate, W_1. If a minimum wage of W_2 is imposed, the effective supply curve facing the firm becomes W_2RS and the corresponding MO_L-curve is coincident with the supply curve over the range W_2R, becomes discontinuous at R, and then becomes TV. If the firm is to maximize its profit, it will hire L_2 units of labor, since at L_2 the equilibrium conditions are being fulfilled:

$$\text{Below } L_2, \quad MRP_L > MO_L$$
$$\text{Above } L_2, \quad MRP_L < MO_L$$

Since the monopsonist was maximizing profit before the imposition of the minimum wage (and consequently L_1 was the optimum quantity of the factor hired), when the monopsonist hires L_2, profits decline.

It is true that if monopsony exists and if the minimum wage can be set at the level where the supply curve cuts MRP_L, the monopsonist will be forced to pay the higher wage as well as offer more employment. But if monopsony is not often encountered, it would be foolish to set an economy-wide minimum wage to offset it. In more competitive labor markets, the minimum wage will certainly reduce employment in industries paying less than the minimum; this is shown in Figure 12.6.

Further, even if it were true that monopsony pervaded the economy,

FIGURE 12.5

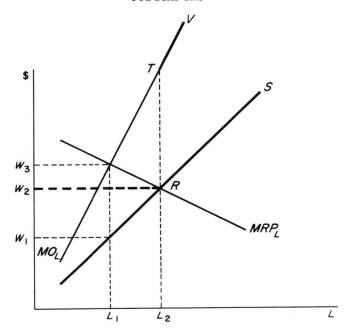

it would be highly unlikely that an economy-wide minimum wage would be for all, or even most, monopsonists that wage which would increase factor employment. If the economy-wide minimum wage were set higher than W_3 in Figure 12.5, this would cause the monopsonist to reduce the quantity of labor hired. We must conclude, therefore, that an economy-wide minimum wage is too gross an instrument for dealing with diverse monopsony.

The Effects of Unions

Unions can affect wage rates and total labor income in several ways, the most important of which are restricting the supply of labor and the determination of wage rates through collective bargaining.

We first investigate the effects of a union on a firm with no monopsony power. In Figure 12.6, we assume W_1 is the competitive wage rate and that the firm hires the equilibrium quantity of labor, L_1. Now assume that, through collective bargaining, the wage rate that the firm must now pay increases to W_2. Consequently, the firm will now employ L_2 units of labor. Thus, the short-run effect of the higher wage is a decrease in

FIGURE 12.6

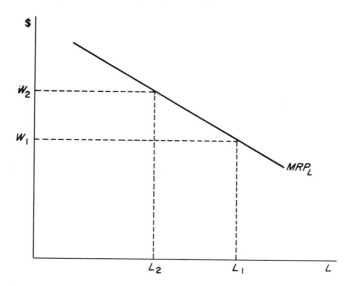

employment. The new total wage bill of the firm, W_2L_2, can be greater than, less than, or equal to the old wage bill, W_1L_1, for labor, depending upon the elasticity of demand. The demand for labor will be more inelastic[3]

1. the more inelastic is the demand for the firm's product.
2. the smaller the percentage of total cost accounted for by expenditure on labor.
3. the more inelastic the supply of other factors.
4. the fewer the factors that can be substituted for labor.

Most likely the elasticity of demand will be greater in the long run than in the short run. This is true because the demand for the finished product will tend to be more elastic in the long run and, since in the long run all factors are variable, the firm will be able to achieve the most economical combination of factors. Furthermore, in the long run, the supply of other factors will tend to be more elastic.

Next, let us assume that the firm in Figure 12.6 is a perfect competitor in the product market and the only one, or one of several, to be unionized. In the short run, the firm's costs will be higher because of the unionization;

[3]See Alfred Marshall, *Principles of Economics* (8th ed.; New York: Macmillan, 1920), pp. 385–386. See also George Stigler, *Production and Distribution Theories* (New York: Macmillan, 1959), pp. 83–87.

however, it will keep producing as long as $P \geqslant AVC$. In the long run, price in a perfectly competitive industry will be equal to minimum LAC; therefore, since the firm's costs will be higher than those of the other firms in the industry, it will be forced to leave the industry.

If the firm in Figure 12.6 is perfectly competitive but all other firms in the industry are also unionized, then the costs of all firms will be higher and in the long run the price of the good will also be higher.

FIGURE 12.7

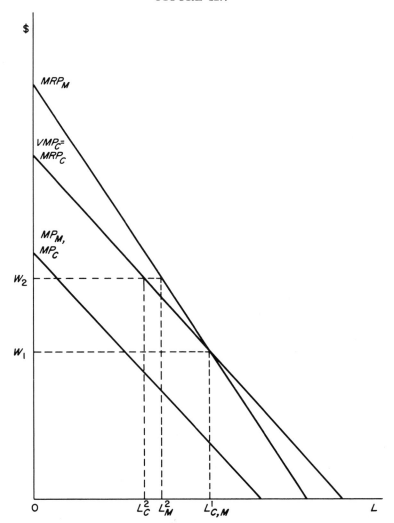

As a result of the higher costs, the long-run industry supply curve is higher and long-run equilibrium output will be reduced. Thus, factor employment will also go down.

Perfectly competitive industries are generally difficult to unionize because of their large numbers of firms. Thus, the most effective unions are in industries where there are a small number of firms and/or industries that are geographically concentrated.

If the union deals with a firm that is an imperfect competitor in the product market, the adjustment of the firm to the higher wage rate will be an increase in the price of the product and a decrease in the quantity of the good sold. In fact, the reduction in employment will be less for the monopolistic firm than for the competitive one. This is illustrated in Figure 12.7, where we assume that both firms have the same marginal productivity schedules. Since the perfectly competitive firm faces a constant market price, the MRP ($= VMP$)-schedule will be parallel to the MP-schedule. The monopolist, however, faces a downward sloping demand curve; therefore, marginal revenue is also negatively sloped. We assume that for the output corresponding to the input $L'_{C,M}$, the MR for the competitive firm is equal to that of the monopolist. Therefore, at $L'_{C,M}$, the MRP's are the same. Since the monopolist has a negatively sloped MR-schedule, for inputs less than $L'_{C,M}$ (and thus for smaller outputs), MRP_M will be greater than MRP_C; and for greater inputs than $L'_{C,M}$, $MRP_M < MRP_C$.

In the absence of unionization and a wage rate of W_1, both firms will hire $L'_{C,M}$ units since, for both firms, $MRP = W_1$. Now let us assume that a union imposes a wage of W_2. The competitive firm will hire L^2_C units of labor; the monopolist, L^2_M units. The reason for the greater reduction in the amount of labor employed by the competitive firm is that a greater burden is thrown on output adjustments — in fact, this is the only adjustment possible for the competitive firm. On the other hand, the monopolist adjusts both price and quantity and, therefore, reduces labor employment by a smaller amount.

In the long run, the ability of the union to keep the wage above its free-market equilibrium level, in the face of resulting unemployment, will depend on the union's ability to maintain its power under these conditions. If the unionized industry is a growing one, the union will be able to accomplish this if it has control over entry into the union. Instead of creating unemployment under these conditions, employment will be prevented from growing as rapidly as it would in the absence of the union wage.

The effect of a union dealing with a monopsony is demonstrated in Figure 12.5. Before the imposition of a union wage rate, the monopsonist hires L_1 units and pays W_1 per unit. A union wage of anything greater than W_1 but less than W_3 will force the monopsonist both to increase labor hire and to pay a higher wage rate. W_2 is the wage rate that maximizes employment. If the union is interested not in the maximization of employment but in the maximization of the total wages paid by the firm, the wage rate selected will depend upon the elasticity of demand for labor.

GENERAL
EQUILIBRIUM

13

The market economy is an interrelated whole and changes in any part of it cause changes and reactions of a greater or lesser magnitude in every part of the economy. Our ability to deal with a large number of economic variables and interrelationships is limited, and so, for the purpose of simplification and to make the analysis manageable, we usually resort to partial-equilibrium analysis. That is to say, we classify our variables into (1) those directly impinging upon the phenomenon in question, (2) those less closely related but of great importance, and (3) those whose influence is much less direct and that can, for the purpose at hand, be ignored. Thus when we write $Q_{d_x} = f\ (P_x,\ ceteris\ paribus)$, P_x represents the prime variable and those assumed to be temporarily constant — income, tastes, the prices of good substitutes and complements — are in the second category of variables; other variables are ignored. In theory, a general equilibrium approach to an economic problem would take into account the interdependence of all economic variables — a change in any of these variables causes ripples of effect to spread throughout the economy. No such complete analysis is possible, given the present state of our knowledge.

The first general equilibrium equation system that demonstrated this general interdependence of economic quantities was presented by Leon Walras in 1874. Although economic analysis is still primarily carried out in a partial equilibrium context, Walras' contribution was to emphasize the interdependence of the sectors of the economy and to give us an overview of the interrelationships.

Although Walras' analysis is in completely general terms we shall be somewhat more concrete, limiting ourselves to an economy of 2000 people and 200 firms, 100 of which produce a good X, and 100 of which produce a good Y. Further, there are two factors of production, A and B, used in the production of both X and Y; these factors are held in initial endowments by the individuals.

Thus we have:

2000 persons	$1 \cdots 2000$
2 goods	X, Y
2 factors	A, B
100 firms producing X	$1 \cdots 100$
100 firms producing Y	$101 \cdots 200$

We use the following symbols:

Consumption of the individuals (including consumption of factors):

$X_1, X_2, \cdots, X_{2000}$
$Y_1, Y_2, \cdots, Y_{2000}$
$A_1, A_2, \cdots, A_{2000}$
$B_1, B_2, \cdots, B_{2000}$

Production of the firms:

$x_1, \quad x_2, \quad \cdots, x_{100}$
$y_{101}, y_{102}, \cdots, y_{200}$

Initial endowments of the factors:

$\overline{A}_1, \overline{A}_2, \cdots, \overline{A}_{2000}$
$\overline{B}_1, \overline{B}_2, \cdots, \overline{B}_{2000}$

Supply of the factors:

$a_1 = \overline{A}_1 - A_1, a_2 = \overline{A}_2 - A_2, \cdots, a_{2000} = \overline{A}_{2000} - A_{2000}$
$b_1 = \overline{B}_1 - B_1, b_2 = \overline{B}_2 - B_2, \cdots, b_{2000} = \overline{B}_{2000} - B_{2000}$

Demand for the factors:

demand for $A = A_x^1 + A_x^2 + \cdots + A_x^{100} + A_y^{101} + A_y^{102} + \cdots + A_y^{200}$
demand for $B = B_x^1 + B_x^2 + \cdots + B_x^{100} + B_y^{101} + B_y^{102} + \cdots + B_y^{200}$

The following unknowns must be determined:

For an individual i, X_i, Y_i, A_i, B_i

There are 2000 persons, giving *8000 unknowns*.

For a firm k, A_x^k, B_x^k, x_k

There are 100 such firms, giving *300 unknowns*.

For a firm l, A_y^l, B_y^l, y_l

There are 100 such firms, giving *300 unknowns*.

With X used as numeraire, so that $P_x = 1$,

P_y, P_a, P_b must also be determined.

This adds *three additional uknowns.*

We have a total of 8603 unknowns.

Given, for each consumer i,

$$U_i = U_i(X_i, Y_i, A_i, B_i) \tag{13.1}$$

There are 2000 of these utility functions.

For each individual there is also the initial endowment of factors $\bar{A}_i, \bar{B}_i$.

There are 2000 of these initial endowments.

Given, for each producer k, the production function:

$$x_k = f_x(A_x^k, B_x^k) \tag{13.2}$$

There are 100 of these production functions.

Also

$$y_l = f_y(A_y^l, B_y^l) \tag{13.3}$$

There are 100 of these production functions.

THE CONSUMER SECTOR

For each consumer, i, maximization of utility function 13.1 subject to a budget constraint will involve fulfilling the equations:

$$\frac{MU_y^i}{MU_x^i} = P_y \tag{13.4}$$

$$\frac{MU_a^i}{MU_x^i} = P_a \tag{13.5}$$

$$\frac{MU_b^i}{MU_x^i} = P_b \tag{13.6}$$

This gives 6000 equations.

Subject to the constraint that the value of the initial endowments of factors must equal the amount spent on goods plus the factors retained for consumption

$$P_a\bar{A}_i + P_b\bar{B}_i = P_xX_i + P_yY_i + P_aA_i + P_bB_i \tag{13.7}$$

This gives 2000 equations.

Once we have A_i and B_i, the demand for factors, for each consumer we then have his supply of factors $a_i = \bar{A}_i - A_i$, and so on.

We may therefore rewrite 13.7 as

$$P_a a_i + P_b b_i = P_x X_i + P_y Y_i \qquad (13.7a)$$

and there are alternatively 2000 of these equations — $13.7a_1$ to $13.7a_{2000}$.

When each individual equation such as 13.4 through 13.7 is solved for X_i and Y_i in terms of P_x and P_y, we have the individual product demands, and when we aggregate the demands over all individuals we have the market demands for the products X and Y.

THE PRODUCER SECTOR

The conditions for long-run equilibrium require that in each of our industries the firms maximize profits and that profits be zero in equilibrium. This amounts to maximizing equations 13.2 and 13.3 subject to the constraint that total receipts from output be equal to total expenditures upon factors — each firm is to move up the long-run expansion path until the point where payment to factors just exhausts the value of output.

For each firm

$$\frac{MP_a^x}{MP_b^x} = \frac{P_a}{P_b} \qquad (13.8)$$

and

$$\frac{MP_a^y}{MP_b^y} = \frac{P_a}{P_b} \qquad (13.9)$$

also

$$P_x x = P_a A_x + P_b B_x \qquad (13.10)$$

and

$$P_y y = P_a A_y + P_b B_y \qquad (13.11)$$

The last two equations are the zero profit constraints. There are 100 of each of these equations, making 400 equations which, along with 200 production function equations, give *600 equations in all*.

For each firm these equations, along with the production function, yield its supply function for the commodity and its demand function for factors; if we aggregate across all firms we have the total supply of goods and the total demand for each of the factors.

Finally we have the condition that both factor and product markets must clear in equilibrium.

$$X_1 + X_2 + \cdots + X_{2000} = x_1 + x_2 + \cdots + x_{100} \qquad (13.12)$$

$$Y_1 + Y_2 + \cdots + Y_{2000} = y_{101} + y_{102} + \cdots + y_{200} \qquad (13.13)$$

$$a_1 + a_2 + \cdots + a_{2000} = A_x^1 + A_x^2 + \cdots + A_x^{100} + A_y^{101}$$
$$+ A_y^{102} + \cdots + A_y^{200} \qquad (13.14)$$

$$b_1 + b_2 + \cdots + b_{2000} = B_x^1 + B_x^2 + \cdots + B_x^{100} + B_y^{101}$$
$$+ B_y^{102} + \cdots + B_y^{200} \qquad (13.15)$$

These market clearing equations *add a total of 4 equations to the system.*

SUMMARY

Unknowns	*Equations*
8000 household unknowns	8000 household equations
4000 product demands	
4000 factor supplies	
600 firm unknowns	600 firm equations
400 factor demands	
200 product supplies	
3 prices	4 market clearing equations

We see that there is one excess equation and that the system is over-determined — if all of the equations are independent, one of them cannot be fulfilled; it turns out, however, that one of them contributes no independent information and can be abandoned.

PROOF OF THE REDUNDANT EQUATION

We may aggregate the right and left sides of equations 13.12 through 13.15.

$$X = x \qquad (13.12')$$

$$Y = y \qquad (13.13')$$

$$a = A \qquad (13.14')$$

$$b = B \qquad (13.15')$$

$$\text{I} = 13.10 + 13.11 \qquad P_x x + P_y y = P_a[A_x + A_y] + P_b[B_x + B_y]$$
$$= P_a A + P_b B$$

$$\text{II} = 13.14' \times P_a \qquad P_a a = P_a A$$
$$\text{III} = 13.15' \times P_b \qquad P_b b = P_b B$$

$$\text{IV} = \text{II} + \text{III} \qquad P_a a + P_b b = P_a A + P_b B$$

$$\text{V} = \text{I} - \text{IV} \qquad P_x x + P_y y = P_a a + P_b b$$

$$\text{VI} = 13.12' \times P_x \qquad P_x X = P_x x$$
$$\text{VII} = 13.13' \times P_y \qquad P_y Y = P_y y$$

$$\text{VIII} = \text{VI} + \text{VII} \qquad P_x X + P_y Y = P_x x + P_y y$$

$$\text{IX} = \text{VIII} - \text{V} \qquad P_a a + P_b b = P_x X + P_y Y$$

If IX is disaggregated, it reads:

$$\text{X} \qquad P_a a_1 + P_a a_2 + \cdots + P_a a_{1999} + P_a a_{2000} + P_b b_1 + P_b b_2 + \cdots$$
$$+ P_b b_{1999} + P_b b_{2000}$$

$$= P_x X_1 + P_x X_2 + \cdots + P_x X_{1999} + P_x X_{2000} + P_y Y_1 + P_y Y_2$$
$$+ \cdots + P_y Y_{1999} + P_y Y_{2000}$$

Now we subtract equations $13.7a_1$ to $13.7a_{1999}$ from IX.

$$\text{XI} = P_a a_{2000} + P_b b_{2000} = P_x X_{2000} + P_y Y_{2000}$$

This is equation $13.7a_{2000}$, a redundant equation, since its information is implied by the other equations. We have, therefore, 8603 independent equations in 8603 unknowns.

In general, if the number of equations is less than the number of unknowns, the information is insufficient to specify a solution (there are rare exceptions). The equality of the number of equations and unknowns by no means, however, guarantees a unique solution (see page 30). It is possible to have inconsistency, so that there is no solution or there are multiple solutions. Checking the number of equations against the number of unknowns is, therefore, only a preliminary step to check that there are a sufficient number of restraints specified. A complete analysis of the conditions under which a unique (and economically meaningful) solution will exist requires rather high-powered mathematical analysis. It has, however, been shown that under certain reasonable assumptions concerning the shapes of the functions, such a solution does exist.[1]

The system of equations we have discussed is static. That is, it does not specify the path by which the economy approaches equilibrium nor whether the equilibrium will be stable or unstable. We can clearly see, then, that a good deal remains to be done in addition to comparing number of equations with number of unknowns. The rudiments of a general equilibrium system as presented here are nevertheless useful to tie together the partial equilibrium study presented in the earlier chapters.

[1] For a further discussion of this proof by Abraham Wald see George J. Stigler, *Production and Distribution Theories* (Macmillan, New York: 1941), p. 243.

INTRODUCTION TO
LINEAR PROGRAMMING

14

Up to this point this volume has dealt with traditional price theory, which is concerned with the explanation of resource allocation in the economy as a whole. At the center of its analytical apparatus price theory has marginal analysis, which is dictated by the assumption that entrepreneurs as a whole desire to maximize profits.

In price theory the usual assumptions made are (1) the firm is given its production function as a technological datum; (2) the firm can substitute factors of production for each other continuously (smoothly continuous isoquants); (3) the firm has knowledge of the demand curve it faces. The usual problems faced by businessmen are not of the type that require a choice between a little more of one factor and a little less of another in order to produce a given output as cheaply as possible, but rather a choice among production processes each of which has fairly rigid factor proportions dictated by its technological character. Economists, interested in prescribing for individual business firms, must take into account the multifarious complexities and diversities of the firms, and in this area (sometimes called managerial economics) marginal analysis often fails them.

Although marginal analysis abstracts from the details of the decision making of individual firms, its very "simplicity" makes it useful in analyzing the allocation of resources for society as a whole. As far as the decisions of the individual firms are concerned, a generally more useful tool is mathematical programming, which deals with the problem of maximizing (or minimizing) some function (called the objective function) subject to constraints that take the form of inequalities. Marginal analysis is also concerned with maximization (or minimization) subject to constraints, but in marginal analysis the constraints are equalities.

In this chapter we shall discuss linear programming, which is the most widely used form of mathematical programming. It is not our purpose to teach the student the technique of solving linear programming problems but rather to acquaint him with the nature of the technique and the problems the technique can best deal with. At the end of the chapter we provide a selective bibliography listing some of the outstanding works in the field.

In linear programming we make the following assumptions: (1) Each input contributes to the fulfillment of the objective function in proportion to its utilization, and each process (to be defined below) uses up the scarce inputs in proportion to its utilization. (2) The prices at which the firm buys its factors and sells its products are assumed constant. In their economic context, these assumptions amount to assuming a linear homogeneous production function and perfect competition in both the product and factor markets. We demonstrate this in Figure 14.1.

FIGURE 14.1

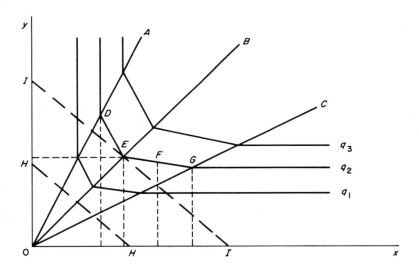

Lines OA, OB, and OC represent three process rays: three different methods of producing a good, each one of which requires a given proportion between the factors. For example, q_2 units of output may be produced at point D on process ray OA, or point E on process ray OB, or point G on process ray OC. q_2 can also be produced by utilizing a combination of processes such as at point F.* When we connect points

---

*It is not intuitively obvious that output at F is the same as at E or G. See Robert Dorfman, "Mathematical, or 'Linear,' Programming: A Nonmathematical Exposi-

such as D, E, F, and G we generate an isoquant. Notice that the isoquant is not the smoothly continuous one of Chapter 7, since there are only a finite number of processes the firm can use.

---

tion," *American Economic Review*, XLIII, no. 5 (December, 1953) 805–806, who has proven this rigorously as follows:

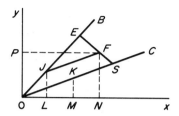

(1) From F on segment EG draw a line parallel to OC that intersects OB at J. Mark off the distance OK on OC so that $JF = OK$.

(2) Assume the firm uses a production plan consisting of process OB at the level OJ and process OC at the level OK. Process OB at level OJ uses OL of factor X. Process OC at level OK uses OM of X.

Thus, the two processes together use $OL + OM$ units of X. However, by construction, $JF = OK$ and JF is parallel to OK. Therefore, $LN = OM$, and together the processes use ON of X. And ON is the X-axis coordinate of F.

(3) Similarly OP represents the amount of Y used by the production plan calling for OJ of process OB and OK of process OC.

(4) Thus F can be interpreted as the combined production plan made up of OK of process OC, and OJ of process OB if we assume that when the two processes are used together, neither process interferes with or enhances the other.

(5) Next it is necessary to show that output at F is equal to output at E and G. Based on the linearity assumption,

$$\frac{\text{output } K}{\text{output } G} = \frac{OK}{OG}$$

and

$$\frac{\text{output } J}{\text{output } E} = \frac{OJ}{OE}$$

Because we assumed output E = output G,

$$\frac{\text{output } K}{\text{output } E} = \frac{OK}{OG}$$

Adding, we get

$$\frac{\text{output } K}{\text{output } E} + \frac{\text{output } J}{\text{output } E} = \frac{OK}{OG} + \frac{OJ}{OE}$$

(Continued on page 240)

FIGURE 14.2

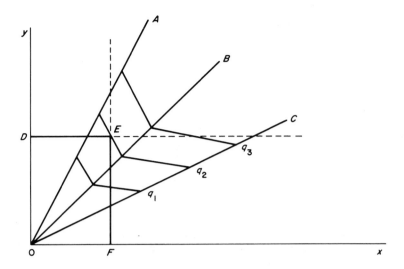

The reader has seen linear expansion paths along which equal proportional increases in inputs resulted in equal proportional increments in output and will identify this as a characteristic of linear homogeneous production functions.

It should be kept in mind that in the linear-programming view of production the firm no longer changes inputs and outputs directly but indirectly by changing the levels at which the various processes are being used. In Figure 14.1 the firm is conceived of as facing only one

---

(Continued from page 239)

But by construction $OK = JF$. Thus,

$$\frac{OK}{OG} + \frac{OJ}{OE} = \frac{JF}{OG} + \frac{OJ}{OE}$$

Since $\triangle JEF \backsim \triangle OEG$ ($\not\lesssim JEF = \not\lesssim OEG$; $\not\lesssim EOG = \not\lesssim EJF$; $\not\lesssim OGE = \not\lesssim JFE$),

$$\frac{JF}{OG} = \frac{JE}{OE}$$

We can write

$$\frac{JF}{OG} + \frac{OJ}{OE} = \frac{JE}{OE} + \frac{OJ}{OE} = \frac{OE}{OE} = 1$$

In words, if [(output K + output J)/output E] = 1, output K + output J = output E. But output F is the sum of output K and output J. Therefore, output E = output F and E, F, and G lie on the same isoquant.

constraint — an expenditure constraint — and wanting to maximize output with this level of expenditure. If the expenditure constraint is II, the firm will accomplish its objective by producing at point E, on the highest attainable kinked isoquant. Graphically, one can see that such an equilibrium will occur at a corner or anywhere along a segment that has the same slope as the constraint line.

The usual situation in which the firm finds itself in the short run is the one in which it is constrained by various limited capacities that may be used in a number of alternative processes to produce a number of products. In Figure 14.2 we visualize the simplest of these cases. We assume the firm produces only one product and that X and Y are its limited capacities in factors X and Y. Thus the feasible area — the one in which the firm *can* produce — is $ODEF$. It should be noted that the constraint is no longer a straight line but an area, and that the boundary DEF represents the maximum combination of the factors the firm can use. With the firm trying to maximize output, it will produce at point E.

A more relevant situation is one in which the firm must decide on a product mix that will maximize its profit and can be produced within the capacity constraints. This kind of problem may be generally stated as follows:

Let $a, b, \ldots, n$ represent the products the firm can produce

$P_a, P_b, \ldots, P_n$ represent the prices at which the firm can sell its products

$A, B, \ldots, N$ represent the fixed amounts of the productive capacities

Let the amounts of the fixed capacities used per unit of output for each product be as follows:

$$A_a\ A_b\ \cdots\ A_n$$
$$B_a\ B_b\ \cdots\ B_n$$
$$\cdot$$
$$\cdot$$
$$\cdot$$
$$N_a\ N_b\ \cdots\ N_n$$

The problem then becomes one of maximizing

$$TR = P_a a + P_b b + \cdots + P_n n^* \tag{14.1}$$

*Note that in this case maximizing total revenue is identical with maximizing profit. Linear programming is based on the assumptions of constant returns up to capacity in the short run and constant factor prices; in other words, marginal cost is constant. The costs stemming from the capacity limitations are fixed.

Subject to

$$A_a + A_b + \cdots + A_n \leq A$$
$$B_a + B_b + \cdots + B_n \leq B$$
$$\vdots$$
$$N_a + N_b + \cdots + N_n \leq N$$
$$A \cdots N \geq 0 \tag{14.2}$$

We now present a specific example of such a problem: Two products: x, y

$$P_x = \$10$$
$$P_y = \$8$$

Four capacities: A, B, C, D

	Inputs needed in		
Input	x	y	Input capacity
A	2	2	1500
B	5	3	3000
C	3	0	1500
D	0	1	600

Maximize: $TR = P_x x + P_y y$ $\qquad$ (14.3)
$\qquad\qquad = 10x + 8y$

Subject to: $2x + 2y \leq 1500$
$\qquad\qquad 5x + 3y \leq 3000$
$\qquad\qquad 3x + 0y \leq 1500 \quad$ and $x \geq 0$ $\qquad$ (14.4)
$\qquad\qquad 0x + 1y \leq 600 \qquad\qquad y \geq 0$

The graphical solution to this problem is shown in Figure 14.3. The A-capacity constraint is shown on the diagram as a straight line with an x-axis intercept equal to the maximum amount of x that the firm can produce if it devotes all of A to the production of x, and a y-axis intercept equal to maximum y production if A is used only to produce y. The B-capacity constraint is determined in analogous fashion. Since the C-capacity is used only in the production of x, the constraint appears as a vertical line at the maximum amount of x that can be produced with full utilization of C. Similarly, the D-capacity constraint appears as a horizontal line at the maximum quantity of y that can be produced with full utilization of D. These constraints delimit the feasible area, $PNKLM$, the area within which the constraints permit the firm to operate.

The objective function that is to be maximized — $TR = P_x x + P_y y$ — is represented by a series of parallel lines with the slope, P_x/P_y. Clearly the firm desires to be on the highest possible isorevenue line permitted by the constraints. This is at point K where the firm produces 375 units of x and 375 units of y. Thus $TR = 375$ ($10) + 375 ($8) = $6750. Note that two of the capacities, C and D, are not being fully utilized. The

FIGURE 14.3

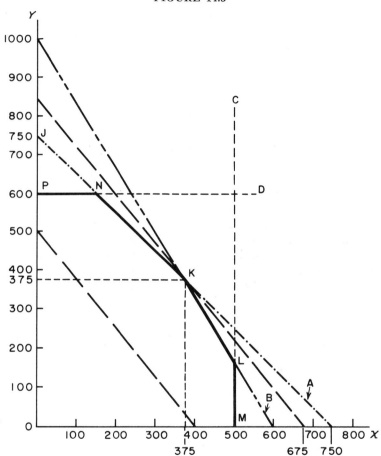

amount of C being used is 1125 (out of 1500 capacity), and $375D$ are being used (with capacity at 600).[1]

At the optimal point, there is no tangency condition being fulfilled and we cannot find this point, therefore, using ordinary calculus methods.

[1]It can be proven that at the maximization level there will usually be as many products produced as there are facilities used to capacity. See W. J. Baumol, *Economic Theory and Operations Analysis* (Englewood Cliffs, N.J.: Prentice-Hall, 1961), pp. 73–74.

Thus, other methods must be used for finding the optimal solution;[2] these methods are iterative methods, the most commonly used being the simplex method.[3]

To every problem of this kind (called a primal problem) there is a corresponding dual problem. To illustrate the meaning of the dual problem, we present the dual form of the primal problem solved above.

Minimize imputed cost: $\quad IC = AI_A + BI_B + CI_C + DI_D \qquad (14.5)$
$$IC = 1500I_A + 3000I_B + 1500I_C + 600I_D$$

Subject to: $\quad A_xI_A + B_xI_B + C_xI_C + D_xI_D \geq P_x$
$$A_yI_A + B_yI_B + C_yI_C + D_yI_D \geq P_y$$
or
$$2I_A + 5I_B + 3I_C + 0I_D \geq \$10$$
$$2I_A + 3I_B + 0I_C + 1I_D \geq \quad \$8 \qquad (14.6)$$
$$I_A, I_B, I_C, I_D \geq 0$$

The terms I_A (imputed value of A), I_B, and so on, require some explanation. Each of these represents the value to the firm of acquiring an additional unit of a presently fixed capacity (the value of the marginal product of a fixed facility). If a facility is not being used to capacity, the worth to the firm of an additional unit of it will clearly be zero, and the imputed value assigned to it by the firm will be zero. If, on the other hand, a facility is being used to capacity, its imputed value will be positive and represents the opportunity cost (in terms of the forgone outputs) to the firm of utilizing the input to produce a particular output. If the sum of the imputed costs of producing a particular commodity is greater than the price of the commodity, this means that the factors can be more profitably used in the production of some other good. (In the primal problem, the output of this product will be zero.) If the sum of the imputed costs is less than the price of the good, this means that the accounting prices (imputed values) assigned by the firm are too low since they do not allocate the total value of the unit of output. Thus, for an output being produced, the sum of the imputed values will just equal the price of the good.

[2]The optimal solution can always be at a corner. This can be demonstrated as follows: If the isorevenue line is not parallel to any of the facets of the feasible area boundary, then clearly the point of contact between the boundary and the highest possible isorevenue line will be at a corner. Furthermore, if the isorevenue line is parallel to one of the segments of the boundary, contact will exist along that segment. Thus, the entire segment — including the corners — will be optimal. Since the optimal solution can always be found at a corner, the simplex method involves searching consecutive corners of the boundary of the feasible region and comparing the values of the objective equation at these corners until no movement away from a particular corner can increase the value of the objective equation.

[3]The student interested in this mathematical technique is referred to the bibliography at the end of the chapter.

In our example, facilities C and D are not being fully utilized; therefore, the imputed values of C and D will be zero. Thus the constraints become

$$2I_A + 5I_B \geq \$10 \qquad (14.7)$$
$$2I_A + 3I_B \geq \$8$$

These constraints are shown graphically in Figure 14.4. Note that the feasible area is the unbounded one lying above the boundary PQR; for all points lying *within* $OPQR$, either or both the constraints are not being fulfilled.

In order to demonstrate why a firm must minimize its imputed cost if it is to maximize its total revenue (and, therefore, profits with our linearity assumptions), we present the following example:

Let us assume that we have two processes, E and F, capable of producing two products, G and H, that have the same prices. The two processes are used to capacity, and the marginal unit of each process is capable of the following additions to output:

$$\Delta Q$$

$$\text{Process } E \quad \begin{cases} 10 \text{ units of } G \\ \quad \text{or} \\ 5 \text{ units of } H \end{cases}$$

$$\text{Process } F \quad \begin{cases} 5 \text{ units of } G \\ \quad \text{or} \\ 10 \text{ units of } H \end{cases}$$

Now if the marginal unit of process F is used to produce G, the imputed cost will be 10 (the 10 units of H forgone when process F is used to produce G instead of H); and if process E is used to produce H, imputed cost is 10.

If production methods were changed so that process E were used to produce G and process F to produce H, output at capacity would increase by 5 units of G and 5 units of H (and, therefore, profits would increase) and the imputed costs would fall from 10 to 5 for both processes. It is therefore clear that, so long as it is possible to reduce imputed cost, profits are not being maximized.

Thus in Figure 14.4 we show parallel isoimputed-cost lines with the slope equal to $-\frac{1}{2}$ (this slope is determined from the objective equation: $IC = 1500I_A + 3000I_B + 1500[0] + 600[0]$). Point Q represents the optimal imputed values for A and B: $I_A = \$2.50$ and $I_B = \$1.*$

---

*In solving the dual problem mathematically, the zero accounting prices for C and D would appear as part of the solution. However, from the primal problem we know that neither of these facilities would have been used to capacity and, thus, both would have zero opportunity cost. Therefore, by assuming $I_C = I_D = 0$, we were able to present the dual solution graphically using two dimensions.

FIGURE 14.4

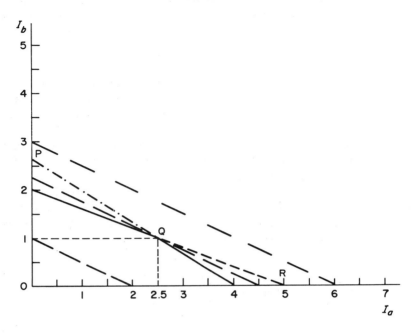

Note that the minimum imputed cost figure derived from the dual solution is the same as the maximum total revenue that was derived from the primal. We can substitute I_A and I_B in the objective equation:

$$IC = 1500(\$0.50) + 3000(\$1) = \$6750 \qquad (14.8)$$

Clearly, from the following conditions,

1. if the sum of the imputed values of the resources used in producing a unit of a good is greater than the price of the good, the good will not be produced, and
2. the price of a good must be imputed completely to the resources utilized,

it follows that the maximum total revenue must be totally imputed.

The following are some types of problems that can be handled by linear programming.

1. Determining the optimum product mix when the firm has some of its facilities at or near capacity. This is the type of problem described above. For example, suppose that a company can produce both automobiles and trucks and that there are certain capacities, some of which

are used exclusively for one product and some of which are required in the production of both goods; what should the output of trucks and automobiles be?[4]

2. The blending problem. For example, minimizing the cost of a diet that fulfills certain minimal nutritional requirements; and minimizing the cost of gasoline with the constraints of minimum octane and certain other quality requirements.

Ice-cream manufacturing, textile production, and metallurgy are other areas in which this kind of problem arises.

3. The transportation problem — minimizing costs of transport subject to certain constraints. For example, if a firm has several plants with fixed capacities and in different locations and has customers scattered geographically, it will want to minimize its costs of transportation subject to the demands of the consumers and the output capacities of the plants.

The dual solution to the linear programming problem that we discussed above is useful, first, because many times the dual problem is easier to solve computationally than the primal problem. Second, the imputed values derived from the dual solution have some interesting applications. One of these is to permit a firm with several plants to use decentralized rather than centralized decision making. If there are certain scarce facilities utilized by all the plants, they can simply be allocated by a central management decision; or the plant managers can be permitted to use as much of the scarce resources as they want but the home office will debit them the imputed value of the resources they use. The managers will be cautioned to avoid losses.

The literature on linear programming is extensive. We list below a few references that the beginning student will find useful.

Baumol, W. J., *Economic Theory and Operations Analysis* (Englewood Cliffs, N.J.: Prentice-Hall, 1961).

Charnes, A., W. W. Cooper, and A. Henderson, *Introduction to Linear Programming* (New York: Wiley, 1953).

Dantzig, G. B., "Maximization of a Linear Function of Variables Subject to Linear Inequalities," in T. C. Koopmans (Ed.), *Activity Analysis of Production and Allocation* (New York: Wiley, 1951).

Dorfman, R., "Mathematical, or 'Linear' Programming," *American Economic Review*, XLIII, no. 5 (December 1953), 805–806.

Dorfman, R., P. A. Samuelson, and R. Solow, *Linear Programming and Economic Analysis* (New York: McGraw-Hill, 1958).

[4]See Dorfman, "Mathematical, or 'Linear,' Programming," *loc. cit.*

INDEX

Index

Agricultural price supports,
elasticity and, 54–56
purchase program, 54
subsidy program, 55–56
Algebraic representation,
functional relationship, 6–7
American Stock Exchange, 39
Antitrust legislation, 207
output and, 210
Attitudes, conditioned, demand
and, 31
Auction markets, 39
Average concept, demand
and, 44–62
Average revenue, defined, 45

Baumol, W. J., 243n, 247
Blending problem, 247
Budget line, equation for, 84–85
equilibrium, 84
indifference curve and, 82–84
slope, 84, 86
slope monomania, 89
wall (plane), 83

Cardinal utility (*see* Utility,
cardinal)
Ceteris paribus assumption, 231
defined, 31
demand and the, 33
supply and the, 35, 36, 37
Charnes, A., 247
Cobweb theorem, elasticity and,
60–62

Collusion, absolute, 197–199
oligopoly without, 202–207
tacit, 199–202
kinky demand curve and, 199
price leadership and, 200
umbrella price leadership
and, 202
Commodity markets, 39
Competition, antitrust legislation
and, 207
imperfect and perfect, 207–211
products and, 211
monopolistic, 111
long-run equilibrium, 194–196
output and, 192–211
price and, 192–211
products and, 193
selling activities and, 193
short-run equilibrium,
192–193
perfect, 38
as economic model, 39
demand and, 31–43
factor price determination in,
212–230
imperfect and, 207–211
in products market, 220–223
long run supply schedule and,
166–174
monopoly vs., 207–211
output and, 154–174
price and, 31–43, 154–174
products and, 211
profits and, 154–166

Competition (*cont'd.*)
    supply and, 31–43
    pure, 38–39
Competitive market, stable
    equilibrium and, 40
Constant-cost industries, 168
Consumer equilibrium, 66–67
Consumer sector equations, 233
Consumption possibility schedule
    (*see* Budget line)
Continuous function, marginal
    utility, 64
Continuous marginal revenue,
    defined, 46
Contour line, 117
Contour map, 7
    utility function, 81
Cooper, W. W., 247
Cost(s), average, 21–23
    long-run, 145
    relationship between long-run
        and short-run, relationship
        between marginal and,
        151–153
    curves, 137
    fixed, 137, 139
        average, 140
    imputed, 244
    long-run, relationship between
        average and marginal,
        151–153
    relationship to short-run,
        147–153
    marginal, 23–28
        average, 140
        continuous, 26–27
        defined, 140
        long-run, 145
        relationship between long-run,
        short-run, and average,
        151–153
    output and, 212

Cost(s) (*cont'd.*)
    output and increases in, 168
    production, economic efficiency
        in, 130
    long-run, 130–135, 145–147
    short-run, 139–144
    technological efficiency, 130
    short-run, relationship between
        average, marginal, and
        long-run and, 151–153
    relationship to long-run,
        147–153
    total, 19–20
        average, 140
        continuous marginal costs
        and, 26
        defined, 139
        long-run, 145
    variable, average, 140
        defined, 159
Cournot, Augustin, 204
Cross elasticity, arc elasticity
    and, 52
    defined, 52
    point elasticity and, 52
Curve(s), contract, defined, 106
    cost, 137
    demand, kinky, 199
    envelope, 149
    expansion path, 132n
    income consumption, 97–101
        demand schedule, 97
        income elasticity, 98
    indifference, 78–82
        budget and, 82–84
        equilibrium, 89
        income effect and, 101–103
        indifference effect and,
        101–103
        marginal rate of substitution
        and, 79
        properties of, 81–82

Curve(s) (*cont'd.*)
　utility approach and, 87–88
　indifference equilibrium, 84–87
　"nonnormal" indifference,
　　88–91
　price consumption, 91–97
　demand schedule and, 94
　profit maximization, 156–157
　ridge lines, 132n
　supply, labor and, 219–220
　negative sloping, 174
　profit maximization, 160–163

Dantzig, G. B., 247
Demand, aggregate, 32
　average concept and, 44–62
　competitive industry and, 108
　complementary goods and, 31
　cultural attitudes and, 31
　curve, individual's, 31
　elasticity, defined, 46
　time and, 48
　elasticity concept and, 44–62
　functional relationship notation,
　　31
　income and, 31
　marginal concept and, 44–62
　psychological, sociological,
　　cultural attitudes and, 31
　quantity and, 31
　revenue and, 44–51
　schedule, in competitive
　　industry, 108
　derivation of, 67–68
　income and, 97
　individual producer and, 108
　individual's, 31
　monopolist and, 108, 111–112
　oligopolies, 112–113
　price-consumption curve
　　and, 94
　total, 32

Demand (*cont'd.*)
　shifts in, 33–35
　substitute goods and, 31
　taste and, 31
　theory, classical utility approach,
　　63–77
　indifference curve approach,
　　78–107
　total concept and, 44–62
　utility and, 63–66
Depreciation, exchange-rate,
　elasticity and, 59–60
Discrete function, marginal
　utility, 64
Discrete marginal revenue,
　defined, 45
Dorfman, Robert, 238n, 247
Duopoly, 204

Economic analysis, graphical
　techniques of, 3–30
　mathematical techniques of,
　　3–30
　models used in, 39
Economic behavior, 154
Economic models, use of, 39
Economic problems, resources
　and, 1
　society and, 1
Economic variables, equilibrium
　approach to, 231
　interdependence of, 231
Economics, external, 172
　government and, 1
　market, 1
Edgeworth box, 185
　free trade and, 105–106
Efficiency, economic, production
　costs and, 130
　technological, production costs
　　and, 130

Elasticity, applications of, 54–62
  arc, 15–19
    formula, 18
  average revenue and, 114–115
  coefficient of, 48
  concept of, 14–19
    demand and, 44–62
  cross, 52
  demand, defined, 46
  demand curve, individual
    producer, 111
  determinants of, 46
  durable commodities and, 47
  formula, 16, 17
  income, income-consumption
    curve and, 98
  marginal revenue and, 114–115
  market structures and, 114–115
  nondurable commodities and, 47
  point, 15–19
    formula, 17
    geometrical interpretation of,
      51–52
  price equals constant and, 52–53
  quantity equals constant and, 53
  results from, 16
  revenue and, average, 49–50
    marginal, 49–50
    total, 48–49
  special cases of, 52–54
  supply, 52
Envelope curve (*see* Curve(s),
    envelope)
Equations, simultaneous, solution
    of, 28–30
  straight-line, 10
Equilibrium, as approach to
    economic problems, 231
  budget, 84
  competitive market and, 40
  consumer, 66–67
    indifference curves and, 84–91

Equilibrium (*cont'd.*)
  consumer sector equations, 233
  determination of unknowns for,
    232
  factor price determination and,
    224
  long-run, monopolistic
    competition and, 194–196
  price change and, 72
  producer sector equation, 234
  short-run, 135–138
    monopolistic competition and,
      192–193
  stable, 39
  unstable, 39
Exchange-rate depreciation,
    elasticity and, 59–60
Excise tax, elasticity and, 56–59
Expansion path, 132, 133

Factor market, factor price
    determination in, 212–230
  perfect competition, factor price
    determination in, 217–219
Factor price determination,
    equilibrium conditions, 224
  monopolistic exploitation as
    factor in, 219
  monopoly, 223–224
  monopsony and, 223–226
  monopsony in factor market and,
    220–223
  monopsony in products market
    and, 217–219
  perfect competition in factor
    market, 217–219
  perfect competition in products
    market and, 220–223
  supply curve of labor in, 219–220
  unions and, 226–230
Fixed cost, 137
  average, 140

Fixed cost (*cont'd.*)
  defined, 139
Free enterprise, American economy
      and, 2
  defined, 1
  system, 2
Free trade, gains to be derived
      from, 105–106
Function(s), demand as a, 31
  notational form, 10
  production, 117–138
    linear and homogeneous,
      125, 240
  slope of, 8–14
    continuous changes, 13–14
    discrete changes, 8–13
  supply as, 35
  tabular form, 9
  treatment of nonlinear, 12
Functional relationships, algebraic
      representation of, 6–7
  among variables, 3–14
  average concept of, 21–23
  defined, 4
  example, two variables, 6–8
  graph of function in, 5
  graphic, representation of, 6–7
  simple, 4–6
  simultaneous equation and,
      28–30
  total concept of, 19–21
    continuous function in, 20
  two variables or more and, 6–8

Giffen good, 73, 104, 105
Government
  control, direct, 187–191
    indirect, 186
  economic choice and, 1
  monopolies and, 186–191
  price regulation by, 187–191

Government (*cont'd.*)
  regulations on monopsony,
      225–226
  taxes, 186
Graphical representation, contour
      map, 7
  functional relationships, 7–8
Graphical techniques, economic
      analysis, 3–30

Henderson, A., 247
Hicks, J. R., 102

Income and substitution effect,
      Hickian analysis of,
      102–104
  Slutskyian analysis of, 102–104
Income-consumption curve, 97–101
Income effect, price change and
      the, 71–73
Income elasticity (*see* Elasticity)
Indifference curve approach,
      income-consumption curve
      and, 97–101
  price-consumption curve and,
      91–97
  theory of demand, 78–107
Indifference map, utility function,
      81
Industries, blocked entry to, 194
  constant-cost, 168
  decreasing-cost, 172
  free entry to, 195
  monopolization of, costs and,
      210–211
  perfectly competitive, demand
      schedule and, 108
  long-run supply schedule of,
      166–174
  See also Monopolies; Producers
Isocost lines, 130
Isoquant, 117

Isoquant (*cont'd.*)
  characteristics of, 118–120
  noninteresting, 120
  ridge lines, 120
Isoquant map, 130
Isorevenue line, 244

Kindleberger, Charles P., 60

Labor, marginal outlay for, 220
  outlay for, 220
  supply curve for, 219–220
    backward bending, 220
Law of diminishing marginal
    utility, 65
Line of attainable combinations
    (*see* Budget line)
Linear homogeneous production
    function, 125, 126
Linear programming, expansion
    paths, 240
  homogeneous production
    functions, 240
  price theory and, 237–247
Long-run costs (*see* Costs, long-run)
Long-run production (*see* Produc-
    tion, long-run)

Marginal analysis, 237
Marginal concept, 8–14
  demand and, 44–62
  total concept and, 23–28
Marginal cost (*see* Costs, marginal)
Marginal quantity, defined, 23
Marginal rate of substitution,
    defined, 79
Marginal utility (*see* Utility,
    marginal)
Market structures, average revenue
    and, 114–115
  elasticity and, 114–115
  marginal revenue and, 114–115
  types of, 108–115

Marshall, Alfred, 73n, 227n
Marshall-Lerner condition,
    defined, 60n
Mathematical technique, economic
    analysis, 3–30
  functional relationships, 3–14
Minimum wage legislation, 225
Monies (*see* Revenue)
Monomania, budget line slope
    and, 89
Monopolies, average cost pricing
    and, 178–179
  conditions for, 175
  control of, government and,
    186–191
  costs and, 210–211
  defined, 108
  demand schedule and, 108,
    111–113
  elasticity and, 115
  exploitation as factor in price
    determination, 219
  factor price determination in,
    223–224
  "natural," 185–186
  output and, 175–191
  perfect competition vs., 207–211
  price and, 175–191
  product market, factor price
    determination in, 217–219
  profit maximization, long-run,
    178
    short-run, 175–177
  public utilities, 185
  pure, 175
  regulated, 185–186
Monopsony, defined, 219
  factor price determination in,
    223–224
  in factor market, 220–223
  government regulation of,
    225–226

Monopsony (*cont'd.*)
power, measurement of, 222–223
relevance of, 224–225
unions and, 229

New York Coffee and Sugar
Exchange, 39
New York Stock Exchange, 39

Oligopoly, characteristics of,
112, 196
absolute collusion and, 197–199
tacit, 199–202
Cournot's treatment of, 204
demand curve and, 112–113
output and, 192–211
pricing and, 192–211
types of, 196–197
unsophisticated behavior by,
202–207
without collusion, 202–207
Oligopsonist, defined, 220
Optimum product mix, 246
Ordinal utility (*see* Utility, ordinal)
Output, antitrust laws and, 210
cost schedules and long-run
supply schedules and, 166
costs and, 212
costs increases and, 168
long-run, perfect competition vs.
monopoly in, 209–210
monopolistic competition and,
192–211
oligopoly and, 192–211
perfect competition and, 154–174
short-run, perfect competition vs.
monopoly in, 207–209

Partial-equilibrium analysis, 231
Percentage changes, ratio of,
elasticity and, 15–16

Perfect competition (*see* Competition, perfect)
Point elasticity, geometrical
interpretation of, 51–52
Price-consumption curve, 91–97
Price line (*see* Budget line)
Price theory, assumptions in, 239
defined, 1
intermediate, 3
traditional, defined, 237
Price(s), ceiling, 187
change in, and income effect,
71–73
and substitution effect, 71–72
competitive factor market, 212
determination, 38–43
equilibrium and, 39–43
perfect competition and, 38
pure competition and, 38–39
determination of factor, 212–230
discrimination, defined, 179
imperfect, 181–185
take it or leave it, 180–181
equilibrium, 39–43
monopolistic competition and,
112
equilibrium market, perfectly
competitive industry
and, 111
leadership, tacit collusion and,
200
umbrella, 202
long-run, perfect competition vs.
monopoly in, 209–210
perfect competition and,
154–174
profit-maximizing, monopolistic
competition and, 192
short-run, 192
regulation, 187–191
ceiling price and, 187
profits and, 187–189

Price(s)
  short-run, perfect competition vs.
    monopoly in, 207–209
  support, agricultural, 54–56
Pricing, average cost, monopoly
    and, 178–179
  monopolistic competition and,
    192–211
  oligopoly and, 192–211
Producers
  individual and demand curve,
    110
  demand schedule and, 108
  See also Monopolies; Industry
Product market, factor price
    determination in, 212–230
  monopoly, factor price
    determination in, 217–219
Production
  costs, long-run, 145–147
    short-run, 139–144
    supply curve and, 116
  function, defined, 6
  long-run, 124–126
    costs, 130–135
    decreasing returns and, 125
    increasing returns and, 125
    profit maximization, 164–166
  short-run, 120–124
    diminishing returns and, 121,
      122, 123
    increasing returns and, 121
    negative returns and, 121
    profit maximization, 156–164
  symmetry of the stages of, 126–130
  theory, 117–138
    long-run, 124–126
    short-run, 120–124
  See also Product(s)
Production function, 133
  defined, 116
  linear and homogeneous, 125

Production *(cont'd.)*
  notation, 116
Product(s)
  marginal physical, diminishing
    returns and, 121, 122, 123
    increasing returns and, 121
  negative returns and, 121
    slope of isoquant and, 123–124
  monopolistic competition and,
    193
  oligopolistic industry, 196–197
  total physical, output, input and,
    121
  See also Production
Profit(s), curve, profit maximiza-
    tion and, 156
  least-costs condition, 215
  maximization, assumption of,
    154
    long-run, 164–166, 178
    perfect competition and,
      154–166
    short-run, 156–164
    short-run notation, 175–178
    supply curve, 160–163
  short-run, marginal, 157
Public utilities, 185

Resources, economic problems
    and, 1
Revenue
  average, defined, 45
    elasticity and, 49–50, 114–115
    graph, 45
  market structures and, 114–115
  continuous marginal, defined, 46
  discrete marginal,
  defined, 45
    graph, 45
  factor price determination and,
    212–213

Revenue (*cont'd.*)
marginal, elasticity and, 49–50,
    114–115
    market structures and,
        114–115
    total, defined, 44
    elasticity and, 48–49
    graph, 44
Ridge lines, 132n, 133

Samuelson, A., 247
Short-run costs (*see* Costs, short-run)
Short-run production (*see* Produc-
        tion, short-run)
Simultaneous equations (*see*
        Equations)
Slope
    budget line, 84–86
        monomania, 89
    concept of, 8–14
    continuous changes in, 13–14
    discrete changes in, 8–13
        notational form, 10
        tabular form, 9
    elasticity and, 16
    of function, 8–14
        continuous changes, 13–14
        discrete changes, 8–13
    marginal concept, 8–14
Slutsky, E., 102
Society, institutions of, economic
        problems and, 1
Solow, R., 247
Stigler, George, 39, 139n, 200n,
        227n, 236
Stock markets, 39
Substitution effect, price change
        and, the 71–73
Supply, curve, 37
    defined, 35
    elasticity, arc elasticity and, 52
        defined, 52

Supply (*cont'd.*)
    point elasticity and, 52
    as function, 35
    functional notation, 35
    price and, 35
    schedule, aggregate, 37
        cost schedules, output and, 166
        curve form, 37
        long-run, perfectly competitive
            industry, 166–174
        tabular form, 36
    shift in, 37

Taxes, excise, elasticity and, 56–59
    profit, 186
    specific, 186
Total concept, functional
        relationships
    demand and, 44–62
    marginal concept and, 23–28
Total cost (*see* Costs)
Total revenue (*see* Revenue, total)
Total utility (*see* Utility, total)
Transportation, 247

Umbrella price leadership, 202
Unions, effect of, 226–230
    imperfect competitive industry
        and, 229
    monopsony power and, 229–230
    perfectly competitive industry
        and, 226–227
Utility, cardinal, defined, 65
    income effect, indifference
        curves and, 101–103
    indifference curve approach
        and, 87–88
    law of diminishing marginal, 65
    marginal, defined, 64
    ordinal, defined, 78
        function, 81
        indifference curves and, 78–82

Utility (*cont'd.*)
    substitution effect, indifference
        curves, 101–103
    total, defined, 63

Variable costs (*see* Costs)
Variables, continuous, 3
    defined, 3
    demand and, 31
    dependent, 5

Variables (*cont'd.*)
    discrete, 3
    independent, 5
    relationship between two, 5
    two or more, 6–8
    value of, 4

Wald, Abraham, 236n
Wall (plane), budget, 83, 84
Walras, Leon, 231